THE
METROPOLITAN
REVOLUTION

THE
METROPOLITAN
REVOLUTION

How Cities and Metros Are Fixing Our Broken Politics and Fragile Economy

BRUCE KATZ AND
JENNIFER BRADLEY

BROOKINGS INSTITUTION PRESS
Washington, D.C.

Copyright © 2013
First paperback edition 2015
THE BROOKINGS INSTITUTION
1775 Massachusetts Avenue, N.W., Washington, DC 20036
www.brookings.edu

The Library of Congress has cataloged the hardcover edition as follows:
Katz, Bruce.
    The metropolitan revolution : how cities and metros are fixing our broken politics and fragile economy / Bruce Katz and Jennifer Bradley.
        pages   cm
    Includes bibliographical references and index.
    ISBN 978-0-8157-2151-2 (hardcover : alk. paper)
  1. Metropolitan areas—United States. 2. City and town life—United States. 3. Municipal government—United States. I. Bradley, Jennifer. II. Title.
    HT334.U5K38 2013
    307.76'40973--dc23   2013016820
    ISBN 978-0-8157-2659-3 (pbk. : alk. paper)

9 8 7 6 5 4 3 2 1

Printed on acid-free paper

Typeset in Sabon and Univers

Composition by Cynthia Stock
Silver Spring, Maryland

CONTENTS

To the memory of my father, Alan Katz

To Leon and Matthew Wieseltier

FOREWORD

How does one measure a city? By the buildings that fill its skyline? By the efficiency of its rapid transit? Or, perhaps, by what Jane Jacobs called the "sidewalk ballet" of a busy street?

Certainly these are the memorable hallmarks of any modern city or metropolitan area. But a city's true measure goes beyond human-made structures and lies deeper than daily routine. Rather, cities and metro areas are defined by the quality of the ideas they generate, the innovations they spur, and the opportunities they create for people living within and outside the city limits.

These are the elements that will be increasingly important as more people flock to cities than ever before. We have already passed the tipping point: a majority of people on the planet now live in metropolitan areas. In the developing world, 1 million people move to cities and metros every five days. At this pace, by 2050 three-quarters of the global population will call urban areas home.

Our language has not yet caught up with the realities. Often when we refer to cities we are actually referring to the broader economic, environmental, and infrastructure networks of the entire metropolitan region of which a city is a part. In this sense, it is difficult to separate the city from its larger metro region—or to separate the metro from the city. In today's world, the two are inextricably linked.

But by any name, metro regions' ability to build resilience and achieve economic growth will have a profound impact on the future of our planet as a whole. This is something I have come to believe strongly as the president of the Rockefeller Foundation, and as the president of the University of Pennsylvania before that. And we have been reminded of this fact as a nation in just the past few years—that just as cities are a source of strength, they are often vulnerable to the shocks and disruptions of our modern world. When Superstorm Sandy barreled up the East Coast of the United States, making a direct hit on New York City, economic activity and commerce felt its impact all over the world. When Bangkok flooded in 2011, many global supply chains ground to a halt. Cities themselves are weakened by vulnerabilities in individual communities within the city. When one part of the city loses connection to a critical system, the stability of the entire region can be threatened.

But examples of innovation happening all over the world give us good reason for optimism. In London's rundown East End, the site of the 2012 Olympic Games, stadiums are giving way to schools, arenas are being converted into affordable housing, and thousands of new jobs are slated to come to the neighborhood. Rio de Janeiro is working with IBM to streamline its emergency response services, including state-of-the-art systems to help monitor weather and traffic, greatly improving response times and the quality of life in Brazil's frenetic metropolis. On the outskirts of Abu Dhabi, a new zero-carbon, zero-waste metropolis, Masdar City, is springing up from the desert, drawing its energy from solar power and other alternative technologies.

A similar movement is happening in metropolitan areas across the United States, where creativity and innovation—two of the nation's greatest resources—are most concentrated. The timing is no coincidence. As has happened many times throughout American history, many of the greatest innovations have come at times of great challenge, and this moment, on the heels of a string of economic troubles, is no exception. The financial crisis and the Great Recession proved that we could no longer apply old solutions to new urban problems, nor could cities exclusively rely on the action of the federal government. Rather, local governments and civil society as well as business leaders and urban planners have come together to chart their own course to spark job creation and catalyze long-term economic growth.

In *The Metropolitan Revolution*, Bruce Katz and Jennifer Bradley describe, in good detail, many examples of how this economic, social, and political transformation is playing out across the United States. The authors are more than just passive narrators. Rather, through the Brookings Metropolitan Policy Program, which Bruce founded, both he and Jennifer have been actively shaping a future that will be powerfully and distinctly urban. They are supremely suited to tell these stories and help us put this revolution into greater context.

Here are just a few of the stories you will encounter.

In Denver, elected officials have joined with civic and business leaders to transform the mountainous urban area into a world-class city, including one of the largest transit system expansions in the country, to attract new visitors and potential residents with its high quality of life.

In Northeast Ohio, leaders from philanthropy, private business, and nonprofit organizations are working across four metropolitan areas to create the necessary connections for a new age of advanced, innovative manufacturing and production, working as a cohesive unit for collective progress.

In Houston, a 100-year-old settlement house bridges the gap between isolated neighborhoods and the metropolitan scale of the economy.

In Los Angeles, the city's efforts to compress thirty years of transit and transportation infrastructure construction into ten years have catalyzed a successful nationwide push for federal transportation finance reform.

In New York City, a global metropolis highly dependent on the financial services sector, the city is working toward a more diversified, technologically innovative economy, creating new Applied Sciences campuses that are marrying new technology to established industries, creating a new field of urban science.

Although they hail from different places, different economic backgrounds, and different political parties, the actors you will meet in these pages are part of a pragmatic caucus, acting decisively to grow jobs in the near term and retool their metropolitan economies for the long haul. They are integrating their economic growth strategies with their unique assets and their competitive specializations, creating metro economies that export more and waste less, have sectors that serve as engines for both innovation and job creation, manufacture and ship more of what their workers invent and build, and create spaces where families can live, work, and prosper.

For much of its 100 years, the Rockefeller Foundation has supported the transformation of cities as part of its mission to promote the well-being of humanity around the world. From smart financing of large-scale infrastructure to new, citizen-centered e-governance to some of the great work described in this book, we are proud to be a part of the metropolitan revolution that Bruce and Jennifer are helping to lead and hope you will join them in supporting these triumphs and replicating their successes in cities across America and around the world.

JUDITH RODIN
President, Rockefeller Foundation

ACKNOWLEDGMENTS

There is no better example of the benefits of agglomeration than the Brookings Metropolitan Policy Program. Our colleagues have made us smarter, sharper, more thoughtful, more careful, and more generous. They have freely and happily shared their time, their resources, and their ideas. And every single day they make us eager to come to work.

This book would not exist but for the outstanding, tireless, and imaginative research efforts of Allison Courtin, Peter Hamp, Siddharth Kulkarni, Joseph Parilla, and Owen Washburn. They were true partners in this undertaking, breaking intellectual logjams with brilliant ideas or exactly the right data. They not only answered every research question we put to them, they answered questions we had not even thought of yet. And they worked unbelievably hard day in and day out. Any words of praise fall far short of capturing the importance of their work to this book. Julie Wagner's deep experience in domestic and global metros was invaluable in helping us think through the exciting possibilities of innovation districts and trading cities and greatly informed the shape, structure, and content of chapters 6 and 7. Hilary Robinson brought her keen insights on the past, present, and future of federalism to bear on chapter 8.

We also benefited from outstanding interns: Ethan Ebinger, Irene Garcia, Kevin Howard, Elisabeth von Hammerstein, and especially Susan Charlop and Sam Vitello, who were nominally interns but quickly became more like peers.

We would especially like to thank Alan Berube, Carrie Kolasky, Amy Liu, Mark Muro, and Rob Puentes for their engagement, leadership, and encouragement during the long process of writing this book. They corrected mistakes, suggested significant improvements, and have made this book much better than it otherwise would have been. Shyamali Choudhury, Kenan Fikri, Jeanine Forsythe, William Frey, Alec Friedhoff, Marek Gootman, Emilia Istrate, Elizabeth Kneebone, Jessica Lee, Nick Marchio, Mariela Martinez, Brad McDearman, Carey Nadeau, Martha Ross, Jonathan Rothwell, Neil Ruiz, Devashree Saha, Chad Shearer, Audrey Singer, Adie Tomer, Jennifer Vey, and Jill Wilson also contributed to this book through their research, which we have cited throughout, their editorial eye, their sharp questions, and their willingness to review drafts and help whenever we were stuck on a particular point.

Marikka Green somehow manipulated the time-space continuum to give Bruce the weeks and days necessary to write. Dana Chieco, Carrie Collins, Jody Franklin, Rachel Harvey, Ellen Ochs, Amelia Shister, and Karen Slachetka, as well as Leah Frelinghuysen of Monarchy PR, have devoted their considerable energy, skills, and wit to making sure that this book finds its audience.

Laura Mooney, the Brookings interlibrary loan librarian, was tireless in finding articles and books, no matter how obscure, from Ács to Ziegler. Every intellectual traveler should have such a diligent quartermaster. Bob Faherty, Chris Kelaher, and Janet Walker at the Brookings Press were exceedingly patient in waiting for this book to be written and exceptionally gracious when we said, "We know the manuscript is months overdue, but now that it's done, how soon can we publish?" We are grateful for their guidance.

Strobe Talbott, the president of the Brookings Institution, is in many ways the godfather of this book. His persistent encouragement got us started and kept us going.

Research that we and our Brookings colleagues have done under the auspices of the Brookings-Rockefeller Project on State and Metropolitan Innovation inspired the stories and concepts presented in the book, and we are grateful for the Rockefeller Foundation's contributions. The Ford Foundation, the John D. and Catherine T. MacArthur Foundation, the Heinz Endowments, the George Gund Foundation, the Kresge Foundation, and the Surdna Foundation provide general support for the research and policy efforts of the Metropolitan Policy Program, and those research and policy efforts are the foundation on which this book rests. We would also like to thank the Brookings Metropolitan Leadership Council, a network of individual, corporate, and philanthropic investors who also provide the Metropolitan Policy Program with financial support but, more important, are true intellectual partners. Cheryl Cohen Effron, Rick Kimball, Jim Robinson, and Jamie Rubin have been particularly engaged with this process and generous with their ideas and encouragement. Finally, we would like to thank Jim Johnson, who established the urban and metropolitan affairs presence at Brookings almost seventeen years ago and has guided the program ever since.

We would also like to thank the people in each of the metropolitan areas who helped us understand their stories so well and patiently responded to our many questions. In New York City: Benjamin Branham, Johanna Greenbaum, Steven Koonin, Eugene Lee, Seth Pinsky, Kevin Ryan, Deputy Mayor Robert Steel, Charles Vest (based in Washington), and Kathryn Wylde. In Denver: Colorado governor John Hickenlooper, Mayor Michael Hancock, former mayor Federico Peña, Centennial mayor Cathy Noon, former Centennial mayor Randy Pye, Tom Clark, Michael Dino, Tami Fischer, Ismael Guerrero, Peter Kenney, Shepard Nevel, Mike Turner, and Bill Van Meter. In Northeast Ohio: David Abbott, Rebecca Bagley, Robert Jaquay, Molly Schnoke, Baiju Shah, Chris Thompson, and Brad Whitehead. In Houston: Adonias Arevalo, Angela Blanchard, Ray Chung, Oriana Garcia, Roberta Leal, Margie Pena, Claudia Vasquez, and the staff at Neighborhood Centers, Inc. In Detroit: Dave Egner, Steve Hamp, and Benjy Kennedy. In Portland: Michael Gurton, Chris Harder, Derrick Olsen, Sean Robbins, Noah Siegel, and Mitsuhiro Yamazaki. In Miami: Janet Jainarain and Manny Mencia. In São Paulo: Denerson Mota. In addition, Xavier de Souza Briggs and Bob Weissbourd read chapter drafts and helped us clarify and, when necessary, correct our arguments. Kristen Grimm of Spitfire Strategies suggested a one-word title change early in the process that changed everything for the better.

We could spend page after page praising and thanking our outstanding editor, Wylie O'Sullivan. Without her, this book would be twice as long and half as readable. Wylie gently corrected our policy-wonk prose and made sure that we did not bury our ideas in jargon and statistics. She was as eager to find the good in the manuscript as to fix the bad. Working with her was a pleasure from start to finish.

Bruce would like to thank Roberta Achtenberg, Andy Altman, Richard Baron, MarySue Barrett, Ricky Burdett, Henry Cisneros, Deb McKoy, Jeremy Nowak, Wolfgang Nowak, Neil Peirce, Anne Power, Nic Retsinas, Michael Stegman, and Julie Wagner for their friendship over the years and their profound influence on his intellectual evolution.

Jennifer would like to thank friends and family members who listened as she talked about little else but this book for months, asked great questions, and enabled her to see old ideas with fresh eyes. Others helped without even knowing they were helping, by providing her space to collect her thoughts: Evan Bradley, Pam Bradley, Steve Bradley, Thea Wieseltier, Joshua Fattal, Isabel Fattal, Rick Boeth, Stacy Burdett, Shari Diamond, Tova Jaffe, Sonja Johansson, Lindsay Kaplan, Howard Rosen, Emma Saal, Kristen Silverberg, Martina Vandenberg, and Heather Way.

Bruce is also humbled by his family's love and support throughout the process of creating this book. They were ever patient and encouraging during the litany of shortened vacations, disrupted weekends, and hourly distractions.

Bruce dedicates this book to his father, with whom he spent decades exploring cities, history, politics, and ideas. Jennifer dedicates this book to Leon Wieseltier and Matthew Wieseltier, to whom she owes so many discoveries and so much joy.

1

A REVOLUTION UNLEASHED

I will not tie this city's future to the dysfunction in Washington and Springfield.

—RAHM EMANUEL, *mayor of Chicago*

A revolution is stirring in America. Like all great revolutions, this one starts with a simple but profound truth: Cities and metropolitan areas are the engines of economic prosperity and social transformation in the United States.

Our nation's top 100 metropolitan areas sit on only 12 percent of the nation's land mass but are home to two-thirds of our population and generate 75 percent of our national GDP. Metros dominate because they embody concentration and agglomeration—networks of innovative firms, talented workers, risk-taking entrepreneurs, and supportive institutions and associations that cluster together in metropolitan areas and coproduce economic performance and progress. There is, in essence, no American (or Chinese or German or Brazilian) economy; rather, a national economy is a network of metropolitan economies.

Cities and metropolitan areas are also on the frontlines of America's demographic change. America's population—and its workforce—will be much more diverse in the future than at present, and soon no single race or ethnic group will be the nation's majority. Many of our metros are already living that

The term city is frequently used to describe a metropolitan area, region, and urban agglomeration—interconnected local economies that represent the hubs of larger state and national economies. In this book, we distinguish between cities and metropolitan areas. A metropolitan area or metropolitan region is typically a collection of municipalities that together form a unified labor market and is often defined statistically by the commuting patterns of its residents between home and work. For instance, the Chicago metro area consists of hundreds of municipalities and fourteen counties that stretch across the U.S. states of Illinois, Indiana, and Wisconsin; the city of Chicago accounts for less than one-third of the metro population. The São Paulo metropolitan area includes not only the city of São Paulo but also thirty-eight surrounding municipalities within the Brazilian state of São Paulo. The geographic extent of these broader regions takes in economic activities that are often found outside cities themselves, such as manufacturing, logistics, and agriculture.

future. In fact, every major demographic trend that the United States is experiencing—rapid growth, increasing diversity, an aging demographic—is happening at a faster pace, a greater scale, and a higher level of intensity in our major metropolitan areas.

Empowered by their economic strength and driven by demographic dynamism, cities and metros are positioning themselves at the cutting edge of reform, investment, and innovation. In traditional political science textbooks, the United States is portrayed neatly as a hierarchical structure—the federal government and the states on top, the cities and metropolitan areas at the bottom. The feds and the states are the adults in the system, setting direction; the cities and metropolitan areas are the children, waiting for their allowance. The metropolitan revolution is exploding this tired construct. Cities and metropolitan areas are becoming the leaders in the nation: experimenting, taking risk, making hard choices, and asking forgiveness, not permission.

Like all great revolutions, this one has been ignited by a spark. The Great Recession was and continues to be a shock to the American zeitgeist, a brutal wake-up call that revealed the failure of a growth model that exalted consumption over production, speculation over investment, and waste over sustainability. A new growth model and economic vision is emerging from the rubble of the recession, a next economy where we export more and waste less, innovate in what matters, produce and deploy more of what we invent, and build an economy that works for working families.

The default proposition in the post–New Deal era is that the restructuring of a national economy as complex and diverse as America's would be led by the national government. Indeed, in the immediate aftermath of the Great Recession, the federal government stepped in, and stepped up, with a stimulus package that kept the economy from collapse and stabilized state and local governments reeling from the housing-market freefall.

But now, four years after the recession's official end, it is clear that the real, durable reshaping is being led by networks of city and metropolitan leaders—mayors and other local elected officials, for sure, but also heads of companies, universities, medical campuses, metropolitan business associations, labor unions, civic organizations, environmental groups, cultural institutions, and philanthropies. These leaders are measuring what matters, unveiling their distinctive strengths and starting points in the real economy: manufacturing, innovation, technology, advanced services, and exports. They are eschewing fanciful illusions of becoming the next Silicon Valley and instead are deliberately building on their special assets, attributes, and advantages, using business planning techniques honed in the private sector. They are remaking their urban and suburban places as livable, quality, affordable, sustainable communities and offering more residential, transport, and work options to firms and families alike. And they are doing all these things through coinvention and coproduction.

Similar to the Tea Party and the Occupy movements, the metropolitan revolution is a child of the Great Recession. Yet it is reasoned rather than emotional, leader driven rather than leaderless, born of pragmatism and optimism rather than despair and anger.

Like all great revolutions, this one has been catalyzed by a revelation: Cities and metropolitan areas are on their own. The cavalry is not coming. Mired in partisan division and rancor, the federal government appears incapable of taking bold action to restructure our economy and grapple with changing demography and rising inequality. Recent Supreme Court decisions have also circumscribed the ability of the federal government to respond to national challenges. States are a varied lot. Some, often under the leadership of mayors-turned-governors, are aligning policies and programs to meet the needs of their metropolitan engines; some are too broke and broken to engage and, in fact, are scaling back investments in critical areas like education, redevelopment, and community health; still others have a long history of antagonism toward their urban and metropolitan engines.

With each illustration of partisan gridlock and each indication of federal, and also state, unreliability, metros are becoming more ambitious in their design, more assertive in their advocacy, more expansive in their reach and remit. To borrow from Pogo, metro leaders have met the solution, and it is them.

With innovation the clear driver of economic growth and productivity and federal innovation funding at risk, metros like New York are making sizable commitments to attract innovative research institutions, commercialize research, and grow innovative firms. With human capital the necessary ingredient for successful firms and places, metros like Chicago are overhauling their community college systems to ensure that students are trained for quality jobs that offer good wages and benefits. With infrastructure the platform for global trade and investment and no national freight policy in place, metros like Miami and Jacksonville are modernizing their air, rail, and sea freight hubs to position themselves for an expansion in global trade.

With companies and consumers demanding communities that are more spatially efficient and federal funding for transportation uncertain, metros like Los Angeles, Denver, and Chicago are largely self-financing the building and retrofit of their own transit systems. With global demand rising and the future of federal trade policy unclear, metros like Portland, Syracuse, and Minneapolis–St. Paul are reorienting their economic development strategies toward exports, foreign direct investment, and skilled immigration.

With the world undergoing a systemic shift toward sustainable growth (a third industrial revolution) and federal energy and environmental policies under siege, metros like Seattle and Philadelphia are cementing their niches in energy-efficient technologies. And with immigration altering the social fabric of American society and national immigration reform seemingly impossible to achieve, metros like Houston are taking innovative steps to integrate tens of thousands of new immigrants into economic and community life.

The metro revolution reflects the maturing of U.S. cities and metros in terms of capacity and focus. Over the past three decades, these communities have innovated on the form of their places, regenerating downtowns, revitalizing waterfronts, restoring historic buildings, inspiring grand architecture, expanding transit and transportation choices. Now they are focusing on their function and the very shape and structure of their economies, taking on the core elements that drive economies: innovation, human capital, infrastructure, advanced industry.

Over the past three decades, these places have labored to improve the delivery of core services such as education and public safety to ensure good schools, safe streets, and a high quality of life. Now they are innovating in the service of a grander ambition and necessary purpose: a local economy that generates wealth and shares prosperity.

For fifty years, metropolitan areas have relied on their biggest single investor—the federal government—to finance infrastructure, housing, innovation, and human capital. They have dutifully competed for federal grants and aligned their visions and strategies to the federal focus du jour. Now cities and metros are driving the conversation, making transformative investments in the public goods that undergird private investment and growth.

The tectonic plates of power and responsibility are shifting. Across the nation, cities and metros are taking control of their own destinies, becoming deliberate about their economic growth. Power is devolving to the places and people who are closest to the ground and oriented toward collaborative action. This shift is changing the nature of our leadership—who our leaders are, what they do, and how they govern. The metropolitan revolution has only one logical conclusion: the inversion of the hierarchy of power in the United States.

A REVOLUTION IN TUNE

The metropolitan revolution is accelerated by the twinned failure of the economy and Washington. But what is happening in the United States today is also rooted in timeless and quintessential American values and is uniquely aligned with the disruptive nature of this young century and the manner and places in which people live their lives. The emerging revolution is not just a cyclical reaction but also a structural shift.

Our federal republic alternates between an emphasis on the "republic" and the "federal." Power is at once centralized and diffuse, among states as constitutional partners and, in this century, among cities and metropolitan areas as de facto engines of the economy and social change. This diffusion, endlessly varied, often chaotic, is central to the American entrepreneurial strain and cultural narrative. Like Chicago's mayor Rahm Emanuel, local politicians and other leaders have long held an ambivalence toward Washington. This reflects an ingrained American suspicion of institutions that are remote, removed, and far from home. Leaders in cities and metropolitan areas are close to the ground. They shop in local stores, eat at local establishments. They are seen and accessible, open to informal, everyday conversation rather than the formal interactions of legislatures and bureaucracies. Cities and metros aggregate people and places in a geography that is large enough to make a difference but small enough to impart a sense of community and common purpose.

Yet the metropolitan revolution is not only about the local and traditional. It is also thoroughly attuned to the pace and tenor of modern life driven by technology and globalization. We are living in a disruptive moment that worships speed, extols collaboration, rewards customization, demands differentiation, and champions integrated thinking to match and master the complexities of modern economies and societies. The metropolitan revolution is like our era: crowd sourced rather than close sourced, entrepreneurial rather than bureaucratic, networked rather than hierarchical.

In a world in which people live, operate, communicate, and engage through networks, metros have emerged as the uber-network: interlinked firms, institutions, and individuals working together across sectors, disciplines, jurisdictions, artificial political borders, and, yes, even political parties. In the process, a new kind of metropolitan leadership is being spawned. It is, at its core, a pragmatic caucus, which puts place over party, collaboration over conflict, and evidence over dogma. As New York mayor Michael Bloomberg observed in remarks to the Economic Club of Washington, D.C., "As a result of [the federal] leadership vacuum, cities around the country have had to tackle our economic problems largely on our own. Local elected officials are responsible for doing, not debating. For innovating, not arguing. For pragmatism, not partisanship. We have to deliver results at the local level."[1]

Members of this pragmatic caucus share common traits. They are impatient. They do not tolerate ideological nonsense or political bromides. They are frustrated with gridlock and inaction. They bristle at conventional pessimism and focus on constructive optimism. They are risk takers. They do not have a partisan allegiance; they have a political attitude.

With its broad-based membership, the pragmatic caucus defies easy political categorization. In Houston, a network of Republican business leaders supports and champions one of the most advanced immigrant integration efforts in the nation. In Salt Lake City, a far-reaching effort to curb sprawl and promote reinvestment is taking place in a state that has not voted for a Democratic presidential candidate since 1964. In Portland, Oregon, a metropolis best known for its commitment to smart growth, a diverse set of leaders are embracing an ambitious agenda to boost trade, exports, and foreign direct investment.

The contrast between the federal and state governments and metropolitan networks is stark. The federal government and the states are legacy institutions: hyper political and partisan, hopelessly fragmented and compartmentalized, frustratingly bureaucratic, and prescriptive.

The federal government and the states are present oriented. They govern, administer, and legislate in two-year cycles, aligned more with the timeline of political elections than with social or market dynamics. By contrast, the new metropolitan leadership is intensely focused on, in the words of John Hofmeister, a former president of Shell Oil, "getting the future right."[2] They think in the long term, act in the short run. Twenty of the top fifty metropolitan areas in the country now have formal planning efforts to achieve specific growth targets by 2040.[3]

The federal and state governments, at their core, establish laws and promulgate rules. In so doing, they reflect the curse of the twentieth-century Weberian state: highly specialized, overly legalistic, prescriptive rather than permissive, process oriented rather than outcome directed. They reward consumers who play by the rules, check the box, and confine their innovations to tightly circumscribed boundaries. Cities and metropolitan areas, by contrast, are action oriented. They reward innovation, imagination, and pushing boundaries. As networks of institutions (for example, firms, agencies, schools), they run businesses, provide services, educate children, train workers, build homes, and develop community. They focus less on promulgating rules than on delivering the goods and using cultural norms rather than regulatory mandates to inspire best practice. They reward leaders who push the envelope, catalyze action, and get stuff done.

The federal and state governments are organized as a collection of hardened silos, fragmented executive agencies overseen by separate legislative committees. These agencies look down at challenges, conforming and confining the reach of solutions to the powers and resources at hand. A transportation agency responds to transportation challenges (for example, congestion) with transportation solutions (for example, widening a road), affirming the old adage "If the only tool you have is a hammer, everything looks like a nail." Cities and metros are, by contrast, organic communities. Multiple public, private, and civic actors are empowered to look across challenges, naturally connecting the dots between related issues. Resolving a transport challenge, for example, might most effectively and efficiently be achieved through a shift in housing or jobs location or alternative means of transportation. Metros are integrated rather than compartmentalized.

The federal and state governments focus on atomistic firms and workers and silver-bullet tax and regulatory solutions. Cities and metros, by contrast, blend the ecosystem and the enterprise. They focus not just on a singular transaction, firm, or solution but rather on building effective structures, institutions, intermediaries, and platforms to give dozens of entrepreneurs and firms what they need: skilled talent, strategic capital, stable governance, reliable rules, functioning infrastructure, collective branding, and marketing.

The federal and state governments, driven by outworn notions of legislative horse-trading, prefer one-size-fits-all solutions that serve to frustrate rather than placate. They spread resources across the landscape of the nation and their states like peanut butter on a slice of bread, diluting return on investment and diminishing public confidence in public action. Cities and metropolitan areas are, by contrast, aligned and attuned to the differentiated nature of their economies. They build on their distinctive strengths, buttress and leverage their specific assets, attributes, and advantages. They follow Dolly Parton's maxim: "Find out who you are and do it on purpose."[4]

The federal and state governments constitute passive, representative democracy; citizens' only active role is to vote at designated intervals. Cities and metropolitan areas constitute active, participatory democracy: tens, if not hundreds, of thousands of leaders who collectively steward their places, guide their regions, and coproduce their economies.

The federal and state governments think in terms of constituencies competing against one another for scarce resources and routinely practice divide-and-conquer tactics. Because they are dominated by legislatures that are divided by party and ideology, they reward those who rely on partisan calculus and engage in partisan combat. There, good politics is good policy—for individuals seeking to move up the legislative ladder. Cities and metropolitan areas think in terms of networks that act together to achieve common goals and encourage collaboration and teamwork. They have a different disposition toward progress and continuous improvement. There, good policy is good politics—for individuals seeking to gain community trust and commitment.

Metropolitan leaders, in short, own challenges in ways that representatives of higher levels of government do not. Problems like congestion, educational performance, or economic progress are experienced rather than studied. Leaders live daily with the consequences of their decisions. Metropolitan success is tangible and almost tactile: it can be tasted, touched, and felt in ways that abstract national actions cannot.

A REVOLUTION'S PROMISE

The metropolitan revolution offers the United States its best chance to revive its national economy, reboot its national competitiveness, and restore purpose to its politics and civility to its commons. For a national economy stuck in first gear, the metropolitan growth model offers the promise of more jobs (to resolve America's employment deficit), better jobs (to make work pay), and more accessible jobs (to ensure workers can get to those jobs). Against all odds, cities and metros are working to restructure the economy away from tantalizing illusion (endless consumption and irresponsible speculation) and back toward hard fundamentals: talent-fuelled production and innovation. The prerecession economy, driven by consumption and amenities, celebrated the uniform. The next economy, driven by production and innovation, rewards the distinct.

For a nation undergoing profound demographic transformation, the metropolitan model of education and social integration provides a path toward managing growth and diversity in a way that lifts all boats. Cities and metros understand intuitively what the nation fitfully remembers and often contests: the United States is demographically blessed, and diversity is its greatest competitive advantage and strength.

For a nation paralyzed by hyper partisanship, the metropolitan model of collaboration offers a sensible counterpoint. Cities and metros are honoring the lessons learned at early age in the sandbox: those who play well together reap mutual rewards and benefits.

For a nation confronting new global realities, the metropolitan model of global engagement reveals another lesson: places that link together grow together. In many respects, cities and metros are guiding the world back to the pre-Westphalian era, when networks of trading cities—the ancient Silk Road, the medieval Hanseatic League—provided the platform for relationships of mutual benefit and exchange.

The lines, in essence, between the macro and the metro, the global, the national, and the local, have become blurred. Cities and metros, lacking any choice, are innovating on the big stuff: policies and practices that drive the wealth-generating, tradable sectors of the economy; commercialization of innovation; support for advanced manufacturing, export promotion, and foreign direct investment; public-private financing of advanced transport and energy infrastructure; upgrading the education and skills of a diversifying workforce; attracting foreign-born talent and assimilating immigrants; engaging globally on the seamless movement of people, goods, services, ideas, and capital; forging strong relationships with trading partners in mature and rising economies alike.

If American history is any guide, these metropolitan innovations will not begin or end in isolation. We know that innovations naturally replicate "horizontally" across multiple cities and metros, adapted and tailored to the unique circumstances of disparate places. Cities and metros are fast, eager learners, ever observant of their peers, able to move quickly to spot innovation elsewhere and apply it at home. A smart export strategy in Portland will inform thinking and action in Phoenix within months, given easy access to information and the tendency of smart ideas to spread virally in a political market.

The natural metropolitan propensity for innovation and replication is being sped up by market adoption, technological progress, and global urbanization. The metropolitan revolution is inventing new ways of financing and delivering transformative infrastructure investments and game-changing initiatives, partly to substitute for declining government resources, partly as a result of the growing sophistication of public-private techniques. The revolution is being televised by twenty-first-century means, deploying the disruptive technological tools of the young century, particularly the Internet and the social media it has enabled. Metropolitan ideas and practices are leapfrogging state and even national borders, moving across borders with the speed of a click or the concision of a tweet. Ideas are also being spread, face to face, metro to metro, by the new globalists—multilateral institutions and multinational corporations, for sure, but also transnational philanthropies, associations, think tanks, and intermediaries that are now focused on the rise of cities as the dominant trend worldwide.

Local and metropolitan innovations also tend to scale up vertically, at the state and then the national level. City and metropolitan innovations today (government reinvention, school reform, smart growth, infrastructure finance) become federal and state innovations tomorrow. This is a time-honored tradition in the United States. It occurs partly because successful mayors and metro leaders tend to move up the political ladder (bringing their pragmatic ethic and favored reforms with them), partly because local innovators gain political legitimacy and currency, and partly because the political class is perennially hungry for new ideas and initiatives.

The scale-up of metropolitan innovation is also a product of raw politics. The political power of cities and metropolitan areas has long lagged their economic primacy. Governmental fragmentation within metropolitan areas and historic city-suburb divisions have been a challenge, as have differences in priorities among metropolitan areas, within and across states. Yet this is changing. The extent of policy innovation at the metro scale, and growing frustration with the dysfunction of higher levels, is yielding new cross-jurisdictional, bipartisan, multisectoral coalitions that, in turn, are clamoring for federal and state reforms that, at a maximum, support and extend local efforts and, at a minimum, do no harm.

The logic of today's metropolitan revolution is unveiling a third path for progress. The revolution is occurring at the very time that the United States is having its most vital and virulent debate in decades about the size and scale of the federal government. The federal government will scale back in the coming years. But the current debate, largely framed around deficit targets, entitlement spending, and programmatic budgets, is not sufficient. This is not a mathematical exercise but a choice about core national priorities. We face fundamental decisions, about not just the size of the federal government but also its purpose, not just the scale of the federal government but also its scope, not just federal focus but also federalist delivery.

As cities and metros step up, states and the federal government may be moved to do less but do it better, to cut speculative spending, invest in productive activity, and place their resources and policies fully in the service of metropolitan America. The United States is on the verge of a historic re-sorting, in which responsibilities once reserved for higher levels of government are being fully shared with, even shifted to, cities, metropolitan areas, and the networks of leaders who govern them. The federal government and the states could shift responsibilities de jure, as Germany did to its states with housing policies in the early years of this century, or, more likely, de facto, as metros rush in to fill financing gaps left by federal cutbacks. In any event, the federal government and the states will be motivated to do more with less by giving cities and metropolitan areas greater flexibility to design and allocate what are likely to be shrinking levels of resources.

REALIZING THE REVOLUTION

This is a book about fully realizing the metropolitan revolution, a manifesto for change and action. In 2013 we find ourselves at a crossroads. On one hand, the United States has grown a network of metropolitan economies and metropolitan polities that are endowed with assets, rich in leadership, and fundamentally oriented toward problem solving and progress. On the other hand, we have a federal government (and, unfortunately, a hefty number of states) that is paralyzed by ideological division, and driven more by short-term political gain than long-term national progress. The metropolitan revolution could not be further—in spirit, in tone, in constitution—from the farce currently being played out in Washington, D.C., and in many state capitals.

We intend, in the first instance, to chronicle a revolution in motion by exploring metropolitan areas that illustrate a mix of individual leadership and institutional heft, of idealism and pragmatism, of affirmative vision and realpolitik. We will look, for instance, at economy shaping in New York City and Northeast Ohio, society building in Houston, coalition building in Denver and Los Angeles. These and other places we visit in this book are a repudiation of the current national myth that America lacks leadership at the very time we confront supersize challenges and Solomonic choices.

Yet cities and metropolitan areas, even if they are largely on their own, cannot go it alone. Federal and state governments are dysfunctional but powerful actors. If the states are an irresponsible parent, the federal government is a distant, often clueless relative—who nonetheless controls the family money. Washington also has a crippling hoarding disorder: everything is collected, nothing is discarded. After decades of growth, the government has become an accretion of program over program, regulation over regulation, law over law. As Washington struggles with deficit reduction, it is not enough to get the federal fiscal house in order. It is time for a housecleaning of epic proportions—and for a national policy in the service of cities and metropolitan areas in order to fully realize and leverage the competitive assets and advantages of our national engines.

The metropolitan revolution under way in the United States is a step change in political consciousness and collective action. The transformative actions taken by metros today are innovative and promising. But they are not uniformly applied, and there is much work to be done to ensure that the metropolitan revolution is the norm rather than the exception.

Metropolitan areas *can* situate themselves economically. They can understand who they are, how they are special, what they invent and trade, and whom they trade with and then decide to measure what matters by charting progress, keeping score, and assessing effort.

Metropolitan areas *can* innovate locally. They can act on their distinctive strengths in strategic ways. They can stop subsidizing the stupid stuff and start investing in those things that create jobs and generate wealth, a metropolitan version of the cut-to-invest strategy we recommend for the federal government and the states. They can get back on track and stay on track.

Metropolitan areas *can* network globally. Knowing their trading partners, they can structure intimate and sustained relationships across governments, firms, and institutions to undergird the seamless flow of goods, services, people, capital, and ideas. This is what will fuel exchange and commerce in our urban age.

Finally, metropolitan areas *can* advocate nationally. On paper, they are a supermajority in the nation and a supermajority in most states. There is nothing—*nothing*—that can stop metropolitan political coalitions that are organized, focused, and engaged.

They can do all these things with precision and granularity, with ambition and vision, with persistent dedication and hard work.

We do not believe in fairy tales. The federal government will not heal itself any time soon. The states are political artifices, not natural markets. We do, however, believe in metropolitan pragmatism, metropolitan power, and metropolitan potential.

This book explains why.

PART **I**

THE LIVING LABORATORY
The Metropolitan Revolution Today

2

NEW YORK:
INNOVATION AND THE NEXT ECONOMY

No amount of savings and investment, no policy of macroeconomic fine-tuning, no set of tax and spending incentives can generate sustained economic growth unless it is accompanied by the countless large and small discoveries that are required to create more value from a fixed set of natural resources.

—PAUL ROMER, *professor of economics, New York University*

In January 2009 the shock of the Lehman Brothers implosion had only just started to reverberate through the global economy. Over the course of the year, global economic activity would shrink by half a percent—the worst downturn since 1945.[1] By the end of the year, 7 million Americans had lost their jobs, and an additional 8.8 million were involuntarily working part-time. The unemployment rate had reached 10 percent nationwide.

New York's large financial sector made the city uniquely vulnerable to the fortunes of the industry where the crisis began. The collapse of Lehman Brothers was a watershed moment for New York City's economy, as it was for the global financial sector. After it became clear that there would be no buyers or bailouts for Lehman Brothers in September of 2008, the city began to lose jobs rapidly from other financial firms and in other sectors across the economy. In the fifteen months between August of 2008 and November of 2009, New York

City lost 36,000 jobs from its financial services sector alone.[2] As a result of those and other job losses, city tax revenue shrank by more than $2 billion in fiscal year 2009 and by another $1.4 billion the following year, exacerbating a budget gap of more than $4 billion. Lower government and consumer spending contributed to a recession that erased 139,000 jobs from city payrolls, with the brunt of the losses borne by workers outside the financial services industry.

In the days and weeks after Lehman Brothers fell, New York City's government had taken some immediate actions to mitigate the damage, expanding workforce training efforts and business loan programs and starting a job-search and information-sharing website for suddenly unemployed entry- and mid-level workers.[3] In early 2009 the city rolled out another suite of initiatives intended, at least in part, to keep former financial services employees from leaving the city in search of a job elsewhere. In hopes of turning investment bankers and analysts into new entrepreneurs, the city established new business incubators, a start-up investment fund, and a couple of boot camp–style programs for people who wanted to join a start-up or create one themselves.[4]

But even as they were promoting these efforts, Mayor Michael Bloomberg and other city leaders understood that they would have to take much more aggressive and creative steps than they had previously to diversify and rebalance New York's economy.[5] The Bloomberg administration and other groups had long recognized the importance of economic diversification and the city's overreliance on the financial industry, but following the collapse, they realized that the slice of the financial services industry that was hit hardest by the downturn and was likely to be weakest in the future, capital markets, was exactly the one in which the city had the highest concentration of jobs. The sectors that were likely to emerge the strongest were the ones in which the city lagged. So New York could not wait for the financial services sector to get back to normal. City leaders had no reason to believe that there would ever be a back to normal.

Figuring out what the postrecession economy might look like was a central focus not only of the mayor's office but also of the New York City Economic Development Corporation (NYCEDC), a nonprofit corporation that works closely with the city government to catalyze economic growth. The corporation was implementing many of the city's new entrepreneurial efforts, and it realized that trying to support new businesses and thereby bring new ideas and innovations to life was an approach that could do more than help financial services workers reinvent themselves. Innovation and entrepreneurship could be a path to reinventing the city's overall economy.

With this idea in mind, the NYCEDC started to work on what it called a game-changers initiative. Staffers wanted to test their hypothesis that New York's future economic strength depended on the capacity of its residents and firms to innovate and the availability of a talented workforce to implement those innovations and come up with new ones. They also wanted to make sure that they were not overlooking other possibilities.

The inquiry started with a question: Imagine there are no funding constraints. What can or should we do to increase economic activity? All ideas, no matter how impractical or far-fetched, were welcome. Staff at the NYCEDC started by brainstorming among themselves and then spent months reaching out to 325 chief executive officers of companies of all sizes, more than twenty-five community groups, and more than a dozen deans and presidents of New York universities. These audiences were shown a short presentation about the direction of the city's economy and were then invited to imagine what should come next: How can New York City best retain and attract the talented people who make it thrive? What key aspects of our physical infrastructure are holding back growth? How can we do things differently to get more out of our limited resources? How can we employ our existing community resources to create good jobs for New Yorkers?

In early 2009 people all over the country were asking the same kinds of questions, both about their local economies and about the nation's economy. While New York struggled with the collapse of Lehman Brothers and related shake-outs in other sectors, cities and metros in Nevada and Florida wondered how to move ahead from the loud and painful bursting of the real estate bubble that had inflated their economies to wondrous but unsustainable size. Communities in Ohio, Kentucky, and Michigan were suddenly mired in their own foreclosure crises, compounded by another deep slide in the auto industry as General Motors and Chrysler wobbled on the precipice of bankruptcy. There was broad agreement that the postrecession economy needed to be very different from the real estate- and consumption-driven economy that had run aground. The United States needed, as Richard Florida calls his book about life after the crash, a "great reset."

There was also general consensus on the key elements of that reset or new strategy: innovation in science and technology, exports, and sustainability and new energy. For example, Jeffrey Immelt, the chairman and CEO of General Electric, told an audience in Detroit in June 2009 that the United States should have three priorities: "become a country that is good at manufacturing and exports," "win where it counts in clean energy," and "invest in new technology."[6] Lawrence Summers, the director of the National Economic Council, said one month later, "The rebuilt American Economy must be more export-oriented and less consumption-oriented, more environmentally-oriented and less fossil-energy-oriented, more bio- and software-engineering-oriented and less financial-engineering-oriented."[7]

In its meetings with business, civic, and academic leaders, the NYCEDC gleaned more than 100 ideas about how to move the city's economy forward, covering everything from generating electricity from subway turnstiles to immigration reform to better waterfront access. One of the themes that emerged consistently was that the city and the region needed more—much more—science and technology talent to drive its future. The NYCEDC was getting the same kind of feedback from people involved with its new incubators, investment funds, and related entrepreneurial efforts. "We were getting this feedback from multiple initiatives," recalled the NYCEDC's president, Seth Pinsky. "Simultaneously, we were hearing, 'We can't find the right talent, we are at a significant disadvantage to other areas.' It was more validation."

UNIVERSITIES ⟶ INNOVATION ⟶ CLUSTERING ⟶ MORE INNOVATION

Innovation is closely intertwined (although not synonymous) with new developments in science and technology, either breakthroughs that create entirely new systems or products or new applications of existing technology.[8] A historical survey of 220 famous entrepreneurs and inventors, reaching as far back as the nineteenth century, finds that these individuals were most likely to have engineering backgrounds (physics and chemistry degrees ranked second and third). Individuals who were both inventors and entrepreneurs overwhelmingly had engineering backgrounds. As technology becomes increasingly more sophisticated, engineering and other highly advanced degrees will be required to continually further innovations in niche fields.[9]

New York City had great strengths in biotech research but was significantly weaker in engineering. Whereas, for example, colleges and universities in metropolitan Boston and San Francisco spent $337 million and $299 million, respectively, on engineering R&D in 2006, New York City's colleges and universities spent less than one-third that amount.[10] Spending on R&D was also much less in the Greater New York metropolitan area than in either the Boston or San Francisco metros. New York's institutions also lagged well behind Boston, San Francisco, and other regions in attracting industry-funded research and development, which is also connected to engineering.[11] The city's top-ranked engineering school, Columbia University, granted 880 graduate engineering degrees in 2006; Stanford's graduate engineering class was almost twice as large and MIT's was 50 percent larger; even Georgia Tech outpaced Columbia.[12] The city also ranked thirty-third in the percentage of the metro area workforce employed in science and engineering jobs, behind not only tech hubs like San Jose, Austin, Boston, and San Francisco but also lagging Hartford, Sacramento, Houston, and Richmond, Virginia.[13]

The lament about too few engineers and similar technical professionals in New York was not new. According to Kathryn Wylde, the president and CEO of the Partnership for New York City, a nonprofit organization of CEOs focused on the city's economic growth, the need for more technical skills in the New York workforce "had basically been the drumbeat since Silicon Alley in the 1990s."[14] As years passed, the city's lack of a particular kind of technological talent was not only a problem for the tech sector but also for more traditional sectors. Recalling conversations about the need for more engineers, New York's deputy mayor Robert Steel said, "Every industry, every company is a technology company today. [Given the] growth rate in Macy's online business, they will have 150 people in their technology department. So Macy's is a tech-driven company." Companies in myriad industries in the city simply could not find the people who could translate their needs into new platforms, programs, and applications. So over the course of a year, from late 2009 to 2010, the NYCEDC researched how the city could best expand its pipeline of technological talent.

Technology strength often clusters around universities. Greater Boston and the San Francisco Bay Area were strong in technology and engineering because highly trained people worked in or graduated from top-ranked science and engineering departments there and tended not to leave. One study of MIT's impact on the Massachusetts economy puts it this way: "As a result of MIT, Massachusetts has for many years been dramatically 'importing' company founders. . . . More than 38 percent of the software, biotech, and electronics companies founded by MIT graduates are located in Massachusetts, while less than 10 percent of arriving MIT freshmen are from the state."[15] Google is in California largely because its founders were at Stanford.

There is, of course, a deep irony in the fact that technology, which was supposed to cut the ties between people and places and allow people everywhere to work from almost anywhere, turns out to flourish in fairly compact geographic concentrations. "Innovations cluster in places like Silicon Valley because ideas cross corridors and streets more easily than continents and seas," as the Harvard economist Edward L. Glaeser puts it.[16] In that respect, technology is no different from the garment industry that flourished in New York City in the nineteenth and early twentieth centuries, film production in Hollywood, music recording in Nashville, computer chip making in Portland, or scores of other examples from around the world and across centuries.

All of these industries benefit from—even depend on—the effects of clustering. Clusters are geographic concentrations of interconnected firms and supporting or coordinating organizations.[17] Silicon Valley has a cluster of professors, researchers, entrepreneurs, venture capitalists, intellectual property attorneys, and engineers who learn from one another, trade ideas, and hop between companies, bringing innovations with them and creating new ones that then spread out to other companies. This movement of ideas and people has the happy effect of making the workers and companies throughout the sector a little smarter and sharper than they would be by themselves. Firms and inventors located in clusters are also significantly more inventive than firms off on their own.[18] A host of studies have shown that clusters spur entrepreneurship and boost the survival chances of start-up firms.[19] Universities do not usually by themselves create clusters, but they can be powerful factors in maintaining and energizing them.[20]

The power of clusters and spillovers, multiplied over and over, explains why metropolitan areas and big cities like New York are the nation's innovation hubs.[21] The spillovers within and across clusters lead to new ideas and inventions. Eighty-two percent of the inventors granted patents in the United States between 2005 and 2012 lived in one of the largest 100 metro areas.[22] But metropolitan areas do not just produce more patents; the patents within metropolitan areas tend to be cited disproportionately by others within the same metropolitan area, meaning that inventors are learning from and building on the ideas immediately around them.[23] In Denver, for instance, many clusters like information technology, telecommunications, life sciences, optics, and aerospace all spill over into one another because the skills of workers and the technologies rooted in the region have many applications. In Rochester, Kodak collapsed but left behind a rich legacy embodied in new companies that are based on applying old skills in new ways, including web design, digital x-rays, military optic technology, and blood analyzers.[24]

THE APPLIED SCIENCES INITIATIVE

For its part, New York City already had a few tech clusters—some quite established, others just emerging. There was what one report called "a better than average foundation of [information technology] and biotech companies that easily could be built upon" as well as a large and growing digital media sector. Since these and many of the city's other clusters, such as fashion, media, and health care, needed engineering and technical talent, the NYCEDC concluded that the game changer they were looking for would be a new science and engineering graduate campus. The efforts of New York City's existing institutions were vitally important to the city's technologically infused future, but by themselves they were insufficient to attract or create the scores of scientists, hundreds of new laboratories, and thousands of graduate students that the city would need to scale up its technological capacities. The NYCEDC decided that building a brand-new institution from scratch was too risky; instead, they reasoned, the city's best bet was to find a capable and highly ranked institution or group of institutions that wanted to come to or expand in New York.

On December 16, 2010, Deputy Mayor Robert Steel unveiled the Applied Sciences NYC competition at Google's Manhattan offices. The city invited all universities in the world to enter a year-long contest to build a new campus in New York City. For its part, the city would provide one of four city-owned sites for the campus, along with a $100 million investment in infrastructure or other improvements. The competition showed that the NYCEDC and the city were willing to look beyond their borders—even internationally—for a source of engineering talent. Local university leaders were not terribly pleased by this decision, particularly after their presidents, deans, and other staff members had spent a considerable amount of time with the NYCEDC and city officials, work-ing through the feasibility of an applied sciences graduate school. "We had to take a courage pill with regard to going outside the city," Steel recalled.

The request for an expression of interest (RFEI) drew eighteen propos-als from twenty-seven institutions, including universities in Finland, India, Korea, and the United Kingdom.[25] In response to its full-dress request for proposals, issued in July 2011, the NYCEDC received seven final propos-als from universities (individually or as members of consortiums) from the United States, Israel, India, Canada, and the United Kingdom.[26] Through-out summer and fall of 2011, local media were reporting that "the contest has created world-wide buzz."[27]

New York's decision to make this an international contest fit with the city's understanding of itself as deeply engaged and enmeshed with the rest of the world. The material that the NYCEDC distributed in Decem-ber 2010 (the RFEI), explaining the Applied Sciences NYC competition and inviting universities to submit preliminary bids, proclaims, "NYC is your connection to the world and your entry to the U.S." and highlights the fact that "the City is the international nexus of the world, with a population that speaks more than 200 languages and hails from 138 coun-tries," including the largest Chinese population of any city outside of Asia and the largest Hispanic population of any city in the United States.[28] A presentation to interested universities also mentioned that the city had a growing share of immigrants from nations with emerging economies and thus had links back to those economies.[29] "Universities from around the country—and some from around the world—have expressed interest in our offer," Mayor Bloomberg said in a speech in mid-2011. "And that's how it should be. Because we are an international city—and a city that believes in free competition. We are open to any person with any dream, any entrepreneur with any idea, any company with any capital, and any university with any proposal."[30]

New York has the sixth-largest proportion of foreign-born residents of all large U.S. metropolitan areas, with more than 37 percent of its population, or 3,066,599 residents, born outside of the United States and a million more immigrant residents than Los Angeles. Metropolitan areas generally are where the United States starts to engage the rest of the world, and that global engagement is an important feature of the next economy. Essentially, metropolitan areas (both cities and suburbs) are where new immigrants and talent enter the country and where the goods, and especially the services, that are in high demand across the world are built and born. When New York City noted, as it did in its Applied Science NYC material, that it has the universities with the second- and third-highest shares of foreign students in the United States, it was highlighting one of its export strengths: the education of international students counts as a service export.

The international competition itself became part of the process of inquiry that taught the city and the NYCEDC what to aim for. The RFEI had detailed information about potential sites but not many specifics about what the city expected from the responding institutions. According to Seth Pinsky, "We were very deliberate in spelling out only what our goals were rather than telling schools how best to achieve them, in order to get from them their best thinking. . . . We were looking for investments universities could make that would have the biggest impact on the New York City economy. We left it open to people as to how big, where, how many faculty, how many students." Once the RFEI process concluded, the city and the NYCEDC had a better sense of what to ask for in the next round of the competition.

The city kicked off the final and most rigorous stage of the competition in July 2011, when it issued the request for proposals. Universities had less than four months to respond to the application packet, which ran to 129 pages and included questions on everything from institutional decisionmaking processes to fund-raising prowess, to number of patents garnered by faculty members, to the utility requirements for the proposed campus, to a thirty-year projection of cash flows to pay for it all. The tight deadlines of the Applied Sciences competition imbued the project with a sense of seriousness and urgency, which helped universities move their own boards to act more quickly. "You don't usually think that the ingredients for fast action are academia and government," Steel laughed. But, he went on, "deadlines create much more positive effects than negative effects. If you're squishy, it seems like a squishy project. We're serious people, and this is how a for-profit business would manage it, too. . . . We needed respondents to be all-in, not dial-in." Seventeen institutions, individually or as part of consortiums, submitted seven final proposals.

Although Mayor Bloomberg would ultimately decide the winner, the city and the NYCEDC continued to draw on outside advice as they evaluated the applications. For example, they asked representatives from schools that had not responded to the request for proposals to serve on an advisory board, alongside private sector representatives. The advisory board included Charles Vest, the president emeritus of MIT and the president of the National Academy of Engineering; Mark Burstein, the executive vice president of Princeton University; Paul Gray, the chair in electrical engineering at University of California at Berkeley; Joseph M. McShane, the president of Fordham University; Kevin Ryan, a long-time tech entrepreneur in New York; Charlie Kim, the founder and CEO of NextJump; Alan Patricof, the managing director and founder of Greycroft; Parag Saxena, the CEO of Vedanta Capital and New Silk Road Partners; and Kathryn Wylde, of the Partnership for New York City. Vest said that the advisory group guided the city on "what kinds of questions you should ask the [competing] institutions and why. They really needed to look for some unique themes in what the applicants wanted to do. As wonderful as Silicon Valley and Research Triangle Park are, this is the twenty-first century, and something different is needed." Based on the advisory board's input, the city and the NYCEDC started negotiating with applicants, asking them to refine or elaborate on particular parts of their proposals.

One year and one week after it first publicly proposed the idea, the city announced that Cornell and Technion–Israel Institute of Technology had won the right to build a new graduate school on Roosevelt Island, a tiny sliver of land in the East River between Manhattan and Queens. The announcement was undergirded by enforceable contracts that Cornell and Technion signed with the city, a $10 million escrow account backing the project, and hard and fast agreements in place with clear deadlines and penalties for failure to meet them. "Everything was mapped out," said Seth Pinsky, the president of the NYCEDC. Control of the campus site will be transferred by the last day of Mayor Bloomberg's term, and construction is scheduled to start in 2014.

Cornell's president, David Skorton, explained the new school's role this way: "We intend to be one more piece of the puzzle of how to further diversify the economy of the commercial center of the country, if not the world. . . . We're in a new phase of the technology revolution— not technology for technology's sake, but technology in the service of commerce."[31] The school, named Cornell NYC Tech, will eventually be home to 280 faculty members and up to 2,750 graduate students doing applied research in "hubs"—not traditional academic departments—of media, health industries, and the built environment.[32] Cornell, Technion,

New York City, and the NYCEDC all hope that graduates will help New York–based companies, nonprofits, and industries—ranging from hospitals to news companies, from museums to real estate developers—use new technologies to work better, more efficiently, or at a grander scale than they can with existing tools.

The school will offer a number of innovative services. For instance, the U.S. Patent and Trademark Office will create a resource center on Roosevelt Island once the campus is finished—the first such close collaboration between the agency and an academic campus.[33] Furthermore, the university will provide legal support for start-ups, establish a pre-seed financing program to support promising research, and create a $150 million revolving financing fund that will be solely devoted to start-up businesses in the city.

In January 2013 a "beta" class of enrollees in a one-year master of engineering program started school in 22,000 square feet of space within Google's New York City headquarters. (According to the *Wall Street Journal*, while the dean of Cornell's New York City campus was a visiting professor at Google one summer, he asked a friend who was in charge of research and special initiatives at Google whether the company could help out with space.)[34] A staff member from the patent office is on site. Twenty percent of each student's coursework consists of classes in entrepreneurship or interdisciplinary work (for example, connecting technology to particular industry concerns). In the spring of 2013, among the courses offered were CS 5091: Entrepreneurial Life and NBA 6850: Tech Enterprises. Fridays are reserved for interdisciplinary workshops. In addition to engineering and computer science professors, the faculty for the first semester included experts in entrepreneurship and a former chief technology officer of Twitter, Greg Pass, who himself graduated from Cornell in 1997.

When the city put multiple sites in play for the competition, they realized that that they could also have more than one winner. In April 2012 the mayor announced that there would be a second Applied Sciences campus. A consortium led by New York University would create this new school in the former headquarters of the New York Metropolitan Transportation Authority in downtown Brooklyn. The campus will be known as the Center for Urban Science and Progress (CUSP). "We are about applying the technologies of big data to urban problems and urban systems," said Steven Koonin, CUSP's founding director. The center's partners include NYU, NYU-Poly, Carnegie Mellon, the City University of New York, the Indian Institute of Technology, the University of Toronto, and the University of Warwick.

The city will provide $15 million in either new funds or abatements of funds due related to the site.[35] Both city and university officials hope that the redevelopment of the transit authority building will create investment and growth at the heart of the emerging "Brooklyn tech triangle," an area bound by downtown Brooklyn, the Dumbo neighborhood along the waterfront, and the Brooklyn Navy Yard, which has become a hub for niche manufacturers, tech companies, set designers, and media production. A first class of students will enroll in a brand-new degree program, the master in applied urban science and informatics, in the fall of 2013.

One early project will address urban noise, which is by far the greatest source of complaints to NYC 311, New York City's public service call system. "Nobody's gone out to map it, measure it, characterize it in terms of the source—traffic, HVAC, construction, and wind—and create a more efficient reporting and enforcement system," explained Koonin. Solving the problem of noise pollution is a massive interdisciplinary undertaking, requiring experts in databases, signal processing, geographic information systems, regulatory processes, and the arcane inner workings of city agencies. The center is designed to bring those types of specialists together. "It's not just about the technology. You really need the social sciences" to solve these problems, Koonin said. You also need data, and CUSP has agreed to work with both the Metropolitan Transit Authority and a host of city agencies to provide free analysis in return for the use of their data.[36] Other potential research projects include building energy efficiency, addressing particulate plumes from heating oil, and solving the perennial urban problem of parking.

Like Skorton at Cornell, Koonin understands that his project is not a typical ivory tower undertaking. "We need to be looking for projects that have a high impact, that can be done in a relatively timely way, [because] we have clocks ticking. . . . I've got contractual obligations with the city about the size of the research staff [and other metrics]. . . . I'm very concerned that we can actually deliver something in the next two years." The center will also work with private industry partners, including IBM, Cisco, ConEdison, National Grid, Siemens, Xerox, AECOM, Arup, IDEO, Lutron, and Microsoft, and government labs, including the Livermore, Los Alamos, and Sandia National Laboratories.

NEW YORK CITY'S APPLIED SCIENCES CAMPUSES

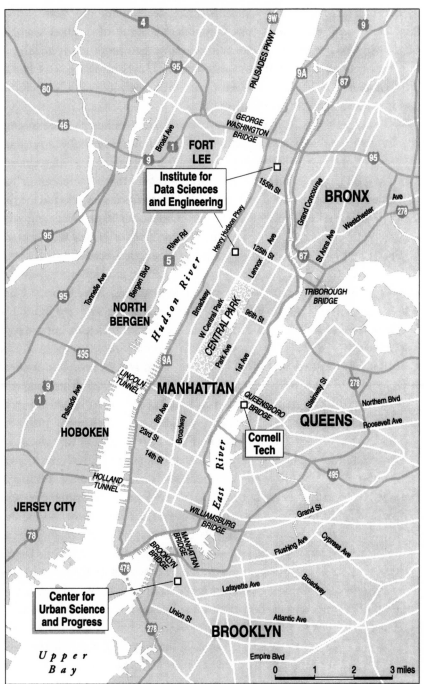

In July 2012 Columbia University's new Institute for Data Sciences and Engineering, located at its Morningside Heights and Washington Heights campuses in New York City, became the third Applied Sciences campus.[37] At Columbia, students and faculty will focus on applications for new media, smart cities, health analytics, cybersecurity, and financial analytics, among other areas. Columbia's deal, like NYU's, includes $15 million in various forms from the city.

In a rapidly urbanizing world, with more than 6 billion people expected to populate cities and metropolitan areas over the next several years, smart and sustainable municipal services, or what NYU is calling "urban science," will be in high demand. Thus it's no surprise to find that a "smart cities" or "built environment" thread runs through all the institutions selected for the Applied Sciences initiative. In particular, innovations in products and processes that use less energy or develop different kinds of energy will be especially sought after in the coming decades. The world economy is moving away from carbon-based fuels and toward new sources of energy, driven in part by state, national, and international goals and agreements.[38] Narrow discussions of the impacts of cap-and-trade regimes or green jobs have obscured how profound a transition this will be. Shifting to new energy sources will affect the source of our energy, the cars we drive, the products we buy, the kinds of homes we live in, the shape and location of our communities, and the way we get from one place to another.[39] This shift will also drive job creation, as the nation will need scientists to invent, entrepreneurs to take to market, and workers to build solar panels, wind turbines, biomass plants, advanced fuel cells, and other energy-efficient products.

Cities and metropolitan areas in the United States are well positioned to continue to be at the center of the nation's clean economy. Although the densest parts of metropolitan areas (typically, central cities) are thought of as dirty, congested, and polluted, their environmental impact per capita is in fact fairly modest.[40] As economist Ed Glaeser has written, "If the future is going to be greener, then it must be more urban. Dense cities offer a means of living that involves less driving and smaller homes to heat and cool. Maybe someday we'll be able to drive and cool our homes with almost no carbon emissions, but until then, there is nothing greener than blacktop."

But cities and metros are also leading the way on the production side of critical sectors of the low-carbon economy. The largest 100 metros in the United States are home to 78 percent of the jobs in solar energy, 80 percent in wind energy, and 83 percent of the jobs in energy research, engineering, and consulting services. They are also the site of fifty-four of the fifty-eight top-ranked high-impact U.S. clean technology firms on the 2010 Global Cleantech 100 list.[41] Three-quarters of clean economy jobs created from 2003 to 2010 are located in large metros. Moreover, the clean economy is innovation intensive and thus plays to metropolitan area strengths.[42]

The city and the NYCEDC believe that the Applied Sciences initiative is already paying off. According to Seth Pinsky, "If you look at the talented individuals and companies moving to the city, the evolving start-up ecosystem, and the number of construction jobs being created—it's already been a huge success. We've leveraged $130 million in public dollars to attract as much as $2 billion in private investment, and we're already seeing the dividends." In addition to construction jobs, there will also be, in the next five years, administrative support and back-office jobs for workers with mid-level skills. (Almost 30 percent of university employees in New York City do not have a bachelor's degree.)[43]

But the real measure of success will not be apparent for years, even decades. "In that first phone call, I said to Deputy Mayor Steel, one thing that's going to be hard to face is, you're not going to know for thirty years whether this is a success. One mistake would be to overpromise immediate results," recalled Charles Vest from MIT and the National Academy of Engineering. "I was astounded to get a response that said, 'Yes, we understand that.'" His comments were echoed by Kevin Ryan, a founder of Gilt Groupe, Business Insider, 10gen, and past president and CEO of Double Click. Ryan served as an adviser to the process alongside Vest and others, and he said,

> Twenty years from now—and it will be hard to prove this exactly—there will literally be tens of thousands of jobs created because of Applied Sciences. I'm imagining a guy, he's brilliant, he comes to Cornell, gets his master's, stays in New York partly because he's here already, his girlfriend is here. He gets a job at Gilt or someplace, and in four years he spins off and creates a company that employs a thousand people. That will have happened because of Cornell [even if] no one will attribute it.

METROPOLITAN AREAS AND THE NEXT ECONOMY

How do we change our economy? That is, in essence, the question that led to Applied Sciences NYC. New growth strategies that move the United States toward the next economy are coming alive not in federal agencies or congressional committees but in New York City and other cities and metropolitan areas. Those are the places where new ideas are created and commercialized, where people get smarter and more skilled, and where the United States reaches out to the rest of the world. Our cities and metros are where the country's next economy is taking root because they are the places that fulfill the next-economy imperatives.

Metros grow by selling goods and services outside their borders. Exports, as Immelt, Summers, and others note, are going to be key to the next economy for the simple fact that the fastest economic growth is coming from rising economies in Asia and Latin America. For the first time in recorded history, more than half of the world's population lives in cities and metropolitan areas. By 2030 the metro share will surpass 60 percent.[44] Rising nations and their rapidly growing metros now power the world economy and drive global demand. More specifically, as these populations in Latin America, Asia, and elsewhere become more urbanized, their demand for U.S.-made goods rises. By 2025, McKinsey & Company estimates, 1 billion more people will have entered the global "consuming class," meaning that they will have enough income to be consumers of global goods. The bulk of these consumers will live in cities outside of the United States and Europe. McKinsey estimates that of these 1 billion new urban consumers, 600 million will live in 440 cities in emerging markets, markets that will be responsible for half of global GDP growth between 2010 and 2025.[45] That growth will contribute to an already large market for goods that exists outside the United States; according to the U.S. International Trade Administration, 70 percent of the world's purchasing power is located outside the United States.[46]

Places that innovate will be able to take advantage of rising global demand for new kinds of products and services. In fact, in high-wage countries like the United States, exporting requires innovation: people outside the United States generally buy what they cannot make or do, cheaply or at all, for themselves. Selling new inventions and efficiencies brings fresh capital to metros, and that capital in turn allows existing businesses, spin-offs, and start-ups to make more new things to sell to the outside world. What a metropolis exports becomes its economic raison d'être—the metropolis exists and thrives because it can do something better, faster, or cheaper than most other places.[47] These strengths in innovation show up in metropolitan areas' export levels. In 2010, according to research by Emilia Istrate and Nicholas Marchio, U.S. metropolitan areas produced some 84 percent of the nation's exports, including 90 percent of service exports.[48] The 100 largest U.S. metropolitan areas produced an estimated 65 percent of the nation's exports, including 63 percent of manufactured goods exported and 75 percent of service exports.

As businesses in a metro earn revenue from exported goods and services, they not only create more exports but also enable the creation of a more diversified and robust set of businesses and companies that meet purely local needs, from selling insurance to building houses to walking dogs. It's true that most of the economic activity in Greater New York, Boston, Portland, or any other metro tends to be focused on meeting the needs of the local market. Real estate is a perfect example of an industry with a local focus. It can create a lot of jobs and, for a time, a nice level of economic growth as furniture stores, garden centers, office cleaning companies, restaurants, and other kinds of businesses spring up to fill and service new houses, new buildings, and new people.

Yet for all its benefits, the locally focused economy does not have the same impact on economic growth that selling goods and services outside the boundaries of the metropolitan area does. Jobs in export sectors have a high multiplier effect, meaning that they create more additional jobs than those that serve purely local markets. Jobs in the high-tech sector have an especially strong multiplier effect. As the urban economist Enrico Moretti has found, each new high-tech job in a metropolitan area leads to, over the long term, two additional professional and three additional nonprofessional jobs.[49] According to Moretti, "Attracting a new scientist, software engineer, or mathematician to a city increases the demand for local services. This in turn means more jobs for cabdrivers, housekeepers, nannies, hairstylists, doctors, lawyers, dog walkers, and therapists. . . . In essence, from the point of a view of a city, an innovation job is more than a job."[50] Businesses that provide local services are important because they are part of what makes a place pleasant to live in: the ability to buy flowers and shoes, coffee and ice cream, legal services and financial advice. But what makes a place prosper is what it offers to people who don't live there.

The cycle of trade and innovation must be relentless for a place to flourish. Detroiters like to point out that their city was the Silicon Valley of the early twentieth century; but at some point Detroit stopped making cutting-edge cars. Now the region is scrambling to deploy its deep reservoir of skilled people, resurrect its distant history of entrepreneurship, and revivify innovation. As Jane Jacobs puts it, "Innovating economies expand and develop. Economies that do not add new kinds of goods and services, but continue only to repeat old work, do not expand much nor do they, by definition, develop."[51] More specifically, if a metropolitan area starts to lose its export orientation and forgets about the need to make things or provide services that are competitive on a national or international scale, eventually even its local market will become stuck.[52]

The Applied Sciences campuses are, in essence, a major push for New York to create more things to sell to the rest of the country and the rest of the world. The vast Greater New York metropolitan area sells only about 7 percent of what it produces to other countries—ranking it 93rd of the largest 100 U.S. metros.[53] But the "built environment" solutions that all of the Applied Sciences campuses are working on could be in tremendous demand across the globe. As more and more people move to megacities in the coming decades, and the demand for energy soars, cities will need ways to build more efficient buildings in more efficient configurations.

Take the smart parking systems that the researchers and students at CUSP in Brooklyn will work on. Rapidly urbanizing cities in Asia "face alarming predicaments over parking," according to one report.[54] Beijing and New Delhi add more than 1,000 new vehicles a day to their roads—without commensurate increases in parking spaces.[55] (Beijing has 740,000 parking spaces for 5 million cars.)[56] Drivers and transportation departments in these places will be very interested in acquiring this technology. Nations like Japan, with a rapidly aging population, might benefit from new technologies that incorporate sensors in smart phones, to monitor the vital signs of homebound people, and nations in which clinics and hospitals are scarce might benefit from the creation of mobile medical devices; the Cornell-Technion campus imagines developing both of these technologies.

The most competitive metropolitan areas are leading the way in the next economy in part because they are hotbeds of innovation and exports. Metropolitan areas concentrate ideas, people, and technology to create a virtuous cycle that generates more innovation, attracts still more people, and makes many of the people and firms that are already there even smarter and more productive.[57] They are to idea generation what heat, enzymes, and pressure are to chemical reactions: they speed everything up.[58]

GAME CHANGERS

It's tricky to use Applied Sciences NYC as a model for metropolitan economic development for the next economy. As New Yorkers are the first to say, their city is not like most other places. For one thing, Applied Sciences had the intense focus and backing of Mayor Bloomberg, who used his special connection with the business community to draw it into the initial game-changers brainstorming exercise. Mayor Bloomberg also drove the project's tight deadlines because he wanted the Roosevelt Island campus to be well on its way by the end of his term in December 2013. Second, New York City has a particular hold on the world's imagination, which enabled the Applied Sciences NYC competition to attract international interest more easily than a similar competition in another city might have. Finally, although it is a vast and complicated place, New York City is a single municipality. Unlike people working at a metropolitan scale (even in metropolitan areas with fewer people than in New York City), Mayor Bloomberg and his administration did not have to coordinate and negotiate with neighboring municipalities to pull off the deal.

But more important, no metropolitan area should blindly copy what New York City or any other metropolitan area does to advance its economy. Applied Sciences purposely builds on New York's unique strengths, industry mix, and existing technology clusters. Other places will have their own set of strengths, and the importance of trade, whether domestic or international, makes the unique features of metros all the more important. Not every metro will be a biotech hub, no matter how many wet labs it builds or enticements it offers. Metros are starting to build deliberately and creatively on their special assets, attributes, and advantages. Metropolitan areas in the aggregate have powerful next-economy strengths, but each metro manifests its strengths in a distinct way. Houston specializes in energy-saving building materials and renewable energy services; Phoenix is strong in air and water purification and solar technologies; Pittsburgh focuses on pollution reduction. The top export from Portland, Oregon, is semiconductors, while Portland, Maine, specializes in aircraft products and parts.

The lessons that other places should learn from New York's Applied Sciences undertaking have less to do with the result and everything to do with the process of inquiry. First, build on your strengths. As Deputy Mayor Steel said of the NYCEDC's game-changers effort, "You can't do [anything] disconnected from what your core skills are. First thing is to audit, what do we have and what are realistic ambitions." Academic studies reinforce this practical, but often ignored, intuition, as did almost everyone interviewed about Applied Sciences.[59] Kevin Ryan explained, "You can't create something out of nothing. . . . We have a building block. New York has enormous advantages in technology, in the Internet space in particular. The rest of the country has been slow to realize it, but there are many areas in which San Francisco is not that relevant, and New York dominates."

As the Applied Sciences competition was building, comparisons to Silicon Valley were ubiquitous in statements from city officials and in news coverage. "We can't just sit here and let Silicon Valley beat us," Mayor Bloomberg told a gathering of tech entrepreneurs in October 2011, as the responses to the request for proposals were coming in.[60] But New York was not, in fact, seeking to transplant an entire industry or create a Silicon Valley East. The NYCEDC and the mayor's office were clear that Applied Sciences NYC would be connected to the particular existing and emerging strengths of the city. As Enrico Moretti points out in *The New Geography of Jobs,* "Universities are most effective at shaping a local economy when they are part of a larger ecosystem of innovative activity."[61] Before launching a major economic development initiative like this, places need a sense of what that ecosystem is.

In 2009 New York City had assets that were underperforming but moving in the right direction. There were the city's existing information technology and biotech clusters and the rapidly emerging digital media sector. Several universities were changing their internal policies to make it easier for researchers, companies, or entrepreneurs to commercialize technologies or innovations developed in their labs; these shifts would spur more new start-ups and encourage entrepreneurship among the scientists and engineers on their faculty.[62] Columbia had a plan to expand its campus and its engineering school, and NYU and Brooklyn Polytech had announced a merger that would strengthen their applied sciences disciplines.[63] NY Tech Meetup, a monthly gathering of local tech professionals that hosted the debut demonstrations of Tumblr and Foursquare, among others, was almost at the 10,000-member mark (it now has 28,000 members).[64] Venture capital deals were starting to rise, and capital for start-ups was about to soar.[65] Most important, the city was a world leader in media, fashion, healthcare, and advertising, industries that were ready for the step change that new technology could provide.

The city also relied on assets that may not have looked like assets at the outset. Koonin, the director of NYU's Center on Urban Science and Progress, said,

> I could have gone to do what I'm trying to do in any one of the country's great universities, anywhere I wanted. I chose to do it in New York, in part because of the commitment that New York had. You can't do [the applied research on urban problems that CUSP will undertake] without the engagement of the government because the government is the beneficiary, and in order to try things out and demonstrate them, you need cooperation and data.

Given Mayor Bloomberg's background, his administration may have been particularly quick to recognize that the wealth of information that city bureaucracies collect and generate could be particularly valuable outside of the realm of government. But other cities and metros can also think about what they have that might be valuable, whether that is specialized data or vacant land or even a particularly thorny problem that an entrepreneur or researcher might be able to turn into a commercial opportunity.

The second lesson other places can take from Applied Sciences is to ask the right people the right questions. Once it understood the city's strengths, the NYCEDC did not jump to thinking about particular transactions—how to get one company or another to locate in the city or expand its operations there. Rather, it started with a big question about increasing economic activity and sought input from literally hundreds of people. One NYCEDC staff member described the effort as "a continual attempt to widen our point of view." The NYCEDC tapped into the broader base of ideas, suggestions, and problem diagnoses that existed outside their offices. Its leaders and staff members did not believe that their expertise alone was sufficient. The NYCEDC staff did generate a lot of creative ideas internally. But in general, casting a wider net makes it more likely that one person's idea will interact usefully with another person's idea and that something beneficial will emerge. Steven Johnson points to fourteenth-century Italian market cities as examples of networked economies: these were the places from which emerged double-entry bookkeeping—the notion of recording each transaction as a debit or a credit, which was one of financial accounting's biggest innovations. This network effect applies to the game-changers approach as well: "They didn't magically create some higher-level group consciousness. They simply widened the pool of minds that could come up with and share good ideas. This is not the wisdom of the crowd, but the wisdom of someone in the crowd."[66] Moreover, a half-year period of brainstorming sessions gave the NYCEDC time to discern common threads and connect different expressions or facets of the same idea.[67]

Cities and metropolitan areas concentrate the expertise of a vast range of people working in myriad sectors. None of these sectors can do the work of economy shaping by themselves, but all have valuable roles to play. Recognizing this crucial fact, the NYCEDC designed a process that allowed for the input of all these sectors. This approach also kept the NYCEDC from steering the project in a direction that would not respond to what business and other leaders actually needed. This point was inadvertently reinforced by Seth Pinsky at a forum about Applied Sciences NYC in late 2012. An economic development official from another city asked him for advice on what city government could do to help small companies merge into larger, more robust companies. Pinsky replied, "Ask them."[68] Once the city and the NYCEDC had narrowed the game-changing idea to an engineering and technology graduate school, they continued to seek outside input. For example, NYCEDC staff members interviewed local university presidents and representatives from national and international universities to gauge their interest in setting up a graduate campus in the city.

The competition itself became part of the process of inquiry that taught the city and the NYCEDC what was possible. Looking back, Steel considered the request for expressions of interest, released in December 2010, "the beginning of the most important part of the process." The RFEI had detailed information about potential sites but not many specifics about what was expected from the responding institutions. The city used the RFEI as another kind of idea-generating exercise. The group of outside advisers who reviewed the RFEI responses was also "invaluable" according to Steel. "In some cases, they would say, 'This is incredible—these guys can't do this, that's just not possible'. . . . The combination of information from the RFEI and the input of the larger [advisory] group was the real secret sauce." Wylde agreed: The city and the NYCEDC "recognized the limits of their own knowledge. If you don't have really thoughtful people [to evaluate ideas], you could waste a whole bunch of money on something that's going to be obsolete in five years. [This process] will be a model going forward for any kind of technology-oriented development." Applied Sciences NYC also incorporates many existing ideas about what the city needs for economic development in an original and grandly scaled way. "The important thing in economic development," said Wylde, "is taking what everybody perceives as a need and figuring out how to craft an action item. I give [the city and the NYCEDC] full credit for that."

"We have a natural tendency to romanticize breakthrough innovations, imagining momentous ideas transcending their surroundings, a gifted mind seeing over the detritus of old ideas and ossified tradition," writes Johnson. "But ideas are works of bricolage; they're built out of that detritus. We take the ideas we've inherited or that we've stumbled across, and we jigger them together into some new shape."[69] And innovative ideas have a much greater chance of being realized if they crop up within a cluster, with a network of supporting services, facilities, and experts.

In an essay titled "Metropolitanism and the Spirit of Invention," Thomas Bender describes how Thomas Edison used such a network in late nineteenth-century New York to develop the light bulb:

> The great gift of the metropolis to Edison was the combination of an older work habitat in which he flourished and direct access to the capital and financial services, corporate leadership, and professional knowledge—especially in law and engineering—that was available in Manhattan. Edison understood this, remarking in his autobiographical notes that other cities "did not have the experts we had in New York to handle anything complicated." Edison was not alone in exploiting the resources of the region. Between 1866 and 1886, 80 percent of the inventors with five or more telegraph-related patents resided in or within commuting distance of New York.[70]

Edison perfected the first commercially viable incandescent light bulb in 1879 in his laboratory in Menlo Park, New Jersey. But his work in rural Menlo Park was the culmination of years of effort that started in New York City, where Edison had secured space in the Laws' Gold Indicator

Company in 1869, and continued in Newark, where Edison moved in 1870.[71] The power of Edison's light bulb was not just that it could illuminate but that it could do so on a grand, commercial scale. To put his invention in front of as many customers as possible, Edison opened a Manhattan office, in 1882, at 65 Fifth Avenue.[72] That same year, Edison created a large generator and demonstration site on Pearl Street in Manhattan, which proved his inventions were useful as public infrastructure, not just private amenities. Five years later, Edison relocated his operations to West Orange, New Jersey, but still maintained close business ties to New York City's financing and legal expertise as he filed and defended patents.[73]

The commercially viable light bulb depended not just on a sole inventor but also on a web of like-minded inventors, craftspeople, engineers, financiers, and lawyers. It required not only a laboratory but also a marketing hub and a large-scale demonstration site. This mix of readily accessible expertise, ingenuity, space, and inspiration could only be found in a great metropolis. Arguably, it took a metro to bring the light bulb into being.

In the more complicated twenty-first century, we need the equivalent of Edison's inventions to deal with carbon emissions and climate change, water scarcity, sustainable food production, new energy sources, new methods of transportation, and other challenges that we have not even defined yet. Crafting the solutions to these problems, bringing them to scale, and taking them through commercialization, demonstration, production, sales, marketing, export, and widespread deployment will draw on the resources and expertise of inventors, investors, universities, private companies, nonprofit organizations, business cluster groups, and an array of governments to provide everything from factory permits to workforce training to access to markets through trade agreements. These challenges, too, will need a metropolis.

3

DENVER:
THE FOUR VOTES

Collaboration is the new competition.
—JOHN HICKENLOOPER, *governor of Colorado*

In a 1940 essay, the historian Arthur M. Schlesinger Sr. describes a "headlong rush into the cities" in the early decades of the twentieth century. Between 1900 and 1930, America's city population grew at more than three times the rate of the rural population, with the result that America became an urban nation: the 1930 census revealed that for the first time, more than half the population lived in cities. But the neat division between rural and urban did not tell the whole story: "In reality, urban preponderance was bigger than [Census Bureau] figures indicate, thanks to the rise of great metropolitan districts in all parts of the nation. . . . The census of 1930 disclosed ninety-six metropolitan districts, composed of one or more central cities with peripheral towns and rural communities, each district comprising a territory united by common social, industrial, and financial interests."[1]

Schlesinger concludes that "these urban provinces, new to the American scene, possess greater economic, social, and cultural unity than most of the states. Yet, subdivided into separate municipalities . . . they face grave difficulties in meeting the essential needs of the aggregate population."[2] In just two sentences, Schlesinger limns the fundamental, paradoxical

DENVER METROPOLITAN AREA

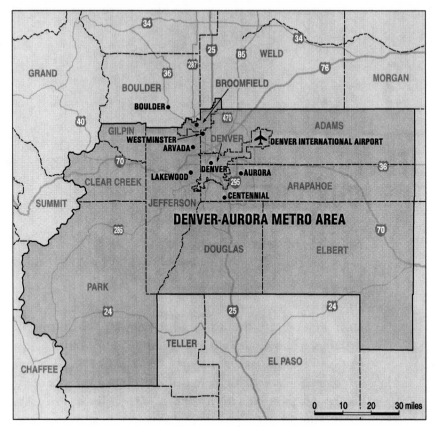

dynamic that has played out between American cities and suburbs: "economic, social, and cultural unity" crashing into political and fiscal separation, making the satisfaction of shared needs incredibly challenging.

The people of the Denver metropolitan area spent thirty years working out the tension between the common and competing needs of different communities, and their progress can be tracked by four critical votes in which citizens decided how closely the city would be tied to the suburbs. Denver's old nickname was the Queen City of the Plains, and in the late 1960s and early 1970s she was seen as something of a high-handed despot by the counties and communities that surrounded her. In 1974 voters in the region, and in fact around the state, decided to cut the queen down to size, in a ballot referendum that reflected deep divisions and mistrust on the part of city and suburban elected leaders and the people they represented.

Almost fifteen years later, in two separate votes, residents of the region expressed a wish for somewhat warmer relations between city and suburbs. A plan to transfer land in one county to Denver's jurisdiction for a new airport received voter approval in May 1988, and in November of that year a measure to support art and cultural institutions in the region, most of which were located in downtown Denver, passed overwhelmingly. These 1988 votes indicated that the people who lived and worked in Denver, Aurora, Littleton, and the other communities that made up the region were starting to understand that they were united for better or worse. The outcome of the last vote in this story, in 2004, represented the culmination of decades of effort to build Greater Denver, literally: by that time, the region's voters had agreed to tax themselves to support their zoo and art museums, build professional sports arenas, and embark on one of the largest transit system expansions in the country.[3] The 2004 vote also signaled that people wanted to build Greater Denver in a psychological, even emotional sense. These big civic infrastructure projects represent people's commitment to the region as a whole rather than to their own small portion of it.

The story of how Denver's disparate communities came to recognize themselves as part of something larger and stronger also says a lot about the geography and infrastructure of daily life in the 366 metropolitan areas that are home to 84 percent of people in the United States.[4] Many of us sleep in one jurisdiction, work in another, go to movies or concerts or games in yet another, and cross countless lines on a map as we go about the business of raising families, earning money, and enjoying the countless small pleasures of the everyday. The community in which we live, big or small, is connected to many others by systems and structures that we take for granted, at least until they break down: hundreds of miles of tracks, roads, water pipes, electric cables, and fiber optic lines; a web of agreements about pollution, public services, construction, and taxes; and incompletely overlapping layers of local governments, school districts, sewer and water districts, and transportation authorities. All of these districts, governments, and authorities are supported by taxpayers and voters and led by commissioners, board members, executive directors, treasurers, and advisers who have to negotiate with one another, pay bills, and jostle along in a way that, if all goes well, is pretty much invisible to the average person.

In metropolitan Denver, decisions about how people from different places get along, what kinds of governments support what kinds of services and amenities, and who pays the bills have not been invisible at all for the last several decades. Looking at Denver is like prying off the cover of the mechanics of metropolitan life. These mechanics—decisions about rail lines, the status of unincorporated territory, sales tax increases of fractions of a percent—matter because they are the practical working out of some very basic philosophical issues: How do people with different dreams and aspirations live together and create a culture that nurtures and an economy that supports them?

THE FIRST VOTE

During the 1960s and early 1970s, when Denver was a city of just over half a million people, it was grappling with demographic change within its borders and troubled by racial tension—what we now know as the familiar story of many U.S. cities at the time. The share of people of color in the city had jumped more than 54 percent from 1960 to 1970. During the 1970s, the share would more than double, and minorities, mostly African Americans and Hispanics, would make up a quarter of the city's population.[5] In 1969 a federal court found that the Denver School Board had a deliberate policy of concentrating black students in a few schools, going so far as to deploy twenty-eight of the school district's twenty-nine portable classrooms at schools in just one neighborhood "to contain an overflow of black students."[6] The court insisted on desegregation, and the school board implemented an unpopular plan to bus students to achieve a different racial mix in schools.[7]

For four years, the city was roiled by busing protests, including the bombing of one-third of the school bus fleet in a parking lot, sporadic outbreaks of violence, and an antibusing boycott of Denver schools led by the school board's president.[8] The rapid population growth of the suburbs during this period, and particularly the movement of middle- and upper-class whites to these communities, made Denver officials anxious that the city would become, as one planning department study put it, "the ghetto of the metropolitan area, containing in its population primarily the poor and uneducated and a few of the very wealthy."[9] In 1970 the city of Denver was home to 47 percent of the region's population but 95 percent of the region's black population and 70 percent of its Hispanic population.[10]

Denver city leaders embarked on an effort to bring the suburban population into Denver by expanding the city and county's boundaries through the process of annexation (Denver is a combined city and county under Colorado law). Colorado law allowed municipalities to grow by adding adjacent unincorporated territory—in other words, tracts of land next to the city line that did not belong to any other municipality. Annexations had a self-reinforcing effect. The more Denver (or any other city) grew, the more it could grow later, as new boundaries became adjacent to more new territory. It may help to imagine annexation as a high-stakes, highly regulated game of Scrabble. When players lay down their tiles, they are both blocking other players from using the squares they have taken and opening up for play new areas that are now adjacent to their new "territory."* Similarly, when a city annexes territory, it takes it out of the reach of another municipality, and it can use the newly annexed territory as a jumping-off point to further extend its boundaries.

The city planned to go to where the growth was happening, or was likely to happen, and capture it. The mostly white families who lived in these areas would be brought into the Denver public school system, thereby easing busing pressures and mitigating white flight by other parents who did not want their white children to be the minority within their schools. Just as important, these land acquisitions would bring more of the region's wealth into the city of Denver. Colorado municipalities depended largely on sales taxes for their budgets. As the annexed territory developed, the department stores, hardware stores, and strip malls within it would contribute to a stronger bottom line for the city.

But many people living in the unincorporated territories, happy with their school systems in Arapahoe County, or Jefferson County, or Cherry Creek, did not want any part of Denver's desegregation battles and busing schemes. And suburban towns like Aurora and Greenwood Village also wanted to be able to grow by taking a share of the unincorporated territory between their borders and Denver's—why should the city reap all the benefits of new development?

Between 1969 and 1974, a flurry of annexations and incorporations ensued, which hardened the boundaries and soured the politics of Greater Denver. Franklin James and Christopher Gerboth, in a 2001 scholarly paper about the annexation battles of the time, report that "the capital city

---

*The board game Blokus is an even closer comparison. While in Scrabble players can take advantage of the new territory that one player opens up on the board, in Blokus each player's territorial gains reduce the amount of territory any other player can enter. Blokus also mimics the way that annexations can cause places to grow toward one another even though they may start out far apart.

used a variety of tactics, including attempts to deny Denver Water Board services to landowners (and developers) who held out against annexation. Fueled by rumors of impending widespread busing, the suburbs employed similarly tough tactics." Residents in the previously unincorporated area of Lakewood, west of Denver, voted to become an incorporated city (Colorado's third largest) in June of 1969, taking 116,000 people and forty square miles permanently out of the reach of Denver. Aurora started to grab territory on its own borders, as did nearby Greenwood Village, and their actions effectively hemmed in Denver's southward expansion. The authors use such terms as "religious zeal" and "war" to describe the intense feelings of leaders and citizens in both the cities and suburbs and refer to a "climate of fear on both sides"—Denver leaders feared being cut off from growth by what one former mayor called "the white noose that surrounds the core city," while suburban leaders and school districts feared being drawn into real or perceived city problems.[11]

In 1973 a resident of the Denver suburb of Greenwood Village proposed a state constitutional amendment that would make it almost impossible for Denver to continue to grow through annexation. Under the amendment, instead of getting the approval of a majority of landowners in the territory it sought to gain, Denver would have to get the approval of a majority of voters in the entire county in which the territory was located. But the city of Denver was hardly well liked by voters and leaders in neighboring counties. They thought that Denver was heavy handed in its approach to annexation; they resented their dependence on the Denver Water Board and believed the city used the independent water board to withhold services and slow growth outside Denver's city limits.[12] Most of all, they wanted to make sure that their children would not be absorbed into the Denver school system.[13]

The state constitutional amendment, known as the Poundstone Amendment, passed in 1974 by a statewide vote of 58 to 41 percent.* The counties surrounding Denver approved it by 70 percent (only 39 percent of city voters approved).[14] One history of that era concludes that the metropolitan area was now "a ring of prosperity surrounding a troubled inner city."[15]

---

*Another amendment, "to prohibit the assignment or the transportation of pupils to public educational institutions in order to achieve racial balance of pupils at such institution," passed 68 to 31 percent.

Circumstances in Greater Denver in the 1970s—the oft-repeated and discouraging story of tensions between city and suburbs—might seem to reinforce what most people think they know about cities, and who lives there, and suburbs, and who lives there, and the great economic and social gulfs between them. But in the decades since busing battles (not just in Denver but across the country), a different story about cities and suburbs has emerged, one that emphasizes the commonality between these neighboring communities, not just their differences.

The truth is, cities and suburbs share an economy and social ties. The strength of those economic ties, in fact, defines the boundaries of a metropolitan area. According to the Census Bureau, a metropolitan area comprises an urban area of more than 50,000 people, the surrounding county, and the adjacent counties that are economically and socially connected, as measured by commuting patterns. (In the 1950s, when commuting data were less reliable, connections were measured by phone calls.)

That bare definition might suggest that a metropolitan area is essentially a big city and its surrounding, subordinate suburbs—bedroom communities. But as the decades have passed, central cities in the United States have tended not to dominate the metropolitan area as they did in the 1950s and 1960s. Today, for example, the city of Denver is home to less than a quarter of the region's total population. Jobs, too, have migrated to communities that once were imagined as residential refuges from the pressures of work. Nationwide, suburbs have more jobs than cities do: about 23 percent of jobs in major metropolitan areas are within three miles of a traditional downtown, and 43 percent are more than ten miles out.[16] Greater Denver shows a slightly less spread-out version of this pattern: a little more than one-fifth of the region's jobs are close to downtown, while 42 percent are within ten miles and another 37 percent in the ten- to thirty-five-mile ring.[17]

Suburbs in the Denver area and elsewhere have also experienced the same kinds of social and economic changes that cities addressed decades ago (and continue to work on). The image of suburbs as everything that America's cities are not—noisy, diverse, striving, poor—no longer applies, at least not to suburbs across the board. Suburban racial demographics are pretty close to those of the nation as a whole: about two-thirds of suburban residents are white, 10 percent are black, 6 percent are Asian, and 17 percent are Hispanic.[18] The antiannexation efforts of the 1970s did not stop racial change in Denver suburbs and school systems.[19] According to the most recent data from the Colorado Department of Education, four of the seven school districts in Adams County, and two of the seven in Arapahoe County, have a majority of students of color. Two other school districts in Arapahoe County have more than 40 percent students of color.[20]

Suburbs are also increasingly where immigrants make their home in the United States. In the largest metropolitan areas, 61 percent of foreign-born residents live in the suburbs.[21] In places like Minneapolis–St. Paul, Sacramento, and Washington, D.C., immigrants are more likely to live outside the city than within its limits.[22] Denver is not quite at that level yet, but it is not too far: 46 percent of the foreign-born residents of the region live in the suburbs.[23] A majority of the poor people in the United States live in suburbs, not in cities. (True, cities have many more poor residents as a share of their population than suburbs do. But in terms of absolute numbers, there are 2.6 million more people living in poverty in suburbs than in central cities.)[24]

Because of the rapid population and job growth in suburbs, not just in the Denver area but in the United States in general, and the much slower growth or even outright decline in many cities, it can seem as if cities and suburbs are locked in an irremediable zero-sum battle for people, office parks, shopping centers, factories, and other sources of jobs and tax revenues. But actually, a handful of recent studies have found that city and suburban fortunes tend to rise and fall together. For example, a 2005 study of population growth in fifty-eight metropolitan areas from 1970 to 2000 finds that suburbs did grow much faster, on average, than cities during that time, and some (about 20 percent) of that growth was at the expense of cities; but differences between metropolitan areas—between, say, Denver and Dayton, or Buffalo and Boston—were much more important in determining overall growth rates than the differences between any of the cities and their suburbs. The study's author, Jordan Rappaport, explains,

> The faster a metro area's city portion grew, the faster its suburbs tended to grow as well. The faster a metro area's city portion lost population, the slower its suburbs tended to grow. . . . For example, Austin and Phoenix each had city and suburban growth rates that were well above average. On the other hand, St. Louis and Pittsburgh each had city and suburban growth rates that were well below average. This shared fortune of cities and suburbs held continuously throughout the 20th century. The positive correlation between city and suburban growth is extremely robust.[25]

Other studies suggest similar correlations between a city's economic growth and that of its suburbs.[26] For example, it is quite rare for a weak city to be surrounded by a strong metro, or a strong city to be set in a weak metro.[27] One study determines that

> during the 1970s, suburban population growth had a positive effect on growth of city employment. Similarly, during the 1980s and 1990s, growth of suburban employment had a positive effect on city employment growth. . . . The results suggested that city growth tended to be strongly tied to conditions within the city, particularly demographics, population density . . . crime rates, and income inequality. . . . Suburban growth, by contrast, tended to be strongly influenced by national and regional factors, such as climate and regional location, although city demographics and city population density were also important [to suburban growth] during the 1980s and 1990s.[28]

It is a central canon of social science research that correlation does not imply causality, and most studies show that city and suburban economic and population growth is correlated but not that growth (or decline) in one causes growth (or decline) in another. In general, however, research suggests that prosperity of cities and suburbs depends on shared conditions in the wider metropolitan area. Most jurisdictions benefit from a strong metropolitan economy, and most suffer from a weak one.

THE SECOND VOTE

In the 1980s the nationwide recession and then an energy bust walloped the economies of the state of Colorado and Greater Denver.[29] Peter Kenney, a former elected official in Clear Creek County and longtime civic leader who now runs a firm that consults on civic engagement and community planning issues, recalled that in the mid- and late 1980s Greater Denver "had very high vacancy rates downtown, a lot of unemployment, people leaving the region." By the mid-1980s it was abundantly clear to the region's business leaders that their communities had a shared economic fate, and it was not looking like a pleasant one. The business community wagered that the region could build itself out of the local recession, or at least try to, much as the federal government would later try to counteract the effects of the Great Recession by pouring money into "shovel-ready" projects. In 1987 the Denver Metro Chamber of Commerce created a new arm called the Greater Denver Corporation (which would later rename itself the Metro Denver Economic Development Corporation) to lead an $8 million, four-year effort to advance its agenda.[30] "The Greater Denver Corporation was created to do three things," said Tom Clark, the head of the Metro Denver Economic Development Corporation: "Get the airport built, put us on the map globally as a location for jobs, and develop a metrowide economic development program."

So the second important vote in the story came in 1988. The ballots were cast in just one of the region's counties—Adams County—but the vote would have a tremendous impact on the economy of Greater Denver.

Building a new airport for the region was an ambitious goal. The existing city-owned airport, Stapleton, was inadequate for the needs of a growing region that needed more connections to the rest of the country and indeed the rest of the world, but expanding it would have required an expensive, lengthy environmental clean-up of land on which the U.S. Army had once produced nerve gas and mustard gas.[31] A study had identified another potential airport site, some twenty mostly unoccupied square miles in Adams County, just north of Denver (eventually the airport would require fifty-three square miles). To build the new airport, the city would have to do what Colorado voters had made almost impossible a decade earlier: it would have to annex territory and extend its reach into a neighboring county.[32]

Federico Peña, who had been elected mayor of Denver in 1983, had strong backing from the business community to move ahead on the new airport, but that was not sufficient to overcome the constitutional restrictions on the city's annexation powers. He needed the support of voters throughout Adams County, and the best way to get that support was to rally Adams County elected officials to his side. "I decided to go visit the Adams County commissioners in Adams County at a restaurant called Bubba's," Peña recalled. "Back in those days . . . whatever Denver wanted it got. I was the first mayor who said, . . . 'Let's go see them.' We didn't tell the Adams County commissioners to come to Denver and have dinner in a Denver restaurant. I decided we were going to be more humble about this."

Over steaks and beer at Bubba's, Peña started negotiating with Adams County commissioners and elected officials, who had previously declared that they were hostile to just about any ideas Denver had.[33] As talks progressed, Peña sweetened the deal, agreeing to build access roads to the airport and pay Adams County so-called impact fees and other fees and pledging that prime parcels for airport-related development would remain in Adams County's hands.[34] Negotiations culminated in an April 1988 agreement between Denver and Adams County, which stated that the city would, along with paying for selected infrastructure development around the airport, also share economic benefits (including jobs) that would result from construction of the new airport and that noise ordinances would be enacted at the airport to protect nearby Adams County residents.[35]

Airport supporters had worried that, as one case study of Denver International Airport puts it, "historic resentment against Denver alone could still succeed in defeating the [annexation]."[36] The case study quotes one former Denver official as saying, "We were fighting images, symbols, and history because Denver had always considered Adams County as a dumping ground."[37] But thanks to the solid support of the region's business community and the deep involvement of Governor Roy Romer, the May 1988 vote to allow Denver to take control of a portion of Adams County and build Denver International Airport passed with 56 percent approval.[38] (Despite this voter approval, however, two of the three Adams County commissioners who supported the annexation were voted out of office in the November elections later that year.)[39]

More important, the vote was a strong signal that two communities that had been deeply antagonistic for decades had been able to forge an agreement that benefited both, and it suggested that the days of bitter fights between city and suburban leaders and voters had come to an end. "That ability of my team and the Adams County team to come together in a way that nobody thought possible, when the media and others said we were archenemies—when that occurred, there was an aha moment," said Peña. "People said, 'Why can't we do this in other areas?'"

THE THIRD VOTE

At the same time that the Denver mayor's office and the Adams County commissioners were involved in the intricate negotiations around the airport and preparing for the annexation election, the city's cultural institutions were rallying voters for another ballot measure, the third key vote in Greater Denver's history. In 1982 Colorado's budget was so battered by declining energy prices that the state stopped funding some of Denver's iconic cultural and scientific institutions, including the Denver Art

Museum, the Botanic Gardens, the Museum of Nature and Science, and the zoo.[40] The city of Denver tried to fill the gap as best it could, but surveys from the institutions showed that most visitors were from the suburbs, not from the city itself.[41] So, in 1983 the big institutions and other smaller groups started an effort to create a new tax district—called the Scientific and Cultural Facilities District and encompassing seven counties in the metropolitan area—that could levy a sales tax of one-tenth of 1 percent. About two-thirds of the proceeds would pay for Denver cultural powerhouses (in 2004 the Denver Center for the Performing Arts was added to the list), and about a third would go to smaller institutions throughout the region, such as the Butterfly Pavilion in Westminster, the City of Aurora Cultural Services Division, and the WOW (World of Wonder) Children's Museum in Lafayette.[42]

Mayor Peña had campaigned on the slogan "Imagine a great city," and not only Denver residents but suburbanites as well seemed to take the suggestion to heart in supporting the institutions that they thought a great city should have. In November 1988, voters were asked to create a roughly $40 million fund to help pay for cultural facilities and organizations in the region. By a margin of 75 to 25, voters throughout the region agreed that arts and culture were worth a tax of about two cents on a pair of movie tickets or twenty-five dollars added to the price of a new car. This vote was a forceful step toward recentering the region that fifteen years earlier was fractured and divided because the institutions that got the most support were located in the city of Denver.

People in the region remember the vote for the Scientific and Cultural Facilities District (referred to locally as the SCFD) as a turning point in the region. John Hickenlooper, the current governor of Colorado and a former mayor of Denver, is widely considered the personification of regional cooperation. When asked in 2012 about the history of collaboration in metropolitan Denver, among the first things he mentioned was not one of his own undertakings as mayor but rather the SCFD, which had been established long before he was elected. He called the SCFD one of the "bedrock foundations of collaboration in metro Denver that you don't see in other places. . . . We now raise $45 million a year, and we have the fourth-most-visited zoo, the highest number of paid memberships to the museum of nature and science [of all museums] in the United States, and the second-largest performing arts center in the United States, all through regional collaboration," he said, still sounding like a proud mayor. Tom

Clark agreed that "the arts district and the [Colorado] Convention Center set the stage for helping us act regionally in terms of job creation."[43]

By the late 1980s, people in the Denver region were not just imagining a great city, they were reaching into their pockets to pay for its construction. The Kansas City Federal Reserve Bank study mentioned earlier points out that "the importance of shared characteristics in driving the growth of both cities and suburbs suggests that there may be considerable benefits to cooperation among a metropolitan area's many local governments," specifically, "in providing some public goods."[44] The study mentions three in particular: goods that have increasing returns to scale—meaning they cost less per user as more people use them, such as sewage systems and airports; amenities such as zoos, museums, and performing arts centers, which are located in one place but whose costs can be shared by many municipalities; and goods that get more valuable to each user as the population or geography served gets larger, such as a mass transit system.[45] During the latter half of the 1980s, the Greater Denver area steadily marched through the first two categories on that list.

In 1989 the region's voters agreed to another small sales tax (again, one-tenth of 1 percent) to fund the construction of a baseball stadium in downtown Denver as an inducement to major-league baseball officials who were considering sending a new team to the region. Tom Clark remembered that, at the time, "there was a perceived failure on the part of Denver, when we tried to portray ourselves as a major-league city without having a major-league baseball team. We decided, 'If you come, we will build it.'" The suburbs went along, he said, because "by this time, the suburbs had begun to realize that a healthy and vibrant urban center was the retail window onto the economic health of the region."

Too many metropolitan areas believe that stadiums and convention centers, by themselves, can be economic engines. That is rarely the case. There is an initial burst of construction jobs, but more often than not, actual economic benefits fall short of expectations, and stadiums can end up being a drag on state and local budgets, sometimes even sitting empty after teams relocate to another city or facility. In rare instances, regions can successfully use massive infrastructure projects, like stadiums, as part of a larger development plan.[46] In a way, metropolitan Denver was lucky. Building its sports stadiums also built social capital and a shared feeling of community. Everyone in the region was literally invested in major projects and institutions in the city.

Buoyed by these successes, the business leaders who supported the Greater Denver Corporation kept pressing for more collaboration, this time from local economic development offices, who were charged with bringing new businesses into their towns or counties. This was the third item on its agenda: to get the communities in the region to stop fighting among themselves when it came to luring new businesses. The corporation's leadership invited local economic development entities to join an entirely new kind of business-attraction network. Rather than competing against one another to lure a company to Aurora, or Arvada, or Littleton, or Westminster, or Denver, local entities would compete together to bring a company to the Greater Denver metropolitan area, trusting that their own communities and residents would benefit no matter where in the region the company chose to locate. "Prior to [this effort], we had forty different economic development corporations all acting independently, each one going after every lead, and each one seeing all the others as their competition," Peter Kenney recalled. All these groups "were asked to come together and sign an agreement that they would no longer compete with each other but against Dallas, Salt Lake, Hong Kong, because the region was the economic engine here." At the time, and even today, this was a radically different approach to attracting jobs and businesses, rather like Coke and Pepsi joining forces to entice people to drink cola, rather than tea, coffee, juice, or any other beverage, and not worrying so much about whether consumers pick one brand or the other.[47]

The many governments within a single metropolitan area are almost designed to fight among themselves because state law makes them largely dependent on locally raised tax revenues. As the local government scholars Gerald E. Frug and David Barron write, "State law organizes localities to be competitors for real estate development rather than participants in a collective endeavor to further the regional economy. . . . The quality of city services largely depends, under state law, on individual localities' ability to raise their own tax revenue. It is not surprising, then, that economic development policy is driven by parochial, rather than regional, interests."[48]

People, pipes, cars, rails, and the nebulous entity known as the economy might flow seamlessly across local boundaries, but sales and property tax dollars rarely do. A dollar spent (and taxed), or a house built (and taxed), or a business located (and taxed) in one jurisdiction is lost to any other. So, in metropolis after metropolis, individual communities that could work together to harness their distinctive assets in innovation, or to bring their region's products and services to new markets abroad, or to integrate new immigrants into their economy all too often compete against one another for sources of tax revenue—usually commercial development and big employers. Sometimes they spend tens of thousands of dollars to entice businesses to move, often just a few miles, across a city line. Local economic development authorities are sometimes divisions of the local government or independent entities or a hybrid of both, but their imperatives are closely aligned with those of local government officials: increase the number of businesses and the tax dollars they generate in their own city or town, and get more than their neighbors.

Metropolitan Denver's economic development professionals held their breath, crossed their fingers, and hoped that their new approach would work. And it did. "We had to prove that we got more opportunities and more jobs came, so we tracked data in a very unusual way," said Tom Clark of the Metro Denver Economic Development Corporation. The network measured how often the region was in the top three metropolitan areas considered by a company seeking to move or build a new facility. In 1985, according to Clark, Greater Denver was among the top three candidates about 30 percent of the time. After the collaboration started, Denver was in the top three about 50 percent of the time. "I could go back to the partners and say, 'This is a huge demonstration of why this works.'" Kenney concurred: "We got ten times more positive responses than the [individual] economic development corporations had received collectively in the prior decade. It was so successful that everybody said, 'This really does work,' and the companies said they'd never seen anything like that, they had never seen that kind of collaboration across the region that made them want to be here."

Perhaps the strongest validation of the success of this regional approach to collaboration is that today, more than twenty-five years after the precipitating economic downturn, the Metro Denver Economic Development Corporation still exists and boasts on its website that it is "the nation's first and only truly regional economic development entity in which many area economic development groups have joined together to represent, and further, the interests of an entire region."[49] Similarly, voters continue to support the SCFD tax, agreeing to extend it in 1994 and again in 2004.

Tom Clark said that cooperation reinforces itself: "If you do this for twenty-five years, people do not want to let go of this level of ethical behavior, more efficient systems, this sense of being cool because they [cooperate]. They don't want to let this go. It is at the heart of business and civic leadership that we are doing the right stuff."

THE FOURTH VOTE

By the beginning of the 1990s, with Greater Denver a different, more collaborative place than it had been twenty years earlier, the mayors of its various communities started to wonder whether perhaps they, too, could work together on a more regular basis and gain from cooperation. In 1993 Peter Kenney helped a handful of mayors from the larger towns and cities in the region form the Metropolitan Mayors Caucus. "Prior to the caucus forming, many mayors might have known the names of other mayors, but they didn't have relationships, and certainly not friendships," he recalled. "A large part of our initial effort was just the social aspect, just building the relationship, getting to know each other. Before [the caucus] a small-town mayor couldn't call the mayor of Denver and say, 'I have this problem, can you or your staff help me figure it out?'" The caucus became a place where mayors started to talk about issues that no single community could solve alone, problems such as air quality, the side effects of rapid population and economic growth, and how to move the millions of people who lived and worked in the region efficiently. Transportation became one of their main concerns.

Transportation is an inherently metropolitan issue—just imagine the chaos if roads stopped at city limits, or subway passengers had to change trains when they crossed a municipal boundary. The Denver region had had two successful rail lines in the early twentieth century, one connecting Denver and Golden to its west (thirty-one stops over twenty-three miles in forty minutes) and one connecting Denver and Boulder, to the northwest. Neither one could survive the rise of the automobile, however; the Boulder line closed in 1923, and the Golden line made its last passenger trip in 1950.[50]

Several decades later, it became clear that Greater Denver needed to return to rails and generally find more ways to move more people from place to place around the metropolis. "We have one road that goes north-south through the region, I-25," explained Randy Pye, the former mayor of Centennial, a suburb in the southeast corner of the metro area. "When you have a bad snowstorm here, you're dead in the water." Economic forecasters predicted that the Denver region would add almost a million residents by 2025, on top of the 2.5 million that already lived there in 2000. More roads were not the solution: studies indicated that they would not be able to reduce congestion (new roads often do not relieve traffic congestion because of a phenomenon known as "induced travel": people take advantage of the new route to go where they might not have gone otherwise or to drive alone when they might have previously taken public transportation or joined a carpool). Business and civic leaders feared that traffic congestion would simply choke the region. They needed a new way to accommodate all the growth that would flow into the region over the next several decades.

Throughout the 1990s, the Metro Mayors Caucus supported the creation of a modern mass transit system in the metropolis. They backed a $6 billion plan called Guide the Ride, which would have built several rail lines at once, paying for them with a significant sales tax hike in the region. Critics complained that the plan was too focused on getting people to the city of Denver, rather than moving them throughout the metropolis, and that the transportation agency in charge of the plan kept vacillating on costs, at one point suggesting that the build-out of the rail system would cost as much as $16 billion, not $6 billion. In 1997 voters in the suburban counties around the city of Denver gave a resounding no to the proposed tax increases (and only a tiny majority of Denver voters supported it), and Guide the Ride failed, 58 to 42 percent.[51] A prominent local pollster looked at the voting and survey data and concluded that "the future of transportation planning in the Denver metro area will depend on a new alliance of business, local government and transportation agencies that are guided by a new philosophy of transit pragmatism."[52]

"Guide the Ride was about as bad an initiative as you could put on the ballot," said Randy Pye, several years later. "It was telling voters to sign a blank check. But almost immediately after that, the business community got together and said we can't allow something like this to happen again." The mayors, too, understood that mere declarations of support for expensive transportation plans were not sufficient. They needed to start behaving like politicians, in the good sense: making deals and meeting people. Pye and other political leaders in the southeast corner of the region got mayors and other elected officials in the northern suburbs to rally voters around a 1999 state bond package that paid for a nineteen-mile light-rail line to the job-rich southeast.[53] The mayors from the southeastern part of the metro promised that they would ask their constituents to support light-rail to the north when the time came. "All the northern communities were afraid the southeast corridor would walk away" after their rail money was secure, said Tom Clark. "All of us [including the business leaders] pricked our fingers and promised [we] would [advocate for] as much funding for the north" the next time transportation was on the ballot.

In May 2003 the mayors, who had built up a deep reservoir of trust and goodwill among themselves through regular interaction, threw their unanimous support behind a new massive transportation plan, called FasTracks. John Hickenlooper was elected mayor of Denver in 2003, and the early days of his administration coincided with the FasTracks campaign. He prided himself on saying, repeatedly, that "the days of Denver making decisions for its own benefit without the suburbs are over." The Saturday before his first term as mayor began, Hickenlooper invited all the mayors and county commissioners in the region to a party in his loft apartment in a trendy neighborhood. "Most of them had never been invited to a political event in Denver," he said.

Pye, for one, was impressed with Hickenlooper. Pye was one of the founders of the town of Centennial, which incorporated in 2001. According to his biography, he "has always campaigned on a simple three-pronged platform of low taxes, contract services, and limited government intervention in a citizen's way of life." He is exactly the type of person who, according to conventional political stereotypes, would be staunchly opposed to light-rail, new taxes, and the Democratic former mayor of Denver. But he's not. "One of the greatest assets we have in this region is Hickenlooper," he said. "He couldn't have been a more regionally minded person. People really admired him, and the way he would always say, 'It's not about Denver.' He talked about regionalism long before he was elected, long before he even thought about running."

The campaign for FasTracks started well before the eventual vote. For some eighteen months before voters went to the polls in November 2004, political, business, environmental, and labor leaders campaigned for the proposal. "We talked a lot about jobs, so the construction industry got behind this big time. Businesses were talking to their employees about how important this was to the economy of the region. We had the environmental coalition. . . . Hearing the conservation side, hearing the job side, and the economy side—it was a pretty strong argument when you put those three together," Pye remembered. "It wasn't just advertising. We had over five hundred individual town meetings, we were in churches, we went everywhere during the campaign." The southeastern mayors kept their word and campaigned hard for FasTracks, even though their constituents already had rail service (FasTracks dollars were slated to improve their lines, and an extensive rail system is more valuable to users than a limited one).[54]

In 2004 the region's citizens went to the polls for the fourth vote in this story of Greater Denver. Voters approved FasTracks, 58 to 42 percent. The plan was in many ways similar to the soundly defeated Guide the Ride plan: expensive, with a $4.2 billion price tag, paid for in part by one of the biggest sales tax increases the region had ever seen; and extensive, with six new rail lines, improvements to the existing lines, and new suburb-to-suburb bus routes. What made the difference this time was partly that more voters had more experience riding and benefiting from the mass transit lines that had been approved earlier and paid for by means other than tax increases. But more than that, the region's business and political leaders were firmly, unanimously, and vocally aligned behind FasTracks. "When you've got your mayors collaborating, that leads to your citizens collaborating," said Pye. "People ask, 'Why should I care about what happens someplace else?' I ask them, 'When you drive out of your driveway, do you know when you're still in your city, or if you have crossed over to another?'"

Almost as soon as the FasTracks tax increase was passed, the cost of materials to build the rail line skyrocketed, and the Great Recession caused the sales tax revenue that funds a significant portion of the project to come in well under projections. FasTracks will be over budget and finished late, but no one can say exactly how much over budget and how late. The Regional Transportation District is constantly reexamining financing options, interest rates change, and materials costs change. Moreover, the simple fact of inflation can dramatically alter cost projections—there is a bigger price tag for finishing the project in thirty years than in twenty. Determining the final cost of the project is a bit like a forty-two-year-old woman trying to nail down, today, what she will have in her individual retirement account or 401(k) account in 2035. Much as she would like to, she really can't. One estimate from spring of 2012, which Regional Transportation District officials said was out of date by February of 2013, put the total cost at $7.8 billion and the projected completion date in 2044.[55]

It's possible that in the next few years voters will be asked a second time for the money to complete FasTracks by 2020. Cost overruns and broken promises can roil the public and fracture coalitions, but the Metro Mayors Caucus continues to support FasTracks and is deeply engaged in figuring out how to solve the financing problem. "Newspapers and the rhetoric paint a pretty bleak picture, but the picture is much brighter than that," said Kenney, who now is one of two staff members of the caucus. "Ultimately, we are going to have to go back to the voters, but the question now is how can we move forward with other resources, and the Metro Mayors Caucus is right in the middle of that." Former mayor Peña was similarly optimistic: "Fights are going to happen, but it's going to get done. People aren't saying 'Let's destroy the system, let's forget about light rail.' People will work out the differences and figure out how to make it work. Every successive mayor and county commissioner has built on that."

As was the case with the business community, the proof that collaboration works for elected officials in metropolitan Denver is that mayors are still at it. Cathy Noon, who was elected Centennial mayor in 2009, said that the caucus helped her from the start of her term. "People were so inclusive, so welcoming, it was very much a culture that was supportive. It's just something that helps elected officials do a better job. A very supportive culture helps us all do things better for our constituents." Mayor Michael Hancock of Denver agreed. "Typically, when we step away from our values [of collaboration], we move very little. There isn't a city in this region that can undertake some of these major [economic development] efforts by themselves. . . . If we don't work together, then the people lose."

POLITICS AND POSSIBILITY

"If you want to persuade someone, listen and listen again, and ask them to restate it several times," said Governor Hickenlooper. "Even if you can't do everything that they want, once you hear the concern, you can hear some other way to solve it without giving up what you don't want to give up. In that process, you build muscle. In any regionwide initiative, by getting all your civic leadership together, you go across the normal boundaries, the normal silos. Every time you do that, you build civic muscle." There are still disputes in metropolitan Denver—about FasTracks, about more development around the airport, about whether the National Western Livestock Show and Rodeo should move from Denver to Aurora. But these rifts are the exception, whereas in many metropolitan areas, these kinds of fights are the rule. Denver-area leaders still practice politics as the art of the possible, building coalitions, learning from defeats, and adhering to a broadly shared vision.

The main lesson that Greater Denver has for metropolitan-area peers is simple to state but often hard to accomplish: understand the importance of compromise. Speaking of her experiences on the Metro Mayors Caucus, Cathy Noon said, "It's often difficult, and we don't always agree. But we go into it with the understanding that it's okay to disagree. Holding the collaboration together is almost the ultimate goal." She added that the mayors understand that, over time, most places will get most of what they want. "It's compromise that holds the collaboration together. We're not looking at each individual issue. It's the overall picture. . . . On every issue [mayors] say they can live with this, realizing that the next time, someone who might feel differently on your issue will say, 'I can live with yours, too.'" The Metro Mayors Caucus makes decisions by consensus, not majority votes, and that makes compromise more palatable. Even when individual mayors are less than delighted with a particular decision, they know that they have been heard, and heard with respect. According to Peter Kenney, "Sometimes we have to talk and talk and talk so that everybody has said what they need to say, and every attempt has been made to find every possible solution. The big-city mayor and small-town mayor sit at the same table, as peers, and [have] the same strength in their voice. That's been very important."

There are several reasons that compromise fuels collaboration in Denver. First, over time, people have come to expect their political leaders to compromise—which is completely the opposite of what seems to be the case at the federal level. At the national level, compromise is regarded with suspicion, as a sign of either weakness or a lack of integrity. At the metropolitan level, by contrast, gridlock has intolerably high and uncomfortably immediate costs with little or no payoff down the line. Denver's elected leaders cannot get caught up in political games because the other members of the metropolitan leadership network, the civic leaders, business leaders, university presidents, journalists, and a range of others, will not stand idly by. The county commissioners in the region, following in the footsteps of the mayors caucus, have created their own forum for conversation, collaboration, and compromise.

Kenney noted that "the business community feels very strongly about the value of the Metro Mayors Caucus and helps make sure mayors understand the value." Mayor Hancock agreed. "None of us want to say to constituents that stuff is not getting done because we're not talking to each other. All you need is one business leader to say, 'We're not going [to tolerate] this mess.'" Pye joked that regionalism "is a little bit of a phenomenon here." He recalled that once, he and other mayors were having dinner in a restaurant with former British prime minister Tony Blair and a delegation from the United Kingdom. "The waitress gave us a five-minute explanation on regional cooperation and regionalism in the Denver area. They were fascinated by this. Everybody kind of gets it. They understand that we don't do well when we are fighting each other."

Second, mayors have built strong relationships of trust and respect. "These guys and women have sat in the room together, they've gotten to know each other," explained Kenney. "If the person across the boundary was a stranger, maybe you wouldn't care if you did something that was going to hurt them. There's this collegiality that exists between the mayors." At the end of 2012, the incoming chairman of the Metro Mayors Caucus was undertaking what Kenney called "the forty cups of coffee tour, sitting down with every mayor one on one, talking about their jurisdiction, the caucus, what the priorities ought to be. . . . That's been wildly successful, and the new mayors really appreciate it." But even more than that, political officials in Denver have learned to relate to one another as people first, rather than as adversaries. That impulse is what sent Mayor Peña to Bubba's restaurant in Adams County, and what led Mayor Hickenlooper to invite his peers to a party at his home.

This culture of collaboration and respect for compromise, like the networks in Northeast Ohio discussed in the next chapter, has to be nurtured. "Collaboration is not always easy," said Mayor Hancock. "It's important not to paint a rosy picture. It's not easy because by definition, you have to put aside your self-interest for the greater good, and at times your vision has to be modified. . . . It's like a sibling relationship. There are times when it goes very well, and times when it doesn't go well."

Kenney talked about how, because of local term limits, the membership of the Metro Mayors Caucus has experienced a rapid turnover; in 2012, half of the region's mayors were newly elected. Kenney did not take the persistence of the caucus for granted, as he notes:

I can imagine a mayor [saying that] he doesn't want to sacrifice [independence] for the benefit of some larger thing that he doesn't fully understand. Any mayor has the potential to say those days of collaboration and the Metro Mayors Caucus are done, it's every man for himself, and I've got to take care of my jurisdiction. The public is aware of the level of collaboration; they read about it in the newspaper all the time, and the benefits that have been achieved, but I wouldn't venture to say that they wouldn't go along with a mayor who said that if we [stopped collaborating] we'd be all better off. We just have to make sure no mayor feels that way.

Kenney, though, is committed to making collaboration continue to work in the region. "It's a struggle; it is a struggle but it's one that is worth dealing with."

4

NORTHEAST OHIO:
THE POST-HERO ECONOMY

*For the first time in history, the basic unit of economic organization
is not a subject, be it the individual (such as the entrepreneur, or the
entrepreneurial family) or collective (such as the capitalist class, the
corporation, the state). . . . The unit is the network, made up of a variety
of subjects and organizations, relentlessly modified as networks adapt
to supportive environments and market structures.*

—MANUEL CASTELLS, *The Rise of the Network Society*

At the beginning of 2009, a new catch phrase seemed to be
everywhere: "You never want a serious crisis to go to waste."[1]
Some crises, such as the collapse of a major New York–based
global investment bank, hit hard and fast, and they galvanize an
immediate response. In many ways, the slow crises that don't
make an economy implode dramatically but that steadily, in-
sidiously drain its vitality are more difficult to address. During
the 1990s, Northeast Ohio faced just such a slow decline—and
because it was slow, it remained invisible for years. Northeast
Ohio's crisis was, in fact, going to waste.

The region had had its share of dramatic shocks. In September 1977 Youngstown was devastated by "Black Monday,"
when Youngstown Sheet and Tube announced the closing of
its Campbell Works steel mill and the erasure of 5,000 jobs.
Within three years, 10,000 steel jobs were gone, along with

thousands of other jobs in businesses that supplied the mills or sold orange juice, haircuts, coats, refrigerators, and other goods and services to steelworkers and their families.[2] In 1978 the city of Cleveland became the first major city since the Great Depression to default on municipal loans.[3] By 1983 one-quarter of the more than 280,000 manufacturing jobs that existed in Cleveland in 1979 had vanished; from 1983 to 1987 an additional 5,000 jobs disappeared.[4] Restructuring in the tire industry took more than a billion dollars out of the Akron economy in the 1980s.[5]

By the early 1990s, however, many in the region thought that the bad times were over and good days were at hand. Cleveland, which was by far the largest city in the northeast corner of the state and whose fortunes seemed to set the tone for the larger region, was widely and loudly hailed as a comeback city. A building boom in the city's downtown produced amenities like the Rock and Roll Hall of Fame and Museum, the Great Lakes Science Center, and three new arenas for the city's professional basketball, baseball, and football teams. In 1995 a headline in the *New York Times* declared, "'Mistake by the Lake' Wakes Up Roaring," and the accompanying article noted that "Clevelanders are cheering for a new downtown, built in the latest fashions in tinted glass and exposed steel," along with the new arenas, a new mall, and of course the Rock and Roll Hall of Fame, "the repository of guitar and glitter . . . [intended to] lift Cleveland beyond the old age of steel and into the age of Steely Dan."[6] A local rabbi wrote, "One couldn't help but wonder if God hadn't had a hand in this whole epiphany."[7]

Unfortunately, the dazzling buildings obscured a larger truth. There was no comeback. The manufacturing industries that had powered the Northeast Ohio economy were in crisis, and no amount of downtown spiffing up could change that fact. Manufacturing businesses shed 25,000 jobs in Akron, 115,000 in Cleveland, and 45,000 in Youngstown. Greater Cleveland, along with its neighbors Akron and Youngstown, had failed—badly— to keep pace with the rest of the country's economy. In terms of economic growth between 1980 and 2005, Akron ranked seventy-third, Cleveland ninety-third, and Youngstown ninety-ninth of the largest 100 metros.[8]

Between 1980 and 2005, the number of jobs in the United States as a whole grew by 43 percent. During the same period, Akron's gain was only 28 percent, and Cleveland's a mere 10 percent. Youngstown, devastated by the steel closures, was the only large metropolitan area that actually had fewer jobs in 2005 than in 1980. Desperate for jobs and tax revenues, Youngstown's leaders welcomed four privately owned prisons to the region between 1992 and 1997.[9] (The *Youngstown Vindicator*'s headline read, "Steel Bars Are Still Part of Big Business in the Region.")[10] But it didn't help: the precipitous decline continued. Between the 1980 and 2010 censuses nearly 48,000 people left the Youngstown region altogether. The housing market flatlined because of the huge imbalance between the people who wanted to leave the region and those who wanted to move there: in the city itself, about a quarter of the housing units were vacant in 2007.[11]

In 2001 and 2002, after the celebratory stories about the area's alleged comeback had petered out, the *Cleveland Plain Dealer* and Ideastream, the region's largest public television and radio station, put out a series of articles, broadcasts, and interviews making the case that Cleveland especially, but the rest of Northeast Ohio, too, was in the midst of a "quiet crisis." This crisis, said the *Plain Dealer* in its opening editorial in the series, was "one that threatens to drain our economic vitality, take our jobs, send our children packing. . . . In many ways it is a crisis more devastating than the usual kind because it is nearly invisible and generates only sporadic headlines."[12]

Articles and roundtable discussions told readers and listeners how weak their region had become and why. Companies that were once headquartered in Cleveland or Youngstown or Akron became branch offices of larger global concerns, severing the strong ties to the local community and broader region that corporate leaders once had. Northeast Ohio wasn't home, it was just one more stop on the corporate train.[13] The region suffered from a manufacturing hangover of sorts, slow to realize that the sector was forever changed and would no longer be a source of secure lifetime employment for people with high school diplomas but little other formal education. The region's universities and medical centers, which in other metropolitan areas served as powerful economic drivers, were inward looking and disengaged from conversations about the direction of the local or regional economy. A new stadium might bring people together on game day, but it did little else to stop the slide.

The *Plain Dealer* told readers that there was a solution: "Talk to civic leaders, entrepreneurs, academics, builders, business people. They all agree: Greater Cleveland must get serious about creating and backing a master plan for economic development or face economic extinction."[14] The problem was, "Greater Cleveland" didn't exist. It was, of course, a real economic entity, a metropolitan area of 2.14 million people supporting a $79.2 billion economy, spread across five counties and 169 separate municipalities. Greater Cleveland bumped right up against, and was also economically linked to, metropolitan Akron (696,000 people, $21.2 billion gross metropolitan product [GMP]), Canton (406,000 people, $12.2 billion GMP), and Youngstown (602,000 people, $16.5 billion GMP).[15] But there was no single, overarching entity charged with creating a plan for Cleveland and its neighbors in the northeast corner of Ohio. It was hard to imagine any single entity that could take on the task. One *Plain Dealer* column captured the challenge:

> No mayor, however persuasive or dynamic, is unilaterally going to transform the northeast corner of Ohio. No lone-eagle innovator, however ingenious, instantly will reverse decades of income stagnation and educational neglect. No single public project, however daring, will make this region a magnet for the smart, industrious people who are the raw material of the Information Age. Instead, lots of people, acting individually and collectively in different arenas and different niches, must step up and lead.[16]

When telling stories of transformation and turnaround, it is tempting to shape them into personal stories about heroes. One charismatic visionary (a mayor, school superintendent, entrepreneur, outraged citizen) steps up and, with unrelenting vigor and inspirational leadership, starts an irreversible cascade of change. But this search for the superhero is misguided. A growing body of research suggests that as a system or a problem becomes more complex, more minds are needed to adjust the system or solve the problem. It is unlikely that a lone genius can come up with breakthrough solutions, whether in technology or the economy or any other area of life. Metropolitan areas are so big, so complicated, and so diverse that they don't need heroes, they need networks.

The word *network* has been used so often that it is in danger of becoming as faded of meaning as its pre-Web2.0 predecessor, community. The popular writer Steven Johnson defines networks as simply "webs of human collaboration and exchange."[17] Through these collaborations and exchanges each individual, or organization, or node is able to be more effective than it would be alone. These networks must be large and diverse enough to connect people to others that they don't know and probably wouldn't have met otherwise. It is not enough for existing cliques or

NORTHEAST OHIO METROPOLITAN AREAS

groups to rebrand themselves as networks without changing anything else. The strongest networks are held together by a multiplicity of weak ties rather than the repetition of strong ones.

Sean Safford's book *Why the Garden Club Couldn't Save Youngstown* compares networks in Youngstown and Allentown, Pennsylvania, from roughly 1950 to 2000 and argues that Youngstown was hindered by a network of elites that were too tightly intertwined and purposely not connected to other groups in the region. These elites lost power as the domestic steel industry declined, leaving behind a fragmented and uncoordinated region. Allentown, by contrast, had looser networks that provided alternative and cross-cutting relationships. Allentown was better able to recover after the decline of steel because there were individuals and organizations that could serve as bridges between different groups, communities, and classes.[18] If everyone knows each other already, it's not a network, it's just another meeting.

But it is hard to describe the particular alchemy of networks because there are so many actors and so many places to start: that's the point. Every actor matters; any particular interaction or transaction can reinforce the network; and breakthroughs tend to come about as the result of a hundred small things.

LAYERS OF NETWORKS

The story of how networks in Northeast Ohio are reversing the quiet crisis could be told in many different ways. One narrative might focus on the actions of CEOs and business groups, who backed efforts to jump-start the manufacturing sector—or advanced energy, or medical device development—and eventually coalesced around a broader, interlinked agenda. Another story would start in the city of Cleveland and describe local leaders' growing realization that they needed to treat their neighbors as equal partners in the region and build a larger, robust economy together. The story that follows focuses on one organization, the Fund for Our Economic Future. The Fund is one node in overlapping layers of networks, so it is a particularly good place to start. One layer consists of the network of foundations that created and still operate the Fund. Another layer is made up of the organizations that the Fund supports, which themselves operate as networks. Yet another layer is the network that these organizations have created among themselves.

In 2003, with the warnings from the *Plain Dealer*'s Quiet Crisis series still resonant, a handful of program officers from foundations in Cleveland, Akron, and elsewhere around the region started talking about how the region's philanthropies, which gave about $300 million every year to various groups and institutions, could play a bigger role in rebuilding the Northeast Ohio economy.[19] Foundations could not by themselves create jobs or shore up weakened industries, but they could support some interesting new endeavors that were just starting to take root in the early 2000s. The state of Ohio had recently launched a new program of grants and loans to help old industries move toward more advanced technologies—for example, helping glass manufacturers move from making car windshields to making solar panels, which often rely on glass; or helping tire makers shift to more advanced polymer production (rubber is a polymer). A handful of new organizations in Cleveland and elsewhere in the region were also trying to do the same things in biosciences and manufacturing and helping start-up businesses find their footing and grow. Perhaps foundations could be both catalyst and connective tissue—providing critical funding to help these new organizations grow and win highly competitive state grants and connecting disparate economic development efforts in a way that would benefit the region as a whole.

In July 2004 a small group of foundations circulated a document titled "Making Northeast Ohio Great Again: A Call to Arms to the Foundation Community." The paper made the case that all philanthropies, whether they supported fine arts or environmental health, had an enormous stake in the economic health of the region: "Economic prosperity goes hand in hand with cultural amenities, education, health, arts, racial diversity, and many other causes that are the focus of foundation activities. In a weak economy, long-term funding for these areas comes under additional pressure and contributing organizations are called on to do even more. Thus, supporting economic development can help foundations that are focused on quality-of-life issues to achieve their mission." The call to arms recommended that every foundation consider how its grant making supported economic development because "the stakes are too high to ignore this issue," and it encouraged them to join something new called the Fund for our Economic Future.[20]

Fund members vowed to raise a $30 million pool of money to support economic development efforts throughout Northeast Ohio. The Fund would provide a vehicle for foundations that addressed primarily social problems, such as the Sisters of Charity Foundation of Canton (focused on social justice issues relating to poor and underserved people), the Jewish Community Federation (which supported social, health, and education issues and strengthening the Jewish community in Cleveland), and the Bruening Foundation (founded to reduce the impact of poverty), to support efforts to strengthen the economy, which it saw as another way to reknit the social fabric of the region.

But the Fund also had a broader promise. As Bob Jaquay of the Cleveland-based Gund Foundation recalled, "We realized that we could collectively commission research, collectively engage in a big public outreach process, we could gather intelligence and voices around this that would help shape [an economic development] agenda and build a constituency." Furthermore, he noted, "By agreeing to collaborate on a mutual agenda, we would create a model for collaborative behavior that might be replicated within a number of sectors within the community."

Operating as a network in a world that is still looking for heroes has taken a significant amount of work. What Brad Whitehead, the president of the Fund for Our Economic Future, called "the network piece" of the Fund's work did not come to the forefront until three or four years after the Fund was created, for several reasons. First of all, Fund leaders felt that creating a strong, shared regional identity had to precede the development of a shared agenda. But there were more subtle dynamics at work, too, that show how much care, patience, and stewardship strong networks require. In the first years, the philanthropies that had contributed to the Fund, most of which had no experience in giving grants to fire up economic growth, were themselves learning how to operate as a network. To ensure a sense of shared responsibility and authority, the members adopted a policy of one member, one vote. Each member—whether it contributed the minimum of $100,000 over three years or $10 million, as did the Cleveland Foundation in the first three years—had one vote. This policy continues to be a key piece of the Fund's design and empowers much smaller foundations to influence the Fund's work.

But a principle of equality doesn't come with an instruction manual on how to get stuff done as a network of equals. For example, Fund members wanted to make grants—that's what philanthropies do. But no grant, however big, was going to reorder a $178 billion regional economy. Achieving the Fund's goal was going to take more than grant making. Regional change requires the capacity to think, plan, and act regionally. That was a hard lesson for the Fund members to learn—it is a hard lesson for any organization to learn. The Fund, in essence, had to get its own network in order, creating its own culture of collaboration for the sake of change, before it could support other entities in doing so. Whitehead described this as creating "a center of gravity" around which the larger network could coalesce.

One of the Fund's earliest projects was called Voices and Choices, a two-year effort to develop a regional economic competitiveness agenda for Northeast Ohio. In 2005 and 2006 the Fund connected with more than 20,000 residents of the region through one-on-one interviews, town meetings, and workshops to elicit ideas from a wide range of people about the region's assets, challenges, and priorities.[21] (This is the New York Applied Sciences process on steroids.) The Fund and its collaborators distilled what they learned from this process into four goals to guide regional action: business growth, talent development, racial and economic inclusion, and government collaboration and efficiency. More than ninety individuals and organizations, including U.S. senators, local chambers of commerce, local governments, universities, hospitals, and business groups, agreed to be partners in this broad and sweeping agenda and planned to orient their activities around those four goals.

That didn't exactly happen. Five years after Voices and Choices, an independent review found that the regional economic competitiveness agenda "has [had] limited influence on the agenda, priorities, or direction of other organizations."[22] Some potential partners felt that the strategy was too general to guide their own actions, and others felt that the challenges were so complex that the Fund was dissipating its efforts by trying to address them all rather than focusing on a few.[23] The Fund is now working with business leaders and others to craft a sharper strategy with clearer responsibilities and goals. The struggle to launch the regional economic development strategy highlights one of the challenges inherent in networks. Even people who are willing to work together, as the region's business community is, have to learn how to do so effectively. It may take several tries before things gel.

But the Voices and Choices undertaking did have an immediate positive, even galvanizing, effect on people in the region. It helped them understand, as they never had before, the potential power in acting as a region, and the need to work collaboratively to direct their economic destiny. Just after the Voices and Choices initiative concluded in 2006, the Fund for Our Economic Future commissioned a study of opinions about its effectiveness so far. Academics, local government officials, heads of Hispanic and African American organizations, labor leaders, and heads of philanthropies, many of whom had participated in Voices and Choices, were broadly supportive of the Fund's work. Academics interviewed made comments such as "The greatest consequence to date is that we are talking as a region. . . . The spirit is pervasive" and "[The Fund] has created awareness and visibility for regional thinking," and "[Fund members] are modeling the type of collaboration they are trying to create." Others were inspired to collaborate with their own peer organizations to see whether they could accomplish more together than separately: One leader of an organization that served mainly Hispanics said, "It has changed my view. I'm thinking more about even my own collaboration with other Hispanic organizations. We are talking about how we can work together to share expertise and consolidate services to save money." Another head of a group that focused on meeting minority-group needs said, "It has become clear to me what is important [is] to have organizations working together."[24]

The Fund for Our Economic Future has been more successful at bolstering a network of economic development organizations that are changing the economy of Northeast Ohio. But this, too, has taken time and great care. In the private sector, companies that want to work with other companies in innovation networks have to up their game so that they are, in essence, good enough to network and can contribute something of value to their partners.[25] This dynamic also played out in Northeast Ohio. Several of the groups that the Fund supported through grants had to get stronger before it made sense for them to be in a network.

BUILDING AN ENTREPRENEURIAL ECOSYSTEM

Over the past decade, the Fund has given more than $60 million to regional economic development organizations. The stories of two of them, BioEnterprise and NorTech, illustrate the intricacies of redirecting major sectors of a regional economy, and because these organizations also operate as networks, they show how critical networks are to the economies of the twenty-first century.

The doctors, researchers, and scientists at Northeast Ohio's many universities, hospitals, and research institutions are constantly developing new technologies. Most universities and hospitals have special offices for technology transfer, meaning that they manage the transfer of these innovations to companies, usually by granting the companies a license to use an idea, process, or product that the university has patented. In practice, this often means letting the highest bidder develop these inventions in factories or office parks somewhere else in the United States or the world. This arrangement can provide abundant revenues for the institutions but does not necessarily do much to advance the regional economy. A 2009 report by the Center for an Urban Future in New York City carefully details how technology transfer offices in New York's major research institutions had been "overly focused on a handful of technologies with the strongest potential to be scooped up by existing pharmaceutical companies, IT firms or financial corporations—at the expense of other discoveries that could be commercialized through forming start-ups." The report notes, "Some say that NYU and Columbia, among others, got so used to earning large royalties from a small number of blockbuster patents that they came to view their tech transfer office as a cash cow. Instead of trying to get large numbers of innovations into the marketplace, university leaders essentially directed tech transfer officials to focus on technologies that have the greatest potential to lead to blockbuster deals and continued high earnings."[26]

In a place like Northeast Ohio, the failure to create a robust local economy makes it harder for hospitals and universities to recruit new staff. So economic development support is ultimately in their self-interest, although not always as immediately lucrative as licensing deals. Executives and board members from the Cleveland Clinic, Case Western Reserve University, Cleveland's University Hospitals, and Akron's Summa Health System realized that their home-grown technologies could be further developed and brought to market by new companies based in Northeast Ohio—thereby creating jobs in the region. So they started BioEnterprise, a nonprofit that helps inventors connect with experienced managers, venture capitalists, production facilities, other inventors, state and federal grants, and whatever else they need to build their companies.

This node of the Fund's network of networks has already proved fruitful, as these companies have coalesced into a new cluster of medical device, biotechnology, and medical services firms in the region. Because being part of a cluster makes an individual company stronger, a number of companies that started elsewhere have moved to Northeast Ohio to be part of this rich network. The cluster also benefits the region's hospitals and universities by making it easier for them to attract and retain bright and inventive people who benefit from working in an idea-rich environment—and who may themselves decide to make the jump from scientist to start-up founder.

Another node in the Fund's network is NorTech, a nonprofit that specializes in technology-based economic development, that is, economic growth through the intelligent cultivation of technology industries. It has developed a specific technique to build and develop technology clusters across twenty-one counties in Northeast Ohio. In addition, NorTech helps set an overall direction for the growth of clusters, identifies new overseas markets for exports, seeks out public funds to support research or business development, and figures out how to train people for jobs in these clusters. It also provides hands-on assistance to individual companies in the cluster, helping them develop new products and find and keep so-called anchor customers, those customers that will establish credibility with other buyers.

Flexible electronics is one of the industries on which NorTech has focused, because key components of flexible electronics were developed or improved on by companies and research institutes in the region. Kent State University has had a special research institute for liquid crystals since the mid-1960s, and in 1969 a researcher there made dramatic improvements to liquid crystal display (LCD) technology. Tire companies made Akron the one-time rubber capital of the world, but a newer generation of companies figured out how to shift from working with rubber to working with other kinds of polymers. When LCDs met flexible polymers, a whole new industry, known as flexible electronics, emerged. Flexible electronics are pretty much what they sound like: very thin electronic components that are attached to flexible, stretchable materials. Their thinness and flexibility allows them to be used in lighter portable electronic devices and integrated into clothing and packaging. The result could be an athletic jersey or flak jacket that monitors vital signs or motorcycle visors that automatically adjust to bright light.[27]

NorTech also supports Northeast Ohio's advanced energy and water technology clusters. The advanced energy industry encompasses a wide range of subspecialties such as energy storage, smart grids, biomass, wind energy, and fuel cells. This cluster arose out of the interactions between NASA's top advanced energy research center, which is in Cleveland, and the companies and people in the region who know how to make big, complicated mechanical things like wind turbines and generators. There's also a bit of geographic felicity at work: the Great Lakes are a superb source of wind energy. The region's water technology cluster develops anticorrosion technologies used in oil and gas drilling, materials known as sorbents that soak up pollutants in water, and automation and controls that manage industrial water–processing systems. The region's expertise in water cleanup is a happy and unexpected outcome of the 1969 Cuyahoga River fire that led to the passage of the federal Clean Water Act.

BioEnterprise and NorTech are both what are known as intermediaries. They provide the links between entrepreneurs and manufacturers, between suppliers and customers, between workers and jobs. As Baiju Shah, who was until 2012 the CEO of BioEnterprise, explained, "You have to be able to energize so many disparate elements to make it work. All sorts of different actors need to get energized to row in the same direction. They will do it as long as you've got an approach that unifies them." The intermediary helps the diverse actors determine their approach, helps actors decide which piece is their responsibility and which needs to be run by the intermediary, and then relentlessly communicates the vision to reinforce it among partners and to attract new partners. More generally, intermediaries are the glue that holds networks and long-term collaborations together.

The Fund's dollars were critical in the early phases of BioEnterprise, NorTech, and similar intermediaries, providing 30 to 50 percent of their operating budgets during those early years when these organizations were still finding their feet. The Fund, along with business groups, universities, and others, helped stabilize these fledgling entities with grants and guidance. After a few years, BioEnterprise, NorTech, and the rest had adequate funding, but they needed more connecting, both to other local groups working on similar issues (bioscience, manufacturing, or entrepreneurship) and to one another.

In the mid-2000s, the Fund started to require its grantees to show how they were participating and building networks in their areas of focus (such as biosciences or advanced energy) and explain what they expected that network to accomplish in the next five years. On top of that, the Fund began to insist that its grantees connect with one another and collectively set broader goals for the region's economic competitiveness. The Fund asked its grantees to create a logic model (increasingly common in the not-for-profit realm) "to show organization's system/network collaboration work at two levels: 1) the level most applicable to your organization's mission (e.g. the formation of a bioscience/information technology/ advanced energy industry cluster); and, if applicable, 2) the level pertaining to the overall economic competitiveness of the region (e.g. across economic intermediaries and/or other government, private or public sector partners, regardless of specific economic development focus)."[28]

The state of Ohio also provided a nudge, because it was increasingly insisting that entities apply for grants as members of a collaboration rather than individually. The Fund created a structure (and the state an incentive) by which the CEO of BioEnterprise could connect regularly with the CEO of NorTech, and both of them could learn from and share ideas with the CEO of JumpStart, another intermediary supported by the Fund.

This structure helped the now-solid intermediaries figure out how to work together, collaborate on grants from the state or the federal government, and work more effectively on their huge shared task of ramping up Northeast Ohio's economy. As Rebecca Bagley, NorTech's CEO, explained, "We're all trying to build the economy. We have a responsibility to the region. If we fight among ourselves, we aren't meeting that responsibility."

Many collaborations collapse because of limited resources, but the Fund has been able to supply those resources in Northeast Ohio. For example, the Fund played a critical role in helping the region win a $30 million federal grant to start a new National Manufacturing Innovation Institute for additive manufacturing, also known as 3-D printing, which could revolutionize manufacturing by making it faster and cheaper to create prototypes and new products.[29] The grant was awarded in 2012 to a huge consortium of universities, businesses, and nonprofit groups (including three Fund grantees) in Northeast Ohio and two neighboring regions, southwestern Pennsylvania and West Virginia. Additive manufacturing works somewhat like inkjet printing, but instead of ink, the printer uses polymers to create 3-D objects based on digital designs. Prices for 3-D printers and materials have dropped sharply in the past few years, and some observers believe that additive manufacturing will become a truly "disruptive technology," with applications across industry and even for individual consumers.[30] *The Economist* recently noted that "some people think additive manufacturing will overturn many of the economics of production because it pays no heed to unit labour costs or traditional economies of scale. Designs can be quickly changed, so the technology enables flexible production and mass customisation."[31]

As exciting as the prospect of 3-D printing was, getting more than forty institutions and organizations to agree on a vision and codify that vision in a grant application was still a significant undertaking. The Fund for Our Economic Future and other philanthropies spent $425,000 over four years to facilitate meetings, organize grant application reviews, conduct relevant research, and generally do what it takes to hold dozens of partners together. "The Fund put $25,000 in to buy the doughnuts," said Chris Thompson, the Fund's director of regional engagement, "and we got a $30 million return on investment." (Thompson's quip is funny, but it points to a larger truth: Consultants who advise nonprofits and others on how to build and sustain networks say that food and drink are an important part of bringing people together to work on common problems.)[32]

As of 2013, nine years into the Fund's efforts, the region is still not where it wants to be in terms of job growth or other indicators of competitiveness, but there are some promising signs of a turnaround. The Fund estimates that, during its first nine years, the work of its grantees helped add 10,500 jobs, $333 million in payroll, and $1.9 billion in investments to the region.[33] More than half of these gains—the millions invested, the jobs created—have come in the past three years. Fund leaders take that as a sign that their efforts and those of other groups are having a compounding effect.

In a specific set of R&D-rich industries, Northeast Ohio gained jobs faster than the national economy between 2010 and 2012. The region has added 1,500 jobs in computer systems design, 1,300 jobs in machinery manufacturing, and 1,300 jobs in scientific and technical consulting. Across a variety of advanced industries, there are thousands more jobs than there were two years ago. Greater Cleveland, Youngstown, Akron, and Canton still have far to go to replace the tens of thousands of manufacturing jobs they have lost since the 1970s, but people are starting to see a new kind of economy in Northeast Ohio, one that marries existing skills in production with a strong base of research to invent and build new technologies.

These efforts to revitalize Northeast Ohio's economy and reverse the quiet crisis are still a work in progress—almost everyone involved in the Fund uses that phrase. Assessing the region's economy in 2012, the Gund Foundation's Bob Jaquay said, "We still struggle with how regional we [should be], and how to deal with the complexity of the fact that a lot of the action that must take place . . . is very localized. We're grappling with how to create patterns of working, ways of communicating, and levels of trust, that morph over different geographies. This is hard stuff because nobody's ever done it before." Jaquay went on to say,

> Here's how I total it up. [Before the Fund,] we had four or five philanthropic organizations making economic development investments, now we have sixty-five funders. . . . Our organizational coming together has modeled behavior for others that are thinking about questions of the economy vis-à-vis families and the people we care about. . . . We've got hospitals, companies, thinking more about collaboration and how to work with clusters than ever before. Our work has revived a moribund pipeline of entrepreneurship and created a robust network that is thinking more

about firm formation, what it takes in terms of finance, lawyering talent, C-level talent, and what it takes to run a company.

The bottom line, Jaquay said, is "I know where we started." And the region looked a lot healthier in 2012 than it had eight years earlier.

Building shiny new stadiums and office towers downtown is infinitely easier than reinvigorating a sixteen-county, four-metropolitan-area, $178 billion economy. That is why there are so many examples of the former and so few examples of the latter. There is no silver bullet for economic growth, only a series of well-informed (or ill-informed) experiments. Given what we know about how economies grow, how they use old specialties to create new strengths, and how knowledge flows between people and sectors, Northeast Ohio is running exceptionally smart and promising experiments.

THE COLLABORATION IMPERATIVE

Northeast Ohio has embraced the network idea out of necessity. According to David Abbott, who heads the Cleveland-based Gund Foundation, "Nobody has the resources to be the one to save anything. It's really at the heart of why we develop networks, alliances, collaborations to accomplish anything. . . . It's not 'kumbaya.' There's a recognition that this is a big, complicated set of issues. Any one of us acting independently isn't going to make a very big impact."

The idea of networks, collaborations, and alliances as imperative for getting things done has also taken root in private sector companies, particularly those engaged in advanced research and production. Since advanced research and production industries are exactly what the people who are trying to change Northeast Ohio's economy want to foster, the alignment seems propitious.

The notion of competition between firms and between people is deeply ingrained, but in fact, innovation is often deeply collaborative and networked. John Seely Brown, a former chief scientist at Xerox, and John Hagel, of Deloitte consulting, explain:

> If we look at historical periods and geographic regions characterized by significant economic growth, we certainly find bright individuals and innovative organizations, but we also find something else. These individuals and organizations come together and

collaborate in evolving networks of creation, or creation nets. They play off each other, appropriating each other's work, learning from it, building on top of it and then watching and learning from what others do with their own creations.[34]

Research and development in firms has alternated between collaborative and innovative and closed off and proprietary. Beginning in the early twentieth century, companies opted for the closed model. They created special divisions populated with brilliant scientists and turned them loose to think and invent, often in a lab in a bucolic setting.[35] (Harvard president James Bryant Conant referred to this model as "picking a man of genius, giving him money, and leaving him alone.")[36] Those men (and women) of genius were not entirely alone: within the lab, researchers interacted constantly, learning from one another and collaborating to solve problems. But outside the lab, there were few intentional efforts to share knowledge or to work together. Companies wanted to maintain tight control over their intellectual property, and their large R&D divisions gave them an advantage over small, upstart firms that lacked these resources.[37] The disadvantage, though, was that firms could not, or would not, commercialize all of their new ideas, and new innovations grew stale if they were not put to immediate use.[38]

During the 1970s, formal R&D partnerships such as joint ventures and contractual agreements surged from about 30 a year at the beginning of the decade to almost 200 a year by 1980. Partnerships continued to grow by huge leaps—500 a year at the end of the 1980s and 700 by 1995—before dropping back to about 500 a year at the end of the 1990s.[39]

It seems that the trend over the past decade or so is toward less strictly defined and formal arrangements and toward the looser ties described by John Hagel and John Seely Brown's "creation nets" concept.[40] A similar trend is apparent in patent data. Two researchers examining patent applications from 1980 to 2005 in the thirty-plus member countries of the Organization for Economic Cooperation and Development (OECD) and a few Asian countries find not only that there are more collaborations—both within nations and across national boundaries—in innovative activities that lead to patents but also that the size of the inventing team is rising consistently. They conclude that their findings are "clearly indicative of worldwide inventive activities moving away from their traditional approach centering on individuals and often being carried out in virtual secrecy."[41]

An extensive scan of research by William W. Powell and Stine Grodal on collaboration specifically for the purpose of innovation in R&D finds that "collaboration across multiple organizational boundaries and institutional forms . . . is no longer rare. Indeed, many analysts have noted that the model of networks of innovators has become commonplace over the last two decades."[42] Powell and Grodal sift through forty years of research from several countries and several industries, and conclude that "the general picture that emerges from research in organizational sociology and business strategy is one in which networks and innovation constitute a virtuous cycle. External linkages facilitate innovation and at the same time innovative outputs attract further collaborative ties. Both factors stimulate organizational growth and appear to enhance innovation."[43]

This uptick in collaborations came about because companies realized that they needed to get smarter and faster, producing more complex, technologically advanced products on a shorter time scale than ever before.[44] Here's how Hagel and Brown describe the shift (in terms more sociological than technical):

> In times of relative stability, what we uniquely know—our stock of distinctive knowledge—is extremely valuable and needs to be carefully protected. . . . If others acquire this knowledge . . . they threaten to erode our distinction in the market place—we are in a zero sum world—so it pays to be extremely protective of our stocks of knowledge. . . . As change accelerates, something interesting happens—and it can be very unsettling to leaders of large, established institutions. . . . Stocks of knowledge become progressively less valuable while flows of knowledge—the relationships that can help to generate new knowledge—become more and more valuable. Rather than jealously protecting existing stocks of knowledge, institutions need to offer their own knowledge as a way to encourage others to share their knowledge and help to accelerate new knowledge building.[45]

The faster a field is changing with respect to scientific and technological development, the stronger the imperative to collaborate, and the more technology alliances are forged.[46]

Some of our colleagues at the Brookings Institution have identified a specific group of advanced industries that are distinguished by their intensive investment in and reliance on research and development and their potential for breakthrough technology development—exactly the kinds of industries that are most likely to be seeking to form networks for innovation. These industries include, among others, pharmaceutical, medical equipment, and supplies manufacturing; specialized machinery manufacturing, such as engines and turbines; computer and communications equipment manufacturing; and highly specialized instrument manufacturing for navigation, measuring, electromedical devices, and electrical equipment.[47] Combined, they make up 8 percent of the overall economy and have created more than 5.5 million skilled jobs.[48]

Advanced industries hold tremendous promise for Northeast Ohio. McKinsey & Company, which is working with Brookings to further understand advanced industries, describes the mix of products, materials, and inventions that are (or will be) characteristic of advanced industries this way: "Enabling clean transport requires light-weight materials—like carbon nanotubes, alloys, and lightweight batteries. Clean power requires rare earths for super-conductivity, polymers and filters for water and gas filtering, and flexible substrates for photovoltaics. Managing the health of an increasingly aged population requires breakthroughs in biopolymers and materials for medical devices."[49] Researchers, manufacturers, and entrepreneurs in the region are working in many of these areas.

The important point about these sectors is that they combine production, intensive research and development, and technological intricacy: there are 10 million lines of computer code running each Chevy Volt automobile.[50] Only about 10 percent of the jobs in these advanced industries are "manufacturing in nature" according to a McKinsey report (which uses a slightly different definition of the sector than our Brookings colleagues).[51] But without a foundation in manufacturing, these industries lose some of their innovative edge. Several studies have documented how innovations bubble up from the shop floor, as engineers learn not only about the products they are developing but also about the limits of existing technology and the need for new processes, materials, and machines.[52] There are several examples of American companies' sending production facilities overseas in search of cheap labor, only to see research and development capacity take root in the countries where production landed.[53] For example, in the electronics sector, 90 percent of R&D now occurs in Asia, owing in large part to the steady offshoring of manufacturing by American companies since the 1980s.[54] Manufacturing and innovation, once thought to be two entirely different aspects of the U.S. economy, turn out to be closely intertwined. Production teams and invention teams need to collaborate with each other.

The Fund for Our Economic Future and several of its partners are creating a more specific collaboration to benefit small companies, called PRISM (Partnership for Regional Innovation Services in Manufacturing). Small and medium-size manufacturers are important not only in their own right but also for the role they play in the long and intricate supply chains of technically advanced products. Innovation further along the supply chain often depends on these companies, yet because of their small size they have little in-house innovation capacity. Because of extreme pressures to keep costs low and productivity high, many of these firms operate as manufacturers for hire, with little or no capability to develop new kinds of products. They also have weak, if any, ties to universities and the wealth of engineering and materials research that happens in university laboratories.[55] The partnership is designed to plug promising small manufacturers into the rich networks of university research in Northeast Ohio. It also connects these manufacturers with business development experts, financiers, management support, and, perhaps most important, their peers with whom they can collaborate and share ideas.[56] It is managed by MAGNET, a regional nonprofit economic development organization that supports manufacturers in ways that are analogous to what BioEnterprise and NorTech do for their more specialized constituencies. MAGNET itself is part of the network of organizations that receive money from the Fund for Our Economic Future (along with funding from state, federal, and other sources, too), and BioEnterprise, NorTech, the Fund itself, and other Fund grantees are all part of PRISM's planning and implementation team.[57]

Business networks are not a twenty-first-century invention. Steven Johnson traces them to the emergence of the market economy itself.[58] But the conditions of twenty-first-century business—speed, relentless cycles of reinvention, ease of movement of capital and labor, and abundant but highly specialized and fragmented knowledge that is too much for most human brains to contain—make networks particularly important now. Collaboration has even become something of a meme in the broader culture. On November 18, 2012, the *New York Times* and the *Wall Street Journal* carried a full-page ad for a new LG smart phone. The ad reads, in part, "True innovation comes from collaboration. That's why we chose to work with some of the best companies in the industry." After outlining

LG's work with other wireless companies, the ad concludes, "Expect more amazing things from us, because we believe that working together achieves greatness, not just for us but for the industry as a whole, and most importantly, for you."[59] The company understands the currency of collaboration. Its customers want the best of everything, or rather the best of everywhere. Collaboration, LG explains, enabled it to put the best, literally, in the buyer's hand.

Northeast Ohio's economic development actors are working to help companies in the region do the same. The Fund and its intermediaries understand this collaborative topography so well because they organize themselves like the businesses they seek to bolster.

NURTURING THE NETWORK

Stewarding this network has been one of the Fund's most important contributions to the region; it is doing what no other entity can do. A 2010 report by the Council on Competitiveness, a nonprofit group of CEOs, university presidents, and labor representatives, states, "It is not sufficient to have multiple organizations that act regionally on specific development issues. . . . What is needed is a systems integrator that primarily focuses on the regional aspect of regional economic development, not just the specific economic challenges. Without such an intermediary, there is no ongoing entity to organize regional action on a regular basis."[60] The organizations that come together in a particular network are not well suited to sustain that network for several reasons. Organizations have to protect their own interests to some extent; otherwise, they are not doing their job. This imperative results in a classic collective action problem: what is good for one organization in one instance may not be what is best for the network and therefore for the organization in the long term. Some entity has to protect the network itself and steer it toward broader regional goals. "For every node [of the network], the first priority has to be their own node," said Thompson. "The beauty of the Fund is our mission to strengthen the network. We're not trying to protect our node, we protect the network's culture."

One of the reasons that the idea of networks is so popular now is that technology makes creating and coordinating them seem so easy. To join the network of Wikipedia creators, for example, all one needs is an Internet connection and self-defined measure of expertise. But making networks like the one in Northeast Ohio work requires tremendous effort on the part of the Fund and its contributing philanthropies. There is a scene in the adventure novel *Scaramouche* in which a fencing master tells his pupil that he must hold his weapon like he would hold a bird: too tightly, and he will crush it, too loosely, and it will fly away. Networks are like that, too. They have to be tended with intelligence without being managed to death.[61]

"I tell people that I'm a professional meeting attender," laughed Thompson. But, in all seriousness, he said, successful networks need people like him whose primary responsibility "is the care and feeding of the network. I have the luxury of going to meetings with the primary objective of identifying what connections need to be made to turn the talk at the meeting into actions that will generate enough value to persuade people to come to the next meeting. Not enough people have my kind of job."

Once the Fund understood that it needed to be in charge of intensive building and stewarding of the network, it took years of persistence to get the network members to come together. Thompson recalled that,

> because collaboration is such an unnatural act for organizations and institutions, it took years for grantees and others in the region to learn how to work together in substantive ways. There were quarterly meetings among the CEOs, monthly meetings among communicators, and dozens of other regular meetings that, over time, literally years, forged trust among key players and provided them with opportunities to identify shared goals and the willingness to assume shared responsibility to achieve them. There was an evolving realization that they could do more together, but it also was clear that collaboration wasn't going to just naturally happen. Collaboration is a skill that takes time to learn, and collaboration demands commitment and effort at all levels.

The length of time it took to get the network to cohere was not a reflection of resistant or uncooperative participants. Brad Whitehead marveled at how well the leaders of the various intermediaries got along and worked together. "We had a set of regional intermediary leaders who respected, trusted, and liked each other. . . . It is a real testament to these individuals how they could put their narrow interests aside and coordinate so effectively. I never saw anything like it in my twenty years of consulting to clients at McKinsey & Company." Some network participants interviewed for this book said that the formal, regular meetings were invaluable in building trust, while others thought that the real benefits came from informal encounters and ad hoc breakfasts between heads of organizations. But they all talked about how much they liked, respected, and trusted their peers. "The leaders of the nodes in the network carry themselves in a certain manner—it's open, collaborative, it isn't trying to be proprietary in terms of resources or claims on results or information. We somehow have that spirit here," said Baiju Shah, who ran BioEnterprise from 2002 to 2012. He added, "It's partly to do with a sense of shared fate: we all know what Northeast Ohio was looking at in 2000 and 2001 in terms of the future, and we quickly got a sense of 'We're in this together.'"

Sometimes an outside force, such as a new grant opportunity or a rules shift, or a crisis is needed to finally catalyze a network that has not yet cohered. For example, board leaders of several of the metropolitan chambers of commerce in Northeast Ohio had been meeting to see whether they might come together for a more coordinated set of regional actions but had not been successful in developing a model that was compelling to the various geographies. The Fund was a part of these conversations. In 2012 the state of Ohio changed how it supported efforts to draw new businesses into the state and help existing ones grow. State officials divided Ohio into regions and chose a private sector business-development organization in each region to develop a plan and coordinate efforts to attract, expand, and retain businesses in the region.* Northeast Ohio business leaders, encouraged and supported by the Fund, used the state mandate as an opportunity to create a plan to draw businesses to the region and help those already there grow and also to develop and sustain the sharper, more focused regional economic strategy described earlier.

In strong networks, participation is relevant and rewarding. That is only possible when the network participants are themselves helping guide and set the agenda. People who run multimillion-dollar organizations are not going to join a network to be bossed around. At the same time, they want to know that participating in the network helps them make

---

*Most cities and metropolitan areas around the country have one or more of these private business-development organizations, which focus on marketing the city or region to companies and recruiting specific businesses to move there. They also play defense, trying to keep companies from leaving the region by matching outside offers and helping companies grow without leaving town. As noted in the previous chapter, it is often the case that organizations from neighboring communities compete fiercely against one another rather than selling the region as a whole.

progress toward a shared goal. It's a difficult balance to strike, and the Fund is still trying to get it right. NorTech's Bagley suggested that they are getting close: "The clarity of focus helps to engage networks," but once there is a common goal and strategy, "everybody goes off and [works] opportunistically."

Too many metropolitan areas are still looking for the next Bill Gates, Michael Dell, or Mark Zuckerberg, the next hero. But there is a growing appreciation of the power of networks. In his 2012 TED talk, "Be the Entrepreneur of Your Own Life," the venture capitalist Reid Hoffman, cofounder of LinkedIn, extolled the power of "network literacy," which is, he said, "absolutely critical to how we'll navigate the world." He continued, "In a networked age, identity is not so simply determined. Your identity is actually multivariate, distributed, and partly out of your control. Who you know shapes who you are."[62]

Northeast Ohio's efforts to use networks to bring about a new economy—built on the foundations of its old economy—are aligned with powerful social, economic, and cultural forces. This feeling of alignment motivates people like Chris Thompson to go to all those meetings and bring all those doughnuts. He believes that his work and the work of the Fund for Our Economic Future reflects "the civic challenge of our time. We live in an era where power is diffuse and value is created through networks built on trust, not hierarchy. We're going to have to learn how to manage in a networked world, where you can't rely on a hero to save the day. That is the challenge, and we are a test bed."

5

HOUSTON:
EL CIVICS

The good we secure for ourselves is precarious and uncertain, is floating in mid-air, until it is secured for all of us and incorporated into our common life.

—JANE ADDAMS, *Twenty Years at Hull House*

As recently as the 1940s, the Gulfton neighborhood in the southwest corner of Houston was not really a neighborhood at all but mostly farmland. Today, Gulfton is the most densely populated neighborhood in the city of Houston. That breakneck pace of change is emblematic of the larger Houston region, which is a perpetual boomtown. (For each of the past four decades, the Houston metropolis has gained residents at a rate that is at least twice as fast, sometimes three or four times as fast, as the nation as a whole.) In the 1950s, Gulfton's farms started to give way to subdivisions, and those single-family houses were themselves rapidly succeeded by large superblock apartment buildings that housed the people who surged into Houston during the oil boom of the 1970s, when the city's population leapt by almost a third and the region's by almost half. The oil boom soon went bust, but the rush of population into Houston, and specifically to Gulfton, continued. Immigrants and refugees from Europe, Asia, the Middle East, and Latin America came to the neighborhood, and families filled the apartment complexes.[1]

Gulfton has little in the way of public amenities—few sidewalks and only one public park. But these immigrants and refugees have tried to make the landscape suit their needs. Some of the houses in the one suburban-style subdivision that remains in the neighborhood have been converted to car-repair workshops and beauty parlors, and some of the ground-floor apartments in the big 1970s complexes are also used as small shops.[2] As an architecture professor at the University of Houston writes, "Irrefutably, the physical landscape of Gulfton speaks of division and neglect," but even so, "Gulfton also defines the image of a self-sufficient, mixed-use community. Residents can find most anything they need within walking distance: furniture, automobile repair, groceries, bank services, laundry, books, medicinal herbs, a Saturday night out, or a Sunday morning service."[3] Physically, then, Gulfton is do-it-yourself urbanism, where necessity and the absence of a zoning code have reshaped the landscape.

In the early 1980s, one of Houston's oldest non-profit groups, Neighborhood Centers, Inc., which had been founded in 1907 specifically to provide care to children from immigrant and low-income families, started an early-childhood development center in Gulfton. As the staff of Neighborhood Centers started to learn more about the neighborhood, the group expanded its work, collaborating with the community on a youth development project in 1990, starting a family literacy project in one of the neighborhood's large apartment complexes in 1998, and taking over a struggling Head Start program that included the Gulfton neighborhood in 1999.[4]

Most of the neighborhood's current residents are foreign born, from eighty different countries, primarily Mexico and Central American nations but also Somalia, Bosnia, Pakistan, and Afghanistan.[5] Viewed through one lens, Gulfton concentrates all the challenges that many immigrants and low-income people in general face. Forty percent of Gulfton children live in poverty, compared with 22 percent of children in the United States as a whole.[6] Fewer than four out of ten of Gulfton's high school graduates seek higher education.[7] The neighborhood is beset by gang activity and a high crime rate.[8]

But the people at Neighborhood Centers don't see Gulfton that way. They see it as a place of promise, a "'new Ellis Island' where 'new neighbors' come to work toward a better life for their families and a better future for their children. These aspirational assets are harder to quantify than indicators of distress, but just as important. The poverty is real, but

HOUSTON'S NEIGHBORHOOD CENTERS

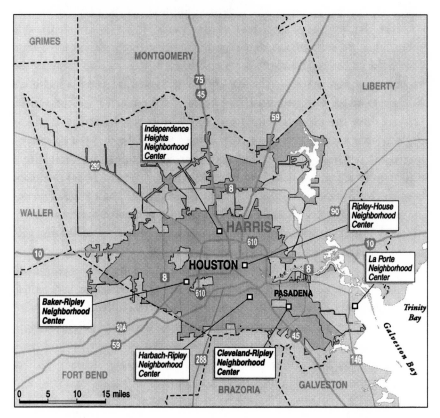

their hopes and dreams are just as real. Crime is high, but so is the sense of community and mutuality that exists. Graduation rates are low, but the work ethic of both students and adults is high."[9]

Gulfton is the home of the Baker-Ripley Neighborhood Center. Five bright, colorful buildings on four acres house a K–5 charter school; a health clinic; a community development credit union and a free tax-preparation center; a citizenship and outreach center where immigrants can start to navigate the naturalization process; rooms for adult classes in English and in health and wellness; an arts center; a business incubator; an outdoor stage; a splash park; a green space for community gatherings and arts and cultural festivals; and a jitney service, called the "magic bus," which stops at grocery stores, health clinics, and other service locations (staffers joke that it is called the magic bus because they count on magic to bring in the money that pays for it). Baker-Ripley opened in 2010, and in its first year and a half, 23,000 people came there to take classes, ask questions, play games, or otherwise participate in the life of the community.[10]

Although it is located in a neighborhood with a substantially higher crime rate than the city of Houston, high juvenile delinquency rates, and considerable gang activity, Baker-Ripley has no security guards or fences to protect the four-acre campus—there has never been a need for them.[11] The facility has no traces of vandalism or graffiti. Neighborhood Centers attributes this to a sense of ownership and pride that Gulfton residents feel about Baker-Ripley. Traditional social services and the way they are delivered, said Neighborhood Centers president and CEO Angela Blanchard, "have turned every form of help into a demeaning experience. If you invest in people, they'll solve things, they'll do things for themselves." Baker-Ripley is the place where people come to solve problems and do things for themselves and their neighborhood.

The suburb of Pasadena is some twenty miles east of Gulfton along Houston's outer beltway. Pasadena's founders imagined it as the market town anchoring surrounding farms and agricultural communities, but it grew and industrialized quickly once the Houston Ship Channel opened in 1914.[12] The city became a hub of chemical manufacturing, ship building, and oil refining. Pasadena's landscape is one of low-slung sprawl, tract housing, fast-food chains, and strip-mall shopping centers. There's no particular neighborhood or retail district or downtown around which the community coalesces. Like Gulfton, Pasadena was once overwhelmingly white and middle class; today, however, about two-thirds of the city's 152,000 residents are Hispanic, and the town's poverty rate is more than 20 percent.[13]

As in Gulfton, Neighborhood Centers' work in Pasadena has changed as the suburb itself has changed. In 1948 Neighborhood Centers created and ran a recreation program for the town after staff members noticed that many Pasadena residents traveled to one of the settlement houses on the east side of Houston for games and activities. By the early 1950s, Neighborhood Centers was running the child care facilities that the federal government had initiated to support female workers during World War II. The Cleveland-Ripley Neighborhood Center opened in Pasadena in 1968. (Houston residents Daniel and Edith Ripley gave Neighborhood Centers, then known as the Houston Settlement Association, money to build a large community center in Houston's East End in 1940. Four of the six community centers that Neighborhood Centers runs carry the Ripley name.)

Now, with the help of the county department of education, Cleveland-Ripley educates more adults and English-language learners than any other place in Pasadena or in the Neighborhood Centers' network. The center provides classes for more than 1,000 students every year in adult basic education, adult secondary education, and GED preparation and in a course called El Civics, which offers government and history lessons for students who are also learning English. The center is the source for services for seniors, tax preparation help, credit union membership, and guidance and support for people seeking citizenship.

The next American society is emerging in central-city neighborhoods like Gulfton, in suburbs like Pasadena, and in metropolitan areas like Houston. Since the Census Bureau began keeping records of the race of the population in 1790, the majority of Americans have been non-Hispanic whites.* But the population growth of minority groups is rapid, and by 2042 no single racial group will constitute a majority of the nation's population.[14] The growing diversity in our metropolitan areas and the nation as a whole during the first decade of the twenty-first century was attributable mostly to children born to Asian, African American, and Hispanic families who were already living in the United States.[15] But new immigrants accounted for more than 30 percent of national population growth between 2000 and 2012. In metropolitan areas, the pace and volume of immigration has been even faster: almost all (95 percent) of immigrants live in America's metros.[16]

These immigrants and their children are the colleagues, bosses, and employees of the coming decades. Over the next forty years, immigrants and their descendants will be responsible for virtually all of the growth in the U.S. labor pool.[17] This diversity can be a huge benefit for the United States. Immigrants are part of America's innovation and entrepreneur

---

*The 1790 census asked respondents to identify the number of free white males sixteen and over, free white males under sixteen, free white females, other free persons, and slaves in their households. The 1850 census asked for the "color" of individuals (white, black, or "mulatto"), and in 1870 the category of "color" was expanded to include Chinese (which encompassed all East Asians) and American Indians. The changing approach to racial categorization through the decades is illuminating. See U.S. Census Bureau, "History: Index of Questions," Department of Commerce, 2012 (www.census.gov/history/www/through_the_decades/index_of_questions/).

economy; immigrants are 30 percent more likely to start a new business; and among individuals with advanced degrees, immigrants are three times as likely as their U.S.-born counterparts to file patents.[18] Recent arrivals have founded or cofounded companies such as Yahoo, Google, Intel, and eBay. Four in ten Fortune 500 companies were founded or cofounded by immigrants or their children.[19]

Studies show that the presence of immigrants can increase wages for U.S.-born workers, in part because immigrants complement, rather than substitute for, the skills of native-born workers. Research by Giovanni Peri and Chad Sparber finds that "immigrants with little educational attainment have a comparative advantage in manual and physical tasks, while natives of similar levels of education have a comparative advantage in communication- and language-intensive tasks. Native and foreign-born workers specialize accordingly. When immigration generates large increases in manual task supply, the relative compensation paid to communication skills rises, thereby rewarding natives who progressively move to language-intensive jobs."[20] Peri finds a similar interaction between highly educated immigrants and native-born workers: "Natives respond to immigration by changing occupations to those with less quantitative and more interactive content than their previous occupations required."[21] Close to 1 million small businesses in the United States are owned by immigrants, and these businesses collectively employ 4.7 million workers, 14 percent of all small-business employees.[22] Immigrant-owned businesses, such as restaurants, retail stores, or warehouses, also hire native-born workers to be waiters, clerks, and stock managers.[23]

But immigrants are also much less likely than native-born residents to have completed high school (30 percent of immigrants lack a high school diploma compared with 9 percent of the native-born population).[24] Immigrants have a slightly higher poverty rate than people who were born in this country.[25] U.S.-born blacks and Hispanics also have lower levels of education and higher poverty rates than native-born whites. The challenge of low educational attainment is not just a personal or family problem, nor is it an abstract national concern. It is a metropolitan challenge because in metropolitan areas a better-educated workforce means more jobs.[26]

Houston is America on demographic fast-forward. More than 60 percent of its residents are people of color.[27] Between 2000 and 2010, the metro area's foreign-born population—already high relative to the rest of the nation—grew 48 percent; in the suburbs alone, the foreign-born population grew by 90 percent (compared with 28 percent for the nation as a whole).[28] More than 42 percent of Houston's children have at least one foreign-born parent, compared with a national rate of 23 percent.[29] In Houston, Neighborhood Centers illustrates just what it means to embrace demographic change and build a new workforce—a new America—at the metropolitan scale.

"YOU CAN'T BUILD ON BROKEN"

Neighborhood Centers traces its lineage back to 1907, when Alice Graham Baker, the civically engaged wife of a prominent Houston attorney (and future grandmother of Secretary of State James Baker III) founded the Houston Settlement Association to create a settlement house in the Second Ward neighborhood. Houston was growing at a mind-boggling pace in the early years of the last century: the population leapt from 45,000 to 79,000 between 1900 and 1910 and almost doubled again between 1910 and 1920.[30] Many of the city's newcomers and poor native Houstonians settled amid railroad yards and warehouses in the Second Ward. Recognizing that the neighborhood's children needed safe places to stay while their parents worked, Baker and her friends created the Settlement Association to provide "educational, industrial, social, and friendly aid to those within our reach."[31]

Today, Neighborhood Centers is one of the largest nonprofit service providers in the United States, with a budget of $275 million a year and an enormous presence throughout Texas. Through its Public Sector Solutions division, the agency manages child-care eligibility and assistance funds and workforce assistance payments for 67 of the 254 counties in the state.[32] Within Harris County, where 69 percent of metropolitan Houston's population resides, Neighborhood Centers offers services at sixty different sites, ranging from Early Head Start to senior care, immigration assistance to tax preparation.[33] From its start as a child-care provider in the Second Ward, Neighborhood Centers now runs some twenty-six Head Start sites serving more than 2,200 children in Greater Houston.[34] Neighborhood Centers also operates five charter elementary schools and one middle school for 1,942 students in pre-kindergarten through eighth grade, including a school within a school where refugee children can learn the rhythms and implicit expectations of an American classroom. (As one staff member put it, imagine walking into second grade and not knowing what a backpack is or what it means to put it in a cubby.) They run a statewide child-care service that provides direct child-care payments for 43,000 families and determines eligibility for subsidized child care for an additional 21,000 families. Neighborhood Centers also offers adults opportunities to bolster their skills, learn English, receive consistent medical care, and gain a firmer financial footing—all of which contribute to their children's success in school and in life.[35]

Working through voluntary tax preparers and a few staff members, Neighborhood Centers facilitated the free preparation of 30,000 tax returns in 2012 and $41 million in refunds (mostly through child-care tax credits and the federal earned-income tax credit) that went back into the Houston-area economy. Neighborhood Centers also sponsors the Promise Credit Union, which serves 3,600 people. The link between the credit union and tax preparation services means that it is easy for members to put a little bit of their tax refund aside in a new savings account. The credit union provides loans, mostly to help people buy used cars to navigate Houston's jungle of freeways, but also for the $680 fee an applicant must pay to become a U.S. citizen. In 2012 Neighborhood Centers educated 7,000 immigrants about their rights and citizenship pathways and helped 350 people become U.S. citizens. The organization provides care and case management to 800 senior citizens and serves 2,200 people in its twenty senior centers. It has provided long-term case management and direct disaster-recovery assistance to 26,000 families along the Gulf Coast affected by Tropical Storm Allison and Hurricanes Katrina, Rita, and Ike. Neighborhood Centers also runs a financial aid office that administers eight different federal programs that help 85,000 Texans find and keep work. And it serves as a single point of contact for financial assistance for veterans and their families in four counties in the Houston metropolitan area.[36]

When Blanchard, the president and CEO of this huge, diverse organization, was asked, "What does NCI do?" she answered, "We keep Houston the way it is—a place of opportunity. We came here for opportunity. We are all here for the same reason." She, her board of directors, her leadership team, and her colleagues work simultaneously at a very small and a very large scale: small in the sense that Neighborhood Centers conducts extensive interviews and listening sessions in neighborhoods to find out what residents want from and can give to their community; and large in that it is present throughout the physically vast Houston metropolitan area and in that it is a supersize, organizationally sophisticated entity (while many social service nonprofits are neither). Neighborhood Centers is an example of the metropolitan revolution that is always in progress, working through networks, continually seeking input and feedback, in a place where constant change is the status quo.

Gulfton's Baker-Ripley Community Center opened in 2010 and immediately became Neighborhood Centers' flagship; it is where staff members take visitors to show them the organization at its best. The center gave Gulfton the community gathering space that residents craved. But the Baker-Ripley center also represents something else: a radically different approach to working in communities, which looks beyond discouraging statistics and incorporates dreams, aspirations, and all the things that are actually working in these neighborhoods.

In 2005 Neighborhood Centers was looking forward to its hundredth birthday, and staff members were thinking about what the next century of work might look like. Blanchard and her colleagues had grown frustrated with the standard descriptions of neighborhoods like Gulfton and the other communities in which they worked. "We got tired of the way people talk about the people that we work with," she said. "We knew we were working with Houston's future. We ourselves had lived that dream [coming from poor or immigrant families]." While others looked at Gulfton and saw poverty, crime, and problems, the residents "don't see themselves that way," Blanchard said. One of her oft-repeated statements is, "You can't build on broken." People in Gulfton are not broken and do not need to be "fixed."

During a conversation with a fellow Houstonian, Blanchard expressed her dismay at the gap between Gulfton's reality and the standard approach to delivering social services, which focused on the "lacks-gaps-needs-wants-broken-stuff." (In speeches and conversations, Blanchard runs this litany together so that it becomes one long singsong word.) She and her colleagues recognized that they were caught in this standard method, she said, but they felt that the approach wasn't working anymore. Her friend told her to look into appreciative inquiry, a method for investigating and implementing organizational change developed by David Cooperrider, a doctoral student at Case Western Reserve University, and others in the mid-1980s.[37]

Cooperrider believed that when businesses and organizations tried to change by starting with a focus on problems and deficits, they were actually limiting the kinds of changes that were possible. "We had really painted ourselves into a picture that argued that organizations are big problems to be solved," Cooperrider told a magazine interviewer. "This problem-analytic set of traditions . . . helps lead to some incremental learning and improvement to find out everything that is holding a system back, but it won't make the breakthroughs that we need today."[38] Rather than honing in on what is broken or deficient and trying to change it, appreciative inquiry starts with what an organization is good at or has done well in the past. As one study of the method puts it, "The tangible result of the inquiry process is a series of statements that describe where the organization wants to be, based on the high moments of where they have been. Because the statements are grounded in real experience and history, people know how to repeat their success."[39]

When Neighborhood Centers staff heard about appreciative inquiry, it resonated. Now they had a method that matched their experience. "Marketing people always wanted us to tell a story about how bad these neighborhoods had been and how great we made them," Blanchard recalled. "We could never bring ourselves to do that. Appreciative inquiry freed us not to tell that story."

Neighborhood Centers started to test the approach in Gulfton. The organization had been working in Gulfton for several years, and Gulfton residents had been asking Neighborhood Centers to build a community center there. But Neighborhood Centers wanted to focus first on the community itself, rather than on the community center. They wanted a better understanding of what Gulfton residents valued and their vision for what their neighborhood could be. Neighborhood Centers started by asking different kinds of questions from those they had asked before. Rather than asking Gulfton residents, "What do you need?" they asked, "What's good about this neighborhood? How do you know you are home? What attracted you to the neighborhood, and what would make you want to work or live here even longer? What skills or abilities can you contribute to make your neighborhood better?" Staff members who worked on this effort recall that they had to ask the questions several times before people understood that they were being asked to talk about good things, not problems.

The questions were asked in eight different languages, but the responses were broadly the same. People were proud of their neighborhood and its diversity, but they wanted a good school for their children, a safe place for their children to play, adult education services, transportation, and a reliable financial institution. This wish list became the blueprint for services at Baker-Ripley.

Adonias Arevalo, a twenty-one-year-old student and restaurant manager who emigrated from El Salvador when he was eleven, said that Baker-Ripley "helped me discover a lot of my talents." For the past three years, he has taught computer literacy and English classes for native Spanish speakers at the center. He also coordinates the work of a handful of other volunteer teachers, helping with their class syllabus, grading, and the like. He started teaching at Baker-Ripley after the instructor of his mother's computer class left unexpectedly. "We made the class more serious, so the students could feel more serious, rather than to just go and sit there. They thought they were really in school. I liked it. I found myself in a position that I never thought I would be, and I thought, 'I like this.' I saw more students coming in." Teaching students, many of whom are old enough to be his parents, has "helped me be more mature," he said, and led him to study education at Houston Community College.

Arevalo is one of the many immigrants who came to the United States without proper documentation as a child, and because of recent changes in federal policy he is eligible to defer deportation for two years. He recalled that during his interview with an agent from U. S. Customs and Immigration Services, he talked about his work at Baker-Ripley. And the agent told him he

> was one of the few who, besides coming to this country to learn, have also helped other people. I like that. It gives me a good image of myself. It's good for other people. . . . When you are willing to help somebody, help somebody grow, no matter how little you do, it helps a lot. Baker-Ripley is an open door. If you want to help others, this is a great opportunity and a great chance. . . . I have something that I can contribute to my community and my neighborhood.

In 2006, when Neighborhood Centers' staff started using appreciative inquiry in interviews with residents, business owners, elected officials, and others in Pasadena, a different set of aspirations and goals from those in Gulfton emerged. People in Pasadena felt that the community's civic institutions did not reflect what Pasadena had become: a home for lower-middle-class Hispanics. Suburbs across the country are facing a similar demographic shift. Slightly more than half of all immigrants (51 percent) live in suburbs, and a majority of the Asians, Hispanics, and blacks who live in metropolitan areas live in suburbs rather than central cities.[40] Suburbs have also become more diverse across income levels. As noted previously in chapter 3, more poor Americans live in suburbs than in cities or rural areas.[41] Immigration and suburban poverty also overlap to some extent, as foreign-born suburbanites have much higher poverty rates than their native-born neighbors.[42] "The emergence of suburbs as places where rich, poor and middle class can all live and work is a quintessential American phenomenon of the last half of the 20th century. Immigrants went along for the ride. So too with the suburbanization of poverty: large shares of low-income immigrants arrived along with the large shares of low-income natives," according to an analysis by Roberto Suro, Jill Wilson, and Audrey Singer.[43]

Roberta Leal, who was interviewed as part of the appreciative inquiry process in Pasadena, said, "What appreciative inquiry did was allow the community to view the strengths of the area, and see the resources we already had. . . . In the last three years, we've seen the full effects of appreciative inquiry. Everybody has started to frame things differently." Leal's mother, an undocumented immigrant from Mexico, first came to Cleveland-Ripley decades ago to use the community food pantry and eventually became a teacher of English language classes to other Spanish-speaking immigrants. Today Roberta Leal is on the community advisory board at Cleveland-Ripley and is pursuing her doctorate in social work. Leal's father and two sisters have also volunteered at Cleveland-Ripley.

Pasadena's Hispanic residents wanted more political influence to reflect their growing population. They also wanted public transportation, which Pasadena did not have, and more adult education options. Cleveland-Ripley staff, volunteer leaders, and members spearheaded the Census Counts Committee to encourage Pasadena's Hispanic residents to participate in the 2010 census so that the town's demographic shift could be clearly documented and eventually reflected in political representation. As a result of the committee's efforts, 74 percent of Pasadena residents participated in the 2010 census, compared with 65 percent in 2000, and the town's two-thirds Hispanic majority was now more accurately reflected.[44] The community advisory board of the Cleveland-Ripley center went to the Pasadena city council to talk about the lack of public transportation, and eventually the county, city, and the neighboring community of LaPorte created a public bus line that links Pasadena and LaPorte to each other and to the city of Houston's public transportation system.

Neighborhood Centers created an alliance with the Harris County Department of Education to provide substantial adult education and English language classes. Leal said,

> One of the things that came out of our vision, because the demographics of Pasadena have changed so much, is the [need] to have multiple [English as a second language] classes. . . . I remember these conversations taking place. Harris County [officials] were saying, "We have the capacity to host the classes, we just can't get to the people." On the other hand Neighborhood Centers is saying "We have the people, we need the resources, the instructors. Let's meet in the middle, let's make this happen.". . . To be able to implement these services, it says we're not upset that you came to this country and you don't speak English. It says, we're glad you're here, come to our home, we can teach you something new and get you out into the community to be your own leader.

Leal works for Communities in Schools, an organization focused on preventing children from dropping out of school. Her organization often works with Neighborhood Centers or refers people to Cleveland-Ripley for services. "The connection with the support networks through Neighborhood Centers is so strong and so important. When you send a client there or send a family there, they can go and have access to all the family services, [whether their request is] 'I need food for today' or 'I want to start my own business' or 'I want to give back to the community.'" Moreover, she said, Neighborhood Centers identifies emerging issues and is often the first to organize other groups to address them. "There is nobody else we can call in Pasadena on immigration. . . . It speaks to their capacity for innovation. As soon as a social issue comes up, Neighborhood Centers is the first one to say, 'You know what, there are these changes coming down the line, let's have a meeting, let's get the school district involved, we need to educate the community about this.'"

Neighborhood Centers' success in Gulfton and Pasadena is inextricably linked to its presence in fifty-eight other places around the Houston region. Appreciative inquiry is hyperlocal, but the systems that realize the dreams and aspirations that it uncovers work best when they are big in reach and resources. Neighborhood Centers has that large scale, in part because of its history of operating all over the Houston region but also because its leaders insist that it be a big, professionally run organization. ("Small is beautiful" just doesn't resonate in Houston.) Neighborhood Centers' size enables it to deal with the complexity of social services delivery and funding in America today. As Blanchard explained, "You need a regional footprint and context. You need muscle. This is not just the scale of dollars, it's the ability, the muscle."

The "muscle" that Blanchard spoke of is necessary to take rigid, compartmentalized, regulation-encrusted funding streams and braid them together to provide the services that new and low-income Houstonians need if they are to flourish. As of the summer of 2012, Neighborhood Centers had grants or contracts from the U.S. Departments of Agriculture, Education, Labor, Health and Human Services, Housing and Urban Development, Treasury, and Energy, the Texas Departments of State Health Services and Aging and Disability Services, and the Texas Education Agency and contracts with the City of Houston, Harris County, and other local government units. Those agencies amount to seventy separate funding sources, with different reporting requirements and spending restrictions. Neighborhood Centers also uses funds from the United Way of Greater Houston and more than 500 private foundations, corporations, and individuals.[45] Keeping track of the dollars and the accountability requirements requires some forty separate database systems.[46]

But for all the administrative complexity, Neighborhood Centers' breadth of work actually enhances its financial stability, since it is not overly dependent on a single agency or program. Blanchard noted that Neighborhood Centers has been asked to or volunteered to take the reins from other organizations that lacked the infrastructure to manage the complexities of funding requirements from a variety of sources or to expand rapidly to meet fast-changing demand. That ability to "go where you're invited, do what you're asked to do," as Blanchard likes to say, is true to the original spirit of settlement-house work. Jane Addams, the cofounder of Chicago's Hull House, probably the best-known settlement house in American history, writes in her memoir that "the one thing to be dreaded in the Settlement is that it lose its flexibility, its power of quick adaptation, its readiness to change its methods as its environment may demand. It must be open to conviction and must have a deep and abiding sense of tolerance. It must be hospitable and ready for experiment."[47]

DIVERSITY, SKILLS, AND THE METRO FUTURE

At the metropolitan scale, demographics and economic success are closely interwoven. It's becoming clear that poverty and economic inequality are likely to act as a drag on economic growth at both the national and the metropolitan level. In 2007 the U.S. Government Accountability Office examined a host of recent studies on poverty and economic growth and found that "some recent empirical studies have begun to demonstrate that higher rates of poverty are associated with lower rates of growth in the economy as a whole. For example, areas with higher poverty rates experience, on average, slower per capita income growth rates than low-poverty areas."[48] The Nobel Prize–winning economist Joseph Stiglitz has written, "The bottom line that higher inequality is associated with lower growth—controlling for all other relevant factors—has been verified by looking at a range of countries and looking over longer periods of time."[49]

The counterproposition, that a more skilled workforce accelerates economic growth, is found in (among other works) Enrico Moretti's book *The New Geography of Jobs,* which came out in 2012. Moretti argues that metropolitan areas with a high percentage of well-educated workers also tend to attract more highly educated people—conversely, those with low levels of well-educated workers tend to bleed highly educated people. Moretti describes three Americas:

> At one extreme are the brain hubs—cities [by which Moretti means metros] with a well-educated labor force and a strong innovation sector. They are growing, adding good jobs and attracting even more skilled workers. At the other extreme are cities once dominated by traditional manufacturing, which are declining rapidly, losing jobs and residents. In the middle are a number of cities that could go either way. The three Americas are growing apart at an accelerating rate.[50]

Moretti also demonstrates significant and increasing differences in length of life, stability of marriages, voting and political participation, and gifts to charity between people in well-educated and less-educated metros.

So here is the challenge facing Houston and other metropolitan areas that are becoming rapidly more diverse and metropolitan areas that are home to a large group of people who have persistently been overlooked or poorly served by education institutions: a large share of their present and future workforce are members of groups who as a whole are less likely to reach high levels of education when compared with native-born whites. Too few minority students (including the children of immigrants) and low-income students go to community or four-year colleges, and that is driving the troubling education gap that leads to Moretti's three Americas.[51]

If research shows anything about immigrants in America, it is that it is difficult to generalize about this diverse group. But there are some discernible trends, at least for some groups of immigrants and their children. Children of two immigrant parents are more likely to be poor than their native-born peers. George Borjas of Harvard writes, "Nearly half of these children live in households that receive some type of public assistance, and about one-third live in poverty."[52] The poverty gap between children of immigrants and children of native-born residents is traceable to the differences in the education level and human capital of their parents.[53]

Being poor, or growing up poor, makes it hard for people to make their fullest contribution to the workforce and hard for them to gain additional skills. The Government Accountability Office's 2007 review of the literature found that "research has consistently demonstrated that the quality and level of education attained by lower income children is substantially below those for children from middle- or upper-income families. Moreover, high school dropout rates in 2004 were four times higher for students from low-income families than those in high-income families. . . . And the percentage of low-income students who attend college immediately after high school is significantly lower than for their wealthier counterparts: 49 percent compared to 78 percent."[54]

A study of children who are themselves immigrants or whose parents are immigrants found that "partly as a result of high rates of Latino school segregation, adolescents from Latin American immigrant families tend to be concentrated in problematic schools, such as those characterized by more conflict, weaker academic norms, weaker ties between students and adults, and larger class sizes."[55] Hispanic immigrant and second-generation college students are more likely than their native-born peers to take remedial classes and to be enrolled part-time, rather than full-time, in higher education, and those factors make it less likely they will complete their degree.[56]

There can be considerable overlap between minority populations and immigrant populations, so some of the achievement gaps and poverty challenges that immigrants and their children experience show up again in broad statistics about achievement gaps and poverty challenges of minorities. High school and college graduation rates for Hispanic and black residents of the United States rose over the first decade of this century, but they still lag far behind those of whites and Asians. Only 61 percent of Hispanics and 80 percent of blacks have a high school diploma, compared with 85 percent of Asians and 90 percent of whites. The gaps in bachelor's degree attainment are much larger: 13 percent of Hispanics, 18 percent of blacks, 31 percent of whites, and 50 percent of Asians have college degrees.

A better-educated metropolitan workforce tends to be more productive and command higher salaries, benefiting not only highly educated people but also workers of varying skills throughout the metropolitan area.[57] By contrast, according to a recent paper by our colleague Jonathan Rothwell, a shortage of educated workers in a metropolitan area leads to higher unemployment—jobless rates are two percentage points higher in metros with too few educated workers to meet demand. Educated workers aren't just creating jobs for themselves and their peers: Rothwell finds that "both less educated and younger workers are much more likely to be working if they live in metropolitan areas with a smaller education gap."[58]

How can metros succeed if their incoming workforce cannot get—because of poverty, race, or the immigration or socioeconomic status of their parents—the education and resources that will make them most productive, most entrepreneurial, and most likely to contribute to job growth? Metros must crack the code of how best to tap into and develop the skills of a more diverse population, one that is not always concentrated in a defined neighborhood but spread out across the metropolitan landscape.

Blanchard said, "If you're poor, you want to be poor in Houston, because there's a ladder here. Our purpose is not to eliminate poverty. People do that on their own. What we're doing is to provide the rungs of the ladder." One of those rungs is education. Children who move from Neighborhood Centers' Head Start programs into Houston schools score higher than most of their classmates in reading and math. Neighborhood Centers' Head Start and Early Head Start programs entice fathers to participate in Head Start–related activities at rates that are much higher than the national average (more than three times the national average in the case of Early Head Start).[59] The third graders at Neighborhood Centers' charter school in Gulfton score better than other students in the Houston school district on tests of reading proficiency—94 percent are rated proficient by state test standards—and early reading proficiency is linked to a higher likelihood of high school graduation. Overall, every grade in Neighborhood Centers' charter schools scored at the average or above-average level on the national Stanford 10 test, and each grade's performance was better than the next lower grade's (for example, fourth graders performed better than third graders, and fifth graders better than fourth graders), suggesting that children in these schools improve their comparative performance with each year they are in school.

Neighborhood Centers offers rungs of the ladder to adults as well. It is a major provider of English language instruction, and nonnative speakers who become proficient in English experience a huge increase in earnings.[60] Neighborhood Centers assists people with the complicated process of gaining citizenship, which also is correlated with an increase in earnings (among foreign-born people, those who are citizens earn, on average, $14,000 more a year than noncitizens).[61]

And that is just a portion of what happens at Baker-Ripley, Cleveland-Ripley, and the other sites in Houston where Neighborhood Centers works. Like the assets of neighborhoods with a bad statistical profile, some of that work is hard to quantify. What is the value of Adonias Arevalo's feeling of competence and maturity and his steady progress toward his teaching credential? Roberta Leal said, "My story is not something that I had shared with very many people. Neighborhood Centers has been the agency that says 'You have the strength to share that with others.' I didn't even realize a few years back that that was a strength that I had." What is the value of people's understanding that their stories and skills matter to their community, and that they, who by some measures have very little, can give something to their neighbors?

THE RIGHT QUESTIONS AND THE RIGHT INVESTMENTS

Neighborhood Centers offers several important lessons in how to help people realize their own assets and raise their education level, their income, and their sense of efficacy and connection to their community. In many ways, these lessons are another application of the lessons from previous chapters. It may seem that there is a great gulf between developing the science and engineering talent that will elevate New York's media, financial, and medical industries and helping a refugee family who has just moved into a large apartment complex in Houston start its journey up the economic ladder, but the approaches are remarkably similar and boil down to this: ask the right questions. And like the people working to redirect the economy of Northeast Ohio, Neighborhood Centers relies on networks and operates at a very large geographic scale. The metropolitan revolution won't play out in the same way in every metro area, but its tools are both powerful and easily adaptable.

The appreciative inquiry approach that Neighborhood Centers uses is a form of crowd sourcing with a crowd that is all too often talked at rather than talked with. The questions are designed not just to enable Neighborhood Centers' staff members to identify the strengths of people in the neighborhood but also to encourage the people themselves to recognize and take pride in what they and their neighbors do well. Neighborhood Centers has written a guidebook to teach other organizations how to use the appreciative inquiry approach, and throughout it there are instructions on how to maintain a cheerful relentlessness in finding what is good and a repeated recognition that "people are rarely asked to reflect on what is working or what they would most like to see. For many, these are new questions that require new thought processes."[62] Neighborhood Centers' staff members say that the appreciative inquiry experience has changed the way people in the neighborhood talk about themselves and their community. "They tell a different story about themselves. They are proud of where they live. They are proud of their neighborhood," said one Neighborhood Centers leader.

Since Neighborhood Centers started using the appreciative inquiry approach, the number of people using their community centers—not just Baker-Ripley but others, too—has soared. In part, this reflects a change in the way community members pay for services. In the past, an individual had to pay $35 to be a member of a community center and then pay extra fees for classes. Fearing a budget shortfall in 2008, Neighborhood Centers started charging $100 for a family membership and eliminated the fees for individual classes. Families who paid more started spending more time at the community centers to feel that they were getting their money's worth. But staff members say that families who had participated in appreciative inquiry also had a greater psychological and emotional investment in the community centers. They had the sense that they themselves had brought this community center into being and were responsible for its flourishing. They needed to invest their time and creativity to teach classes, not just take them. In these ways, the organization helps create networks of neighbors, experts, students, teachers, and families, all of whom shift between various roles. Neighborhood Centers, explained Roberta Leal, "teaches residents, myself included, that there is opportunity out there, and it is okay to take the steps necessary to advance yourself. . . . They say 'Don't give [Neighborhood Centers] credit, give yourself credit, because without you Neighborhood Centers can't function.' I don't think any other agency does that."

Neighborhood Centers' funders also have responded to the new story that appreciative inquiry allows the organization to tell. "There is no energy for change when the story is all about the problems," said Angela Blanchard. "It is much more powerful to have a conversation about investment than charity. I tell [potential donors and volunteers], 'These are people you really want to know.'" Blanchard described how she first went to a major donor with a tale not of Gulfton's woes and shortcomings but of its strengths and possibilities. She said that the donor's eyes lit up. "I've been waiting for this," she remembered him saying. Funders, too, are part of the Neighborhood Centers network, not only giving money but also providing expertise in certain fields and intellectual guidance.

To support its close engagement in neighborhoods, Neighborhood Centers is part of, sometimes the center of, a vast network of organizations with similar goals but different specialties. In any given year, Neighborhood Centers will work with almost a hundred other groups on a range of special events, such as back-to-school days where families can collect school uniforms, get haircuts and dental screenings, and pick up vouchers for school supplies, or a conference on strategies to prevent infant mortality. Neighborhood Centers also has thirty-three separate partnerships (relationships in which a contract or memorandum of understanding lays out different responsibilities) and nine strategic alliances (in which partners provide funding and often share service delivery). It works with the Houston Community College system to provide classes, training, and materials for students of English as a second language. It collaborates with the Houston Center for Literacy on adult education classes; with the Houston Independent School District and Teach for America on Head Start; with Texas Capital Bank on a credit union; with Univision and the National Association of Latino Elected Officials on immigration and civic engagement work; and with Legacy Healthcare and Texas Children's Hospital on clinics at two community centers. Successfully supporting communities and individuals requires a microscope and a wide-angle lens, and Neighborhood Centers uses both.

Many social service and antipoverty organizations understand the importance of close community connections and the necessity of being part of a network of other organizations. Where they stumble, and where Neighborhood Centers is strong, is in the area of support, both financial and professional. Neighborhood Centers has a big budget and a big, powerful, professional back office to support its local work. It streamlines and standardizes overhead and administration, which enables it to be more flexible and responsive to specific neighborhood needs.[63] As noted earlier, big organizations like Neighborhood Centers are also less dependent on any single source of funding and so are not put out of business when a government program ends or a philanthropic organization decides to change its grant-making strategy.[64] Their funding stability allows them to engage in "venture" activities, experiments that can lead to new lines of work and service.[65]

When it comes to building the internal capacity to address the needs of communities, bigger really is better. Neighborhood Centers' leaders estimate that an organization needs to hit an annual budget of about $100 million to both provide services and pay for $6–7 million worth of what they call "internal infrastructure investments," such as advanced information technology and salaries that are roughly competitive with those in the private sector. Those internal infrastructure investments allow Neighborhood Centers to operate as effectively as it does. It is understandable that governments and foundations want their dollars to go to direct services for poor people, not for overhead. But "overhead" can mean sophisticated computer systems to handle the myriad reporting and tracking requirements and data analysis to determine which interventions are most effective. Organizations need internal investment to make smart external investments.[66]

HOUSTON AND THE IMAGINED FUTURE

In his sweeping and irreverent travelogue through the edge cities that exploded on the American landscape in the 1970s and 1980s, the writer Joel Garreau finds America's physical future in Houston. Garreau writes of the massive hotel-mall-office-residential conglomeration called the Galleria, which is about five miles to the north and west of Gulfton and Baker-Ripley:

It raises questions that will resound across America well into the twenty-first century. . . . If Edge City is our new standard form of American metropolis . . . will these places ever be diverse, urbane, and livable? The answers to these questions are of no small moment, for as we push our lives into the uncharted territory of Edge Cities, places like them are becoming the laboratories for how civilized urban American will be for the rest of our lifetime.[67]

Twenty years later, metropolitan Houston is still a laboratory where urgent questions are tested and played out, but these questions are about people. What makes a metropolis is not the mix of buildings, highways, and uses, whether orderly or chaotic; the mix that matters is people and their skills and the opportunities they have to flourish and for their children, and neighbors, and friends to flourish. The real questions are, How do we embrace diversity? How do we manage the cultural differences and the shift in political power that naturally flow from greater diversity? How do we assimilate and integrate tens of millions of new Americans?

Not every metro has a Neighborhood Centers, Inc., with its deep roots in the community and its steady commitment to "go where you're invited, do what you're asked to do," in Blanchard's words. But every metro can learn from the way Neighborhood Centers is embracing Houston's future and weaving it into Houston's history. Angela Blanchard and her colleagues see the people in Gulfton and Pasadena not as impediments to Houston's progress but as the fulfillment of the region's aspirations. In a speech to the United Neighborhood Centers of America (the umbrella organization for the neighborhood centers that grew out of the settlement house movement of the late nineteenth and early twentieth centuries), Blanchard said that the starting point for community change is "looking at your city and the DNA of your city and understanding, what is that city really built around. What are the aspirations here? What is the understanding of what it means to be a Houstonian, or from San Diego, or Orlando? Houston was built to work, and for work." The people that Neighborhood Centers works with "came here to work. Everybody in Houston understands that."[68] Houston is also a region of newcomers. As Blanchard said in her Houston TEDX talk, "70 percent of us weren't born here. We don't share a past, we share a future."[69]

PART II

THE FUTURE OF THE METROPOLITAN REVOLUTION
Ushering in the Metro Age

6

THE RISE OF INNOVATION DISTRICTS

People gathered in concentrations of city size and density can be considered a positive good . . . because they are the source of immense vitality, and because they do represent, in small geographic compass, a great and exuberant richness of differences and possibilities, many of these differences unique and unpredictable and all the more valuable because they are.

—JANE JACOBS, *The Death and Life of Great American Cities*

The American metropolitan revolution, although nascent and evolving, is already inventing new models of economic development (as seen in the Applied Sciences initiative), new approaches to social integration (Neighborhood Centers), and new levels of collaboration (as in Northeast Ohio and Denver). Earlier chapters focused on the revolution as is: how city and metropolitan networks are stepping up in the absence of federal leadership to grapple with the big challenges before the country. This chapter and the next focus on the revolution to be: how megatrends will drive cities and metros to reshape their physical and social landscape within as well as forge new connections with their trading partners abroad.

As the next decade unfolds, profound economic, demographic, and cultural shifts are likely to alter radically the place preferences of firms and people and, in the process, to reconceive the very link between economy shaping and place making.

A confluence of trends is already leading companies and consumers to revalue the physical assets and attributes of cities and make employment centers of suburbia more urban. Our open, innovative economy increasingly craves proximity and extols integration, which allow knowledge to be transferred easily between, within, and across clusters, firms, workers, and supporting institutions, thereby enabling the creation of new ideas that fuel even greater economic activity and growth. Our collaboration-oriented economy is altering how firms and people interact, how ideas flow, and how places—offices, research labs, business incubators, innovation institutes—are actually designed. Our diversified economy and diverse population demand greater choices in where firms locate and where people live—across jurisdictions, neighborhoods, and building types.

The vanguard of these megatrends is largely found not at the city or metropolitan scale writ large but in smaller enclaves, what are increasingly being called innovation districts.[1] Innovation districts cluster and connect leading-edge anchor institutions and cutting-edge innovative firms with supporting and spin-off companies, business incubators, mixed-use housing, office and retail, and twenty-first-century amenities and transport. Some can be found in the downtowns and midtowns of cities like Cambridge and Detroit, where the existing base of advanced research universities, medical complexes, research institutions, and clusters of tech and creative firms is sparking business expansion as well as residential and commercial growth. Others can be found in Boston and Seattle, where underused areas (particularly older industrial areas) are being reimagined and remade, leveraging their enviable location near waterfronts and downtowns and along transit lines. Still others can be found in traditional exurban science parks like Research Triangle Park in Raleigh-Durham that are scrambling to urbanize to keep pace with workers' preference for walkable communities and firms' preference for proximity to other firms and collaborative opportunities.

Innovation districts arise in disparate geographies with different economic drivers. But all of them draw from the best innovations in both industry cluster and place-making strategies to create well-defined communities packed with resources for firms, entrepreneurs, innovators, researchers, and residents. The theory behind business clusters is that the geographical concentration of interconnected firms and supporting institutions leads to more innovation and production efficiencies, shared inputs, thicker labor markets, and collective problem solving; the theory behind walkable urbanism is that dense, mixed-use neighborhoods with cultural, recreational, and retail amenities will attract highly educated, innovative, entrepreneurial individuals and benefit the neighborhood's existing residents. Innovation districts are the physical synthesis of these two ideas, a new nexus between innovation and urbanism.[2]

Innovation districts are a classic case of the whole being greater than the sum of its parts. As Andrew Altman, the former head of the London Olympic Park Legacy Company, has written,

> Innovation and urban-style development (whether in a city, suburb or exurb) have a synergy that can create more value for both together than apart. Innovation without a dynamic environment for its workforce will not be as successful in attracting and retaining the workforce it needs to succeed. And it will not realize the efficiencies that can be gained from a concentration of firms, universities or anchor industries being near one another to exchange ideas or integrate production. Likewise, successful urban development is dependent on a sound economic base with growth potential to justify significant capital investment and risk. With the proper set of public policy and private investment vehicles, these drivers of the innovation economy could reshape growth patterns favoring metropolitan districts.[3]

The early rise of innovation districts could constitute the next phase of what one observer has called the "architecture of technology."[4] In the nineteenth and early twentieth centuries, in Manchester, Torino, the Ruhr Valley, and the industrial Midwest, the United States and other mature economies built industrial districts, characterized by a high concentration of large-scale industrial enterprises commonly engaging in similar or complimentary work, enmeshed in the urban fabric. During the last half of the twentieth century, in Raleigh-Durham, Silicon Valley, and suburban Washington, Boston, and Philadelphia, the United States built science and research parks, characterized by spatially isolated corporate campuses, accessible only by car, that put little emphasis on the quality of place or on integrating work, housing, and recreation. These physical forms were products of their times and their distinctive mix of demographic preferences, cultural norms, and economic imperatives and, in the case of science parks, the exalting of closed innovation systems where ideas were guarded and secrecy was prized.

Innovation districts reflect a new vision of where innovative firms want to locate, where creative and talented workers want to live and work, and how ideas happen. They embody a different vision from that of industrial districts or science parks of both the physical realm (infrastructure, historic buildings, waterfront locations, urban design, and architecture) and the community environment (affordable housing, social activity, cultural institutions and events). They respect the growing penchant for companies in leading-edge sectors to practice open innovation and collaborate with networks of firms, universities, and supporting institutions. They provide the physical and social platform for entrepreneurial growth—incubator space, collaborative venues, social networking, product competitions, technical support, and mentoring. They build on the recent expansion of state-of-the-art transit systems in the United States beyond their original footprint in the Northeast, the mid-Atlantic, and Chicago. Innovation districts cast cities and urban suburbia not just as consumer zones of Starbucks and stadiums, restaurants and retail but also as hubs of invention, collaboration, and entrepreneurialism that drive the broader economy. They are both competitive places (respecting the dramatic impact that innovative, traded sectors have on broader metropolitan economies) and cool spaces (reflecting the revaluation of livability, walkability, and authenticity in neighborhood design).

The rise of innovation districts reflects not only a paradigmatic shift in development patterns but also the manner in which development is delivered. In some cases, one entity is driving redevelopment: the local government, a real estate developer, the manager of the research park. There is a guiding hand, perhaps even a master plan. In other cases, such as Detroit, a passionate network of visionary and stubborn CEOs of companies, universities, hospitals, philanthropies, and nonprofit organizations is catalyzing the market. This is organic place making as jigsaw puzzle, assembled through the simultaneous and iterative actions of dozens of players. In all cases, however, innovation districts are being driven from the ground up, primarily through the actions of local actors. There is no federal or state program or multinational corporation stamping out innovation districts across the country. Rather, the federal and state governments are followers, serving rather than setting the vision of renewal.

MAKING SENSE OF INNOVATION DISTRICTS

Innovation districts represent the physical imprint of profound economic and demographic forces. Chapter 2 described the flow of ideas and the accumulation of knowledge in clusters that fuels New York City's Applied Sciences project. Chapter 4's analysis of economic revival in Northeast Ohio showed the power of networks of innovators to spark more innovation by working in close collaboration and close proximity across a broad spectrum of companies, universities, intermediaries, and other supportive institutions. In key research- and technology-driven sectors of the economy, the confluence of these trends has enormous consequences for the physical location and environment of work.

We have known intuitively for some time that certain creative sectors of the economy place a high value on urban-level density and proximity. Would popular music have had the same transformative impact on our culture without the close-in, collaboration-inducing quarters of Tin Pan Alley or the Brill Building? Would popular advertising be the same without the tightly bound Madison Avenue "Mad Men" cluster of advertising agencies in New York City?[5]

With the rise of open innovation and networked research and idea generation, the imperative to collaborate has expanded to a broader group of knowledge-intensive sectors, including such science- and technology-heavy fields as chemicals, biotechnology, telecommunications, and semiconductors.[6] McKinsey & Company, for example, has noticed a move from internal R&D labs to new "multichannel R&D models," which involve partnerships with "academic centers, partners, competitors, customers, venture-capital funds, and startups."[7] No one company can master all the knowledge it needs, so companies rely on a network of industry collaborators. They must collaborate to compete.

The hunger for knowledge and the imperative to collaborate has spatial implications. Partners want to be near partners for the simple reason that proximity enables constant interaction and knowledge sharing. A study by the British government captures this well: "While the marginal cost of transmitting information across geographical space has fallen significantly, the marginal cost of transmitting knowledge still rises with distance. . . . Therefore, the knowledge spillover benefits of clustering in cities can be large for high-value, knowledge intensive sectors."[8]

Innovation districts capitalize on this difference between information and knowledge. Information is rote, impersonal, a commodity, undifferentiated, one size fits all. Knowledge is subtle, contextual, specific, and is shared between persons. If all we needed was information, we would never leave home; we could all telecommute to work. But firms and workers need knowledge to create and compete, and knowledge is learned, gained through experience, not easily replicable, and enhanced by proximity.

The proximity effect can be staggering: Gerry Carlino has found that the number of patents per capita increases, on average, by 20 to 30 percent for every doubling of employment density, with the greatest increases expected within the most densely populated portions of a metropolitan area.[9] Stuart Rosenthal and William Strange find that the intellectual spillovers that drive innovation and employment drop off dramatically as firms and people move more than a mile apart.[10] At a distance of just over a mile, the power of intellectual ferment to create another new firm or even another new job drops to one-tenth or less of what it is closer in. As Rosenthal and Strange write, "Information spillovers that require frequent contact between workers may dissipate over a short distance as walking to a meeting place becomes difficult or as random encounters become rare."[11] Researchers at Harvard Medical School have found that even working in the same building on an academic medical campus makes a difference for scientific breakthroughs. As one of them explains, "Otherwise it's really out of sight, out of mind."[12]

An economy driven by knowledge bestows new importance on institutions of knowledge such as universities, medical research centers, private research institutions, and innovation institutes. These institutions tend to be disproportionately located in cities and other urban places. More than 1,900 colleges and universities, more than half the nation's total, are located in the urban core of metropolitan areas.[13] Urban universities obviously contribute substantially to local economies through their employment and expenditures on local goods and services. For our purposes, what matters is that urban universities account for roughly 74 percent (about $27 billion in 2006–07) of all research expenditures at U.S. research universities.[14] Brookings has also found a high correlation between the nation's leading biotech clusters and the strength (as judged by, for example, medical research capacity, National Institutes of Health grants, number of PhDs) of local universities.[15]

The technology- and knowledge-driven sectors' renewed emphasis on density is a far cry from the closed innovation spaces of the previous century, isolated labs, and research parks, such as General Electric's Global Research Center in Niskayuna, New York, and Bell Labs in Murray Hill, New Jersey.[16] As the economy evolves and 3-D printing and other disruptive technology enables small-scale manufacturing, the concentration may even extend to the important interplay of innovation and production. It is revealing that the first National Manufacturing Innovation Institute, described briefly in chapter 4, focused on additive manufacturing, is located in the downtown of Youngstown, Ohio, close to the existing base of small and medium-size manufacturing firms. The midtown Detroit location of the watch- and bicycle-making firm Shinola, described later in this chapter, is further evidence of this trend. In many respects, the rise of innovation districts embodies the very essence of cities: an aggregation of talented, driven people, assembled in close quarters, who exchange ideas and knowledge in what the urban historian Sir Peter Hall calls "a dynamic process of innovation, imitation and improvement."[17]

Beyond physical location, innovation districts embrace the broader trends in work that are driving the redesign of buildings and office spaces in support of collaboration and open innovation. The early, highly recognizable model for networked workplaces is the newspaper newsroom, but these principles have been implemented in places ranging from Michael Bloomberg's bullpen in New York's city hall to the campuses of Silicon Valley technology firms. Facebook and Google, for example, have embraced "hackable buildings," in the words of Randy Howder, a workplace strategist at the design and architecture firm Gensler, who led the design of Facebook's recent Menlo Park, California, offices. These offices have open floor plans that can be easily reconfigured to create dense, collaborative spaces for new teams and projects.[18]

The line between private and public spaces is now blurred. When Zappos, the online retail giant that grew to scale in suburban Las Vegas, was looking for new headquarters in 2010, the company's CEO Tony Hsieh decided to create a denser workplace to increase interaction and collaboration. For Hsieh, that meant not only providing open floor plans and amenities within the office but also embedding the new headquarters (and 2,000 Zappos workers) downtown, in Las Vegas's Fremont East neighborhood in the city's old city hall. Hsieh is pairing the move with a new private investment fund (separate from Zappos) called the Down-town Project to build a dense, multiuse and walkable environment; the strategies include luring new start-ups close to the headquarters and creat-ing more housing and co-working spaces in the district. "The idea," said Hsieh said in an interview with *Fortune* magazine, "went from 'let's build a campus' to 'let's build a city.'"[19]

DEMOGRAPHICS ARE DESTINY

Innovation districts are the product of another transformative trend: Americans' changing family structure and the shift to smaller and more numerous households. Over the past century, the average size of a house-hold declined from 4.60 persons in 1900 to 3.38 in 1950 to 2.58 in 2010.[20] Part of this change is attributable to the aging of our population. Yet younger women and men are also delaying marriage and having fewer children. In fact, the share of adults between the ages of eighteen and twenty-nine who are married fell from 59 percent in 1960 to 20 percent in 2010, and there was nearly a six-year rise in the median age at first marriage for both men and women during this period, according to the Pew Research Center.[21] As a result, the prototypical family of the sub-urban era, a married couple with school-age children, now represents 20.0 percent of American households, down from 23.5 percent in 2000 and 40.3 percent in 1970.[22] The move to smaller households will only intensify in coming decades.[23]

This demographic tumult is already changing preferences and behav-ior, in large and small ways. Quality of life is increasingly understood by young people, particularly those who have delayed childrearing, to mean proximity to restaurants, retail, cultural and education institutions, and other urban amenities.[24] They want a vibrant street life, historic neighbor-hoods, and public transit. In fact, between 2000 and 2009, the share of college-educated twenty-five- to thirty-four-year-olds living within three miles of the central business district in the nation's fifty-one largest metro-politan areas increased by 26 percent, double the growth rate of college-educated young adults in the rest of the metropolitan area.[25]

Given these trends it is understandable that the United States is expe-riencing its largest sustained drop in driving, especially among young people. In 1983 nearly half of young Americans had a driver's license; today, only 29 percent do.[26] As Chris Nelson writes in his provocative new book *Reshaping Metropolitan America: Development Trends and Opportunities to 2030,* "When people live within a mile of work, nearly 40 percent walked or biked to work in 2009—up from 25 percent as recently as 1995," and the statistics for running errands are nearly identical.[27] Meanwhile, public transit use increased by 32.3 percent between 1995 and 2011, while the total population growth rate during that time was only half that amount.[28] We are witnessing a virtuous cycle of worker preference and firm demand. Young talented individuals and firms in a growing number of sectors are simultaneously, for distinct but reinforcing reasons, embracing those very attributes of urbanism—what Saskia Sassen calls "cityness"—that were denigrated and often destroyed in the twentieth century:[29] complexity; density; diversity of people and cultures; the convergence of the physical environment at multiple scales; the messy intersection of activities; a variance of distinctive designs; the layering of the old and the new; an integration rather than segregation of uses and activities. If this trend continues, we could be on the verge of a profound, structural shift in the physical landscape of work and living.

INNOVATION DISTRICTS FROM THE GROUND UP

The best evidence for the spatial impacts of economic restructuring, new innovation patterns, and demographic transformation are found not in academic treatises but on the ground. Like differentiated metro economies, distinct types of innovation districts are emerging in cities and metros throughout the county. Some are clustered around powerful advanced research institutions and clusters of technology firms. Others are transforming underused areas of the city, particularly older industrial areas. Still others are remaking isolated, low-density science parks at the periphery of the metropolis.

The power of anchor institutions is best illustrated by the Massachusetts Institute of Technology in Cambridge, Massachusetts. In the mid-twentieth century, MIT was surrounded by acres of abandoned industrial properties and buildings. The university first became actively involved in making the area a high-tech region in the 1960s, when, according to its news office, "MIT and the real estate firm Cabot Cabot and Forbes responded to the request of Mayor Edward A. Crane and used private money to convert a former soap factory into Technology Square, one of Cambridge's first large-scale real estate developments."[30]

Simultaneously, nearby Kendall Square, on the eastern edge of MIT's campus, began to be redeveloped as biotech and info-tech start-ups emerged out of MIT and nearby Harvard. As *The Economist* describes it, "In the 1960s, the entrepreneurialism of the Massachusetts Institute of Technology turned Cambridge, Massachusetts, into a mecca for high-tech startups."[31]

Yet redevelopment at scale in creating a mixed-use district around the university did not begin until the 1980s, when the Forest City Science and Technology Group (a division of the national real estate development firm Forest City Enterprises), in collaboration with MIT and the city of Cambridge, started developing a mixed-use district, University Park at MIT, on a twenty-seven-acre plot in a former blighted industrial area owned by the university and adjacent to the northwest edge of campus. The initial redevelopment involved numerous rezoning fights and required a fundamental rethinking of the community's landscape. A 2005 article in the *Boston Globe* reports that "in 1983 . . . a city master plan for the site established zoning with height and density limits. It called for new utilities, roads, limited traffic, 100,000 square feet of retail space, and rental housing, with 25 percent of the units rented to low and moderate-income tenants. . . . The plan also set design guidelines that MIT and Forest City agreed to follow."[32]

Fast-forward thirty years, and the MIT bio engines continue to hum. University Park now houses more than 1.5 million square feet of scientific research facilities across ten buildings, and it is home to major bioscience firms like Alkermes, Partners HealthCare System, and Millennium Pharmaceuticals. It has 674 residential units, a hotel, a conference center, and an expanding number of retail amenities.[33]

The concentration of biotech and information technology firms and research around MIT now stretches from Central Square, northwest of the campus (close to where University Park at MIT is located), east along Main Street to Kendall Square. This corridor has been described by the Kendall Square Association as "the densest square mile of innovation on the planet."[34]

In the past several years, major biotechnology and pharmaceutical companies (for example, Pfizer and Novartis) as well as tech companies (for example, Google, Microsoft, IBM, and Nokia) have staked their ground in Cambridge with new facilities and expanded operations.[35] This private activity was drawn to the area by the presence of new, world-class research institutes and proximity to the Longwood Medical Area and Mass General. The new penchant for open innovation and proximity is best captured by the story of Biogen Idec, which describes itself on its website as "the oldest independent biotech firm in the world." In 2010 Biogen completed an enormous campus at the intersection of Route 128 and Route 20, in the suburb of Weston, while maintaining a research facility in Cambridge. Barely a year later, under new leadership, the company started the difficult process of abandoning the new Weston facility and moving the entire company back to Cambridge. As the *New York Times* reported in early 2013,

> Pharmaceutical companies traditionally preferred suburban enclaves where they could protect their intellectual property in more secluded settings and meet their employees' needs. But in recent years, as the costs of drug development have soared and R&D pipelines slowed, pharmaceutical companies have looked elsewhere for innovation. Much of that novelty is now coming from biotechnology firms and major research universities like M.I.T. and Harvard, just two subway stops away.[36]

The Kendall Square area is now an enticing place to live and work. Since 2005 nearly 1,000 new housing units have been built, as well as many new restaurants and other retail outlets.[37] As a result, "office space is hard to come by, rents are rising, and it boasts a roster of marquee companies, from Microsoft Corp. to Google Inc. to Biogen Idec that are expanding there."[38]

Other private construction projects, totaling $1 billion, are under way.[39] For its part, MIT has only just started to become actively involved in making this a more mixed-use area. In 2011, nearly thirty years after the University Park rezoning, MIT launched the Kendall Square Initiative, an effort to rezone twenty-six acres and invest $700 million in upgrading and developing eight buildings it owns.[40] The plan calls for, among other things, 1 million square feet of new office space and 240,000 square feet of new housing.[41] After a year of revising the plans, MIT now awaits final approval from the Cambridge city council.

Another innovation district model is being tested on the South Boston waterfront, barely 3.5 miles from Kendall Square. There, the city of Boston is trying to build an innovation district in a former industrial area of 1,000 acres that lacks the strong, driving engine of a world-class research institution like MIT or even, at the beginning of the effort, a robust cluster of entrepreneurial firms. What it does have is close proximity and easy transit access to a city with strong assets—renowned universities, high-level human capital, and a growing concentration of life sciences and tech clusters. This is an innovation district conceived with the supreme confidence that, as Boston mayor Thomas Menino said in 2010, "there has never been a better time for innovation to occur in urban settings than now, and there should be no better place than Boston."[42] As expressed in an initial manifesto titled "The Strategy and Core Principles,"

> Ideas need a tight ecosystem to foster creative growth—distance equals death. The ability for small firms to generate ideas and intermingle with larger firms who have the access to capital and the ability to scale and grow those ideas is imperative in entrepreneurial fields. The tight location clustering leads to job creation as well as more efficient productive and service design. These innovation district clusters become the new economic engines for the region, retaining homegrown talent from the surrounding city and intellectual institutions.[43]

Since January 2010, the city of Boston has implemented a three-prong strategy to transform the waterfront into a thriving center of innovation. First, it has provided public infrastructure and networking opportunities to foster an "innovation ecosystem." The city secured, for example, a vacant, premier office space free of charge for a number of years to lure MassChallenge to the innovation district.[44] MassChallenge is best known for its global competition for entrepreneurship and start-ups. For the winners, the nonprofit runs a three-month accelerator program, which includes on-site mentorships. In its first round in 2010, with 111 companies participating, the effort raised more than $90 million dollars and created 500 jobs.[45] With the help of city leadership and through private funding, a $5.5 million, 12,000 square-foot Innovation Center has been built to provide incubator space outfitted with the latest technology, where new firms can exchange ideas and grow.[46] The district has become a hub for innovation on sustainability. The Fraunhofer Center for Sustainable Energy, a U.S. subsidiary of the German research institution, and GreenTown Labs both have a presence in the district and are dedicating a portion of their facilities to incubate clean-tech companies.

Second, the city has encouraged a range of flexible housing options that would appeal to a unique class of workers, thinkers, and others that are drawn to the area. The Boston Redevelopment Authority, for example, is testing market acceptance of micro apartment units that exist in housing developments with shared amenities and public spaces. Private space is limited to 300 square feet, and the public spaces offer shared work space, large entertainment spaces, and larger kitchens and eating areas.[47] The concept draws from well-known executive learning facilities at Harvard University and Babson College, where similar living spaces were found to stimulate conversations and, ultimately, new collaborations. As a result of negotiations between the city and developers, 15 percent of residential projects, often an entire floor of a building, are dedicated to this type of housing.[48]

The final focus is on attracting clusters of innovative workers. Boston's innovation district offers a distinct approach to clusters, taking an industry-neutral approach but focusing on fast-growing, innovation-driven industries. Boston designed its effort to be "cluster agnostic," explained Mitch Weiss, the mayor's chief of staff, arguing that the best, most productive course is to create the right environment for fast-growing industries and then let them naturally aggregate.[49] A Boston Redevelopment Authority representative explained that the purposefully flexible approach is about "pioneering and re-evolving."[50] Although some companies have overlapping, if not complementary interests, in some cases one field is branching into new, innovative directions as a result of its relationships with companies in other sectors. One example was a clean-energy company working with a microbrewery on developing new energy technologies for the microbrewery.[51]

The initial results of this activity are impressive. As of March 2013, more than 200 new businesses and 4,000 new jobs have been created on the site.[52] New companies fall within the clusters of life sciences and biotech, green or clean tech, architecture and digital design, communications and new media, financial, legal, and a broad category of technology development, which includes manufacturing.[53] Wellesley-based Babson College, the country's highest-ranked college for entrepreneurship, is providing "hatchery space" in the district for Babson start-ups founded by students in its MBA program as well as opening a satellite facility to offer business courses for full-time and evening students.[54] Battery Ventures, one of Boston's oldest venture capital firms, is also becoming part of the new district.[55]

But the psychological impact may be the strongest and longest lasting. The identity and image of a key part of the city have essentially been redefined, and, in the process, its hidden value has been uncovered; and as a result, economic potential and power have been unleashed at a level that was heretofore unexpected and unimagined. This is a true transformative intervention, creating markets in places where markets either did not exist or were only partially realized. As one local observer concludes, "Just a few years ago, the South Boston Waterfront didn't have much to it. Fast forward to 2012 and the area is exploding with activity in what's now known as Boston's innovation district—one of Boston's hottest neighborhoods."[56]

Ironically, the strongest validation for twenty-first-century innovation districts is emerging in North Carolina's Research Triangle Park, perhaps the twentieth century's most iconic high-tech research and development park. The brainchild of visionary business and political leaders in the 1950s, it is widely credited with helping North Carolina transform itself from a low-wage economy dependent on "jobs in the agriculture, forestry and furniture and textile industries."[57] The park grew out of a pine forest strategically located in the triangle between three major universities (Duke University in Durham, North Carolina State University in Raleigh, and the University of North Carolina at Chapel Hill). The complex currently boasts 7,000 acres, 22.5 million square feet of space, 170 companies, and around 40,000 workers, but there are only minimal amenities, and no residential housing, within the park's boundaries.[58] From the park's very origins, its zoning laws helped shape a landscape of isolated corporate campuses sharing little but internal roads and easy access to the Raleigh Durham International Airport and I-40, the major interstate connecting Raleigh and Durham. The park rules insist that buildings cover no more than 15 to 30 percent of a company's total land area, encouraging an expansive parklike setting for corporate tenants and discouraging dense, mixed-use development.[59]

The Research Triangle Foundation began to reconsider its design in response to the development of the downtowns of Raleigh, Durham, and Chapel Hill in the past fifteen years. In November 2012, after several years of review and outreach, it announced a new fifty-year master plan to urbanize the quintessential exurban science park, recognizing that it is no longer the optimal environment to spur innovation and satisfy its younger workforce. The master plan particularly calls for more density and amenities, including the creation of a vibrant central district, more retail, the building of up to 1,400 multifamily housing units at the Triangle Commons area, and the possible construction of a light-rail transit line to connect the park with the larger Raleigh-Durham region, as well as a stronger university presence throughout the park.[60] As Lydia DePillis notes in a piece titled "Dinosaur Makeover," "The current generation of tech workers doesn't want to toil in the soulless *Office Space* complexes surrounded by moats of parking that dot Research Triangle Park's sprawling vastness."[61]

These examples are not isolated. The "anchor plus" model illustrated by University Park at MIT can be found, to a lesser degree, in San Diego (building from the rich base of Scripps Research Institute, Salk Institute for Biomedical Studies, Burnham Institute, and the University of California at San Diego), St. Louis (in the burgeoning life sciences district around Washington University, St. Louis University, the University of Missouri at St. Louis, and Barnes Jewish Hospital) or in Pittsburgh (around the constellation of Carnegie Mellon University, the University of Pittsburgh, and the University of Pittsburgh Medical Center). University Park at MIT is now a model for other Forest City developments including the Science and Technology Park at Johns Hopkins, the Translational Research Lab at the University of Pennsylvania, and the Colorado Science and Technology Park adjacent to the Fitzsimons Life Science District in Aurora, Colorado.

The Cambridge Innovation Center, a technology and life sciences business incubator that has helped launch more than 1,200 companies near MIT since 1999, recently announced that it will expand its operations and start-up support services to Baltimore and St. Louis.[62] The "transform underused areas" model exemplified by Boston can be found in the remarkable development of Seattle's South Lake Union area in the past decade, led by Paul Allen's Vulcan Real Estate and Lennar Urban's ambitious plans for Hunters Point in San Francisco (an expansive former naval facility closed in the 1970s). And the "remake science park" model is sparking serious discussions about redesign in suburban and exurban enclaves as disparate as Route 128 outside Boston, the Dulles corridor outside Washington, D.C., and even Silicon Valley itself. As *Businessweek* observes, "The trend is to nurture living, breathing communities rather than sterile, remote compounds of research silos."[63]

Innovation districts, of course, are not confined to American shores. Many of the U.S. models actually draw from the experiences of 22@Barcelona, the first self-proclaimed innovation district. In less than a decade, 4,500 firms have located in the area, thousands of housing units have been built, and linkages to more than ten universities, twelve R&D technology clusters, and new spaces for start-ups have been created in a highly integrated system of innovation-driven development. As our colleague Julie Wagner has illustrated, the secrets to Barcelona's success are threefold.[64]

First, through extensive public investment and strong, focused public planning, Barcelona has transformed a 494-acre industrial area scarred and separated from the rest of the city by nineteenth-century railroad tracks into a twenty-first-century urban community. To some extent, this was achieved by European-level public funding (more than 180 million euros) to bury train tracks and build a public tram and new energy and telecommunications services. But innovative market mechanisms were used to generate private revenue. After developing a new area plan, the city changed area zoning from industrial (22a) to services (22@) and increased allowable density. Thirty percent of the total land area was transferred to the city: 10 percent was used for affordable housing, 10 percent for open spaces and green spaces, and 10 percent for knowledge-based activities (such as R&D centers or incubators). Property owners were also required to pay funds per square meter of land subsequently developed, and the money was used to build infrastructure and housing.[65] Throughout the area, significant attention was given to the blending of historic and modern architecture and design. The factory of José Canela, for example, which was built between 1898 and 1914, is now a visual focal point and home to the University of Barcelona's Institute of Lifelong Learning.[66]

Second, the transformation of the physical space was paired with efforts to create a new knowledge and innovation hub. After cataloguing the inherent strengths and geographic advantages of the city, 22@Barcelona ultimately settled on five economic clusters to pursue: media, medical technologies, information and communications technology, energy, and design. The city then categorized typologies of cluster magnets—the kinds of anchor institutions and organizations necessary to create gravitational pull, including universities, institutions, companies, meeting and residential spaces for specific industries, a technology center (which would be the driver behind the entire cluster strategy), incubators, and residences for students and workers.[67] Intensive efforts to lure these magnets paid off, as each cluster now has a complete portfolio of these seven magnet typologies. Through investments in districtwide social networking and web updates, firms are apprised of advances in the district that might stimulate new concepts across sectors.

Finally, the district has benefited immensely from its close proximity to Barcelona Activa, considered one of the best entrepreneurial development programs in the world. Among other things, the program offers modules designed for specific economic clusters, such as coaching services for the "bio-entrepreneur," the creative media industry, and even artisans. Activa's 2010 statistics best illustrate their level of impact: 83 percent of all businesses formed survived after the fourth year; 70 percent of coached projects ultimately transformed into a company; and 1,700 companies and 3,200 jobs were created.[68] Barcelona Activa and the 22@Barcelona district leadership meet regularly to find synergies between their activities and efforts.[69]

Innovation districts, whether in the United States, Europe, or elsewhere, are not cookie-cutter models that are easy to replicate. The geography of innovation, unlike the geography of consumption, conforms to the distinctive economic and physical starting points of disparate places. But common lessons cut across these examples, most notably that the new desire for collaboration and integration is coming into direct conflict with conventional norms of specialization and separation.

The challenges to delivering innovation districts at scale are many. Each kind of innovation district, for example, requires a fundamental rethinking of traditional land use and zoning conventions. In the midst of massive economic global change, twenty-first-century metropolitan areas still bear the indelible markings of the twentieth century.[70] In the early twentieth century, for example, government bodies enacted zoning regulations to establish new rules for urban development. Although originally intended to protect access to light and air from immense overbuilding, later versions of zoning added the segregation of uses—isolating housing, office, commercial, and manufacturing activities from one another.[71] The design of a science and research park, as exemplified by North Carolina's Research Triangle Park, was intended to ensure seclusion, isolation, and the protection of intellectual property, often on "research estates," as the North Carolina park's master plan puts it.[72] Thus innovation districts require, at a minimum, variances from the rigid, antiquated rules that still define the urban and suburban landscape.[73] That is essentially what is happening in the Kendall Square area around MIT's campus. In many cases, the new vision of successful districts has become the tool to overhaul outdated and outmoded frameworks and transform exceptions into new guidelines. This is what happened in Barcelona in a very purposeful fashion and what is under way in the Boston innovation district and the Research Triangle Park.

Beyond zoning and land use, innovation districts require integrative thinking and action, seeing and making connections between economic dynamics and urban experiences (for example, transportation, housing, economic activity, education, and recreation), which are inextricably linked in reality but separated in practice. In Barcelona (and, to some extent, exurban Research Triangle Park), this is occurring in a highly structured and planned manner, with particular focus on targeting specific clusters and urbanizing the physical environment. The MIT and Boston innovation district cases, by contrast, appear to be occurring in a more organic way, in which planning acts more as platform than as prescription. As the Barcelona case illustrates, true integrative thinking often involves an empirically grounded vision at the building-block level. Although a unified vision is not a prerequisite to realizing innovation districts, cities and metro areas that proceed without one have a higher probability of making the wrong physical bets, siting them in the wrong places, or ultimately creating a physical landscape that fails to add up to "cityness." It is easy to find such examples around the country, such as isolated megaprojects (a new stadium or convention center) or waterfront revitalization efforts that constructed the wrong projects, having misunderstood the market and the diversifying demographic.[74]

The quest for integration is also present in financing. Innovation districts require juggling multiple, compartmentalized public, private, and civic financing sources. In some respects, that is a natural product of the breadth of discrete and separate activities that take place within the districts. Start-up firms seek venture capital. Housing developers look for financing from banks, tax equity investors, and government. Small businesses want federal small-business loans. Universities and hospitals raise private capital from their balance sheets. Entrepreneurial networks, incubator spaces, cultural venues, and local intermediaries often receive philanthropic or member funding. And governments at all levels make investments in place-based infrastructure (particularly the remediation of brownfields), advanced research and development, skills training programs, and so forth. In addition, achieving social objectives often requires that innovative tax and shared equity approaches be built into particular transactions, so that appreciations in property value can serve higher community purposes (for example, creating affordable housing).

Creating an innovation district, therefore, is not like building an exurban subdivision of single-family houses or a commercial strip mall. Those developments are delivered, for the most part, by standardized and routinized financing vehicles that enable the production of similar products at high volume and low cost. Innovation districts, by contrast, require the layering of multiple sources of financing, placing stress on project design and implementation. As with land use and zoning, the evolution from exceptional transactions to routinized forms of investments is required to ensure that innovation districts become the rule rather than the exception. We return to this challenge later in the chapter.

AN INNOVATION DISTRICT IN THE UNLIKELIEST OF PLACES

Perhaps the most intriguing example of a burgeoning innovation district is in the city of Detroit. In the face of population loss, fiscal collapse, racial division, political dysfunction, and near anarchic conditions, a vanguard of corporate, university, and civic leaders are taking charge and building the city back, from its origins along the Detroit River and around its anchor institutions. Unlike the Barcelona district, there is no unified master plan here. Unlike the London Olympic Park, national government has limited presence. Rather, in Detroit we see the power of networks to crowd source and crowd fund a city and, in the process, transform a metropolis.

The realities of present-day Detroit are grim and well rehearsed. The city has been in free fall for decades. The city population declined 25 percent in the last decade alone and 60 percent since 1950, and, with fewer than 714,000 inhabitants, it is now at its lowest level since 1910. Against such hemorrhaging, the city's sheer size of 139 square miles (Manhattan, San Francisco, and Boston could all fit within Detroit, with 20 square miles to spare) is a daily reminder of past grandeur and failed ambitions. The city resembles a man who has experienced extreme weight loss but is still wearing his old clothes. It has become a land of empty places and ungoverned spaces.

In January 2013 the Detroit Works Project Team, composed of leaders from across the city's public, private, nonprofit, and philanthropic sectors who were appointed by Detroit mayor Dave Bing, released the Detroit Future City report as the culmination of a multiyear effort to provide a new blueprint for the city's resurgence. The report documents the enormous human, physical, and fiscal costs that result when residents flee, jobs disperse, and a city becomes too big for itself:

—Of Detroit's 349,170 total housing units, 79,725 are currently vacant. Roughly twenty square miles of the city's occupiable land area is vacant, including 36 percent of Detroit's commercial land. There are seventy-two Superfund contaminated sites within the city limits.

—Only 35,000 of Detroit's 88,000 street lights work. Of the city's 3,000 miles of road, 27 percent are deemed to be in poor shape.

—The city's water system is only capable of operating at 40 percent of its maximum capacity. As many as 42 billion gallons of water a year are unaccounted for owing to leaks and meter inaccuracies.

—The highest level of education for 82 percent of Detroit's residents is a high school diploma or less. Just 32 percent of those without a high school diploma are employed.

—Detroit ranks second highest among U.S. cities with more than 100,000 people for its rate of violent crime.[75]

—With job decentralization the worst in the nation (over 77 percent of jobs are located more than ten miles from the downtown),[76] 61 percent of Detroiters who have jobs work outside the city limits. Of the jobs within the city, Detroit residents hold just 30 percent.[77]

As Detroit's population declined, its finances worsened. In 2011 Michigan governor Rick Snyder appointed a financial review team to assess the city's financial position and outlook. The team's most recent report in February 2013 reveals a city starved for revenue and addicted to debt, facing a double whammy of short-term cash-flow problems and long-term debt liabilities that exceed $14 billion.[78] On March 14, 2013, Governor Snyder appointed Kevyn Orr, a well-respected Washington, D.C., bankruptcy lawyer, as Detroit's emergency financial manager.[79]

The Detroit that the world knows is what historian Tom Sugrue describes as an "eerily apocalyptic" landscape of boarded-up shops, empty lots, burned-out buildings, roaming packs of dogs, and oddly pristine prairie land.[80] What gets passed over in this harsh portrait is the recovery in the downtown and midtown areas of the city, which, along with the Eastern Market district and the riverfront, make up about 5.2 square miles—3.7 percent and 0.13 percent of the city's and metro's land masses, respectively.[81] It is in this relative dot of a place that a world-class innovation district is slowly emerging, erected through a collaborative network of local leaders, amplified by a pervasive sense of do-it-yourself urbanism. What follows is just a small glimpse of what is happening.

The downtown is being transformed by an idiosyncratic urban evangelist, Dan Gilbert, who happens to be the founder of the mortgage lending firm Quicken Loans and the owner of the National Basketball Association's Cleveland Cavaliers. In 2007 Gilbert moved his firm's headquarters from suburban Farmington Hills to downtown Detroit. Since then, he has brought more than 7,000 employees downtown and purchased more than fifteen buildings and two parking garages in the downtown area.[82] The firm is now the third-largest landholder in the city of Detroit, behind the city government and General Motors.[83] Gilbert's purchases and building plans are all part of his Detroit 2.0 revival vision, "a lively live-work-play district in the heart of the city based around entrepreneurial companies in the digital economy."[84]

Gilbert's acquisitions, of course, built on existing assets: the downtown is a National Register Historic District, and more than fifty buildings are in the National Register of Historic Places.[85] The Kresge Foundation contributed $50 million toward a major public-private reclamation and redevelopment project along the city's riverfront, and public resources helped pay for a portion of the construction and landscaping of two new stadiums—Ford Field and Comerica Park. Several smart private and nonprofit intermediaries—Invest Detroit, the Detroit Downtown Partnership, the Detroit Economic Growth Corporation—have nurtured these deals and the broader revival for years.

But Gilbert's confidence has sparked decisions by other firms, large and small, to expand their downtown presence. Blue Cross Blue Shield of Michigan has moved 3,400 workers from the suburbs; now 6,400 of its employees work in five downtown buildings, with a large share of them at the Renaissance Center complex along the riverfront.[86] Compuware and DTE Energy have had a strong presence downtown. (In fact, Compuware arguably started the downtown trend by building a fifteen-story headquarters in downtown Detroit in 2002, where Quicken Loans now has space.) A new subculture of entrepreneurial, tech-oriented start-ups, such as Digerati, Detroit Labs, and Stik, has emerged in the shadow of larger firms.

All this action has not gone unnoticed by sophisticated investors. In 2010 Connecticut-based Atlas Holdings LLC purchased several companies that separately owned an energy-from-waste facility in the downtown as well as an underground steam loop, providing heating for many large buildings and facilities in downtown and midtown Detroit. A new company, Detroit Renewable Energy LLC, has emerged from these acquisitions, bringing synergies and operating efficiencies to clean-energy supply and distribution for the innovation district.

As Gilbert told *Forbes Magazine* in June 2011, "There's the smell of something special happening. Detroit's going to be a big story here in the next several years for America, and I think [businesses should] want to be part of it."[87]

Sue Mosey, the president of the community development organization Midtown Detroit Inc., is informally recognized as the mayor of midtown. She is a lifelong Detroiter, is a graduate of Wayne State University, and has been the head of multiple redevelopment organizations since 1990. If the downtown strategy was led by corporate relocations and small start-ups, the midtown revival has been led by anchor-driven expansions and Mosey's "slow and steady" restoration of the urban fabric.[88] Midtown is home to four major anchor institutions—Henry Ford Hospital, the Detroit Medical Center, Wayne State University, and the College for Creative Studies. Among the seventy-plus sites on the National Register of Historic Places are the Detroit Institute of Arts, the Whitney Restaurant, and the Detroit Masonic Temple (the largest Masonic temple in the world). Over the past decade, Mosey and a dedicated network of institutional partners have helped drive $1.8 billion in public and private investment in midtown.[89] Here are some of the most noteworthy projects:

—Henry Ford Hospital, a major hospital and research complex that employs about 1,200 physicians, recently finished a $300 million renovation that added more patient rooms and operating areas. In 2010 it announced a $1 billion expansion that would include not only new and enhanced health care and medical distribution facilities but also a community health park with commercial, retail, and housing space.[90]

—The Detroit Medical Center, a major health care center that employs about 3,000 physicians, has its own expansion projects under way on its midtown campus, including a new heart hospital and an outpatient pediatric facility. These projects are parts of the overall $850 million investment that the Detroit Medical Center's parent company, Vanguard Health System, has made in the complex over the past several years.[91]

—Wayne State University, the largest public research university in the city of Detroit, is building a $90 million biomedical research facility to link up with researchers at the Henry Ford Health System. Wayne State has also been home to TechTown, a technology research center and business incubator that since 2007 has provided support to hundreds of companies and thousands of entrepreneurs in industries ranging from life sciences and advanced manufacturing to the arts and alternative energy.[92]

—The College for Creative Studies, one of the top design colleges in the world, expanded in 2008 with a $145 million redevelopment of the 760,000 square-foot historic Argonaut Building (formerly General Motors' first research and design studio). Shinola, a start-up firm that manufactures watches, bicycles, and leather goods, set up production in the Argonaut Building to take advantage of the design talent at the college. As one article notes, "Design drives products, and new ideas from bright young manufacturing designers give Shinola an edge."[93]

And one cultural capstone: in August 2012 voters in Wayne, Macomb, and Oakland Counties approved a property tax increase to raise $23 million annually for the operation of the Detroit Institute of Arts.[94]

The growing economic base in downtown and midtown (including the historic Eastern Market) provides the economic platform for the development of a full innovation district complete with housing, retail, and services. There are roughly 5,400 businesses in the combined area, employing more than 138,700 workers.[95] Add to that the 32,000 students at Wayne State University and more than 9,500 city government employees, and the numbers suggest an opportunity to catalyze the residential market and all that follows. Detroit is rediscovering the fundamental truth of sound economies: housing doesn't create jobs; jobs create housing. And that is what is happening. As of late 2012, both the midtown and downtown areas had rental apartment occupancy rates of at least 96 percent.[96] As housing goes, so goes retail. The in-migration of new inhabitants is spurring demand for restaurants, bars, grocery stores, coffee shops, and other amenities. Mosey has brilliantly spearheaded an effort to ensure that this revival occurs with a keen attention to the details of historic preservation, distinctive design, and neighborhood planning that separate great urban regeneration from the merely good. A Whole Foods Market is slated to open in midtown in mid-2013, the ultimate sign that the innovation district has arrived.

All this activity—corporate relocation, anchor expansion, entrepreneurial growth, housing, and retail—predates the next infusion of energy and capital: the building of the M1 Rail, a 3.3 mile light-rail line from

MIDTOWN AND DOWNTOWN DETROIT

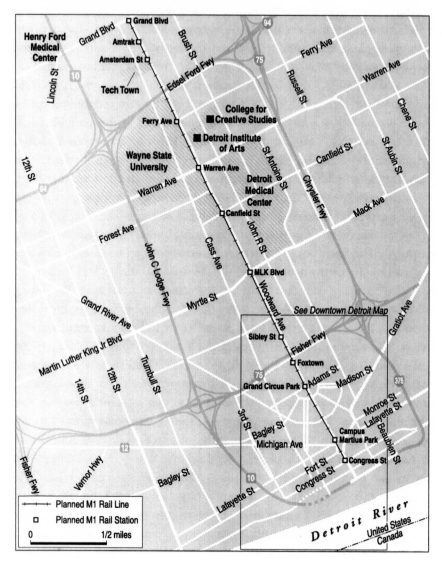

DOWNTOWN DETROIT

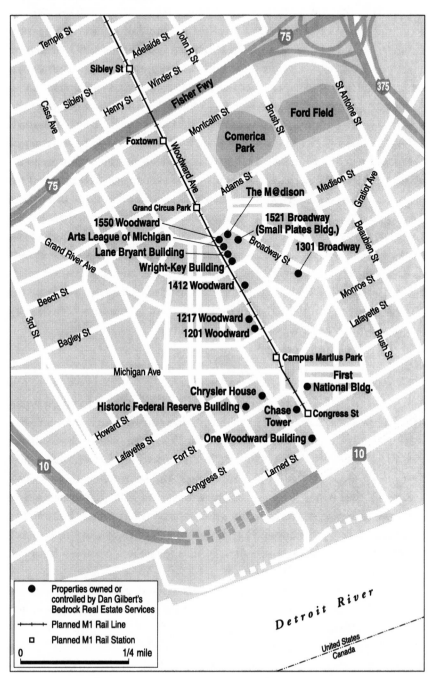

downtown to Grand Boulevard at the upper edge of midtown Detroit. A consortium of public, private, and philanthropic institutions—including General Motors and Chrysler, the Kresge Foundation, and major individual backers such as Dan Gilbert, Roger Penske (the CEO of Penske Racing), and Peter Karmanos (the CEO of Compuware)—has committed more than $100 million to construction of the project.[97] In January 2013 the federal government contributed $25 million, an act made possible only after the Michigan Legislature enacted (and Governor Rick Snyder signed) a law to create a Detroit Regional Transit Authority. As U.S. Secretary of Transportation Raymond LaHood said on making the announcement, "Nobody in America—no community—has ever raised $100 million for a project like this. That is unprecedented. . . . They've done everything we've asked them to do."[98] The symbolism of a sophisticated mass transit system returning to Woodward Avenue (where a streetcar system had run between the 1860s and 1950s) cannot be minimized. World-class transit in the Motor City (financed in part by the major auto companies) sends a signal that mobility in this century will not be driven exclusively by the automobile. The city responsible for the mobility of the twentieth century is adapting to the new mobility of the twenty-first.

WHAT DETROIT TEACHES US

Detroit is drawing a new geography of innovation, tearing down the traditional, artificial borders that have long divided downtowns and midtowns in the United States. Virtually every major city in this country has a strong central business district (mostly for the congregation of government, corporate headquarters, entertainment venues, and some cultural functions), a strong midtown area (where eds and meds and historic museums tend to concentrate), and a state-of-the-art transit corridor, mostly built within the past twenty years, connecting the two. Each of these discrete building blocks brings particular assets that, in turn, provide a platform for a key element of innovation district growth.

Because of their economic, government, and cultural function, the downtown central business districts continue to have large employment bases. They also, as Julie Wagner points out, "have the physical 'bones'— walkable street blocks, the sidewalks, the historic buildings, access to waterfronts and other established infrastructure—that can accommodate a range of residential, commercial, entrepreneurial, retail, and cultural functions."[99] The midtown areas, for the most part, have different strengths—large student populations and the substantial employment, research, and procurement bases of the universities and medical institutions. Transit corridors are the physical tissue that knits disparate parts of a city together. They have the potential, with smart land use and catalytic policies, to be multidimensional in purpose, expanding transportation choices and mobility, to be sure, but also galvanizing new destinations along their routes, including new residential areas, retail clusters, and economic districts.

Across the United States, fledgling innovation districts are beginning to take hold in this new urban geography of innovation. In Houston, a new light-rail system connects the strong central business district (with its phalanx of energy company headquarters) with the Museum District, the Houston Medical Campus, and the University of Houston. In Cleveland, the new Euclid Corridor Bus Rapid Transit system connects the traditional downtown with University Circle (with Case Western, Cleveland Clinic, and key cultural institutions). In Buffalo, the rapid expansion of the Larkin District and the Buffalo-Niagara Medical Campus in the midtown area is also connected by transit with the central business district and the burgeoning waterfront. Similar stories can be told about Atlanta, Denver, Indianapolis, Minneapolis–St. Paul, Pittsburgh, Philadelphia, Phoenix, Syracuse, and even Las Vegas. The physical and economic platform for an innovation district revolution is in place.

Second, the launch of M1 Rail exemplifies the collaborative spirit and integrated nature of economy shaping and place making at the heart of the metropolitan revolution. Detroit's revival is being inspired, accelerated, and supported by an intricate web of philanthropic and business leaders and a remarkable set of nonprofit and quasi-public intermediaries that are painstakingly connecting the dots between hundreds of separate actions and transactions. The New Economy Initiative for Southeast Michigan—a $100 million consortium of ten local and national foundations—is a major investor in Detroit's midtown and downtown. Since its inception in 2007, the initiative has supported or created several investment funds for start-ups and provided capital for significant place-making infrastructure, particularly in TechTown in midtown and its surrounding area, and its grants have helped launch 417 new companies, create 6,700 jobs, and leverage $261 million in additional investment in start-up companies supported by its grantees.[100]

Living Cities, another philanthropic consortium, has invested $22 million in the Woodward Corridor Initiative to "redensify" the corridor and realize the full potential of the transit investment.[101] The Kresge Foundation alone committed $150 million over the next five years to implement the recommendations and strategies outlined in the Detroit Future City report, doubling down on the investments it has already made along the riverfront, in M1 Rail, in the planning for the Detroit Future City effort, and as part of both the New Economy Initiative and Living Cities.[102] In 2011 the Henry Ford Health System, the Detroit Medical Center, and Wayne State University, along with state and philanthropic support, launched the Live Midtown initiative, which provides financial incentives for employees who move to the area and entices existing renters and homeowners to stay and reinvest.[103] Based on the program's success, a group of downtown corporations—Quicken Loans, Blue Cross Blue Shield, Compuware, Strategic Staffing Solutions, Marketing Associates, and DTE Energy—created the Live Downtown Initiative. And, yes, creative individuals and entrepreneurs are taking responsibility for their blocks and streetscape in the absence of local government services.

Finally, the revival in Detroit has been accomplished, for the most part, without deliberate or purposeful action by either the federal government or the state government. The federal government has been a large investor, but most of those investments (for example, National Institutes of Health investments in Wayne State, Medicare and Medicaid reimbursements at Henry Ford Hospital or Detroit Medical Center, Small Business Administration loans) are made through a routine grant- and loan-making process rather than by any intentionality. The state government, for its part, under the strong leadership of Governor Snyder, has smartly focused on fixing the basics and putting the city's fiscal house back in order. Detroiters, in essence, saw the writing on the wall: No one is going to rescue them. They are on their own and must fend for themselves. As a city in extremis, Detroit validates the fundamental premise of the metropolitan revolution. With Washington in gridlock and states distracted, cities and metros are increasingly on their own to devise, finance, and implement the large and small economy-shaping interventions.

Detroit is an incredible living laboratory where the future of American cities is being demonstrated, one project, one investment at a time. As counterintuitive as it may seem, Detroit's intense civic engagement, networked leadership, and reevaluation of assets make it a model for other cities and metropolitan areas.

THE REVOLUTION CAN BE VISUALIZED

At its core, the metropolitan revolution entails disruptive acts that respond to disruptive dynamics. The creation of innovation districts across American cities and suburbs clearly fits the mold. Innovation districts combine the physical, social, economic, and technological in new forms and permutations, reflecting the changing values and preferences of our changing population as well as the shifting demands of leading advanced industries and sectors. They represent a departure from both the development patterns and the economic theories of the last half of the twentieth century that dominated cities (large amenity-driven projects like sports stadiums, convention centers, and performing arts facilities) and suburbs (ubiquitous strip malls and big-box uniformity, isolated corporate campuses far from residential communities, near-exclusive dependence on the automobile for all mobility needs). They require an overhaul, an implosion, of traditional conventions, practices, disciplines, financing, norms, and institutions that still make compartmentalization easy and integration hard. This is a revolution in kind, not in degree.

It is easy to imagine how the revolution would happen. Innovation districts would sprout up in metros across the country. They would continually reinvent and remix our notion of work, recreation, and living spaces, creating a blurring of activities across all hours of the day.

They would instigate innovation by new means of social networking, collaborative ventures, and entrepreneurial incubation. They would spread the benefits of innovation through new partnerships with universities, local schools, and community-based organizations to promote education, workforce preparedness, and business development. In doing all this, they would retain their intrinsic sense of organic growth, aligning with the distinctive strengths of disparate places rather than merely imitating the successes of others.

The private finance sector would conform to the needs and demands of these innovation engines, rather than the other way around. There would be ample supply of early-stage venture capital and commercial lending to support the building and expansion of innovation-related firms, reinforced by real estate, small business, and community lending to create the districts, housing, and mixed-use buildings these firms and their workforce need to thrive. Large commercial banks might establish special innovation district initiatives to bring a spatial coherence to their current aspatial array of products and financing vehicles. Other financial institutions might set up special innovation district funds to invest directly in firms and intermediaries that are at the cutting edge of design, execution, and management of this new form. Philanthropic commitments would be available, from corporate as well as civic organizations, to catalyze the supportive innovation ecosystem as well as efforts to make innovation more inclusive. Crowd-funding entities like Kickstarter, Indiegogo, and others would routinely give entrepreneurs and residents access to pooled capital to pursue their own creative and community projects.

Government would become a true and reliable partner in realizing the potential of the innovation form. Cities and suburban municipalities would revise land-use ordinances and building codes to enable the mixing of uses in districts as well as facilities. To ease design and delivery, disparate government services would be joined together rather than managed separately. The federal and state governments would supply rules and resources that really matter: mortgage standards that encourage mixed-use development and multifamily housing; tax incentives for the preservation of historic buildings and the remediation of brownfield land; sustained investments in basic and applied science and alternative transportation; and sustained support for the commercialization of innovation and the work of regional innovation clusters.

Over time, the people who deliver innovation districts would constitute a new network of metro builders who cut across disciplines, programs, practices, and professions. Modern society has deified specialists and technicians who diagnose and strive to fix discrete problems—say, traffic congestion or slum housing. Metro builders, by contrast, would be fluent in multiple city "languages"—architecture, demographics, engineering, economics, and sociology—and be cognizant of theory and practice. They would see the connections between challenges and work to devise and implement policies that advance multiple objectives simultaneously. Our academies and universities would become central agents in furthering this ambition, breaking down artificial divisions between separate schools, professions curriculums, departments, and self-defeating academic fiefdoms. And new institutions would deliver continuous, multidisciplinary learning, so that professional evolution could respond to new challenges and changing demands.

This is a tall order, no doubt. But megatrends require megachange. The early rise of innovation districts is a sign that cities and metropolitan areas have truly recognized the demands of a new century. The large-scale replication of innovation districts would be a sign that cities and metropolitan areas are ready to master them.

7

TOWARD A GLOBAL NETWORK
OF TRADING CITIES

*If I had to do something different [as mayor] . . . I would be traveling
even more to Asia, to China, Japan, Korea, to Singapore, to Malaysia,
to India, to Mexico, to Latin America, to Brazil than I have previously.
That's the one mistake.*

—ANTONIO VILLARAIGOSA, *mayor of Los Angeles*

The metropolitan revolution described in this book is of domestic origin and, to date, primarily domestic focus. Yet its
future is relentlessly global. The Great Recession unveiled the
limitations of an inward-looking domestic economy driven
by home building, shopping, and excessive debt. The downturn coincided with the culmination of a structural shift in the
global economic order, exemplified when Brazil, India, and
China surpassed the United States' economy as a share of the
global gross domestic product in 2010. With American consumers overextended and middle classes rising abroad, there is
now an imperative for the United States to trade and globally
engage as never before.

There is a metropolitan twist to this macro story: the new
global economic order is a new metropolitan order. The scale
and speed of urban and metropolitan growth across the world
is the defining and unifying thread of the twenty-first century.
Rising metros are fueling the rise of nations. Throughout

history, cities have been the heart of global commerce, forming trade routes, crossroads, switching points, and meeting places. Metropolitan areas are now the origins of global trade, concentrating idea generators, innovation zones, and production hubs. They have become the focus of global investment, responding to the insatiable hunger for the transport, energy, and social infrastructure necessary to grow and develop.

Something profound is happening. The world is being remade in the metropolitan image. The traditional discourse on globalization, for understandable reasons, has focused on countries and companies. Countries set the rules of global exchange and help facilitate global trade and investment. Corporations obviously make the goods and provide the services that are sold abroad. But as the twenty-first century unfolds, the locus of globalization is shifting toward cities and clusters, metros and metro networks. National economies, as we have seen in prior chapters, are really just the aggregation of metropolitan economies. And corporations, as we have also seen, are nested in metropolitan ecosystems of skilled labor, customized support, and supportive infrastructure.

But there is more here. Metros have become both the object and subject of the new trading system. They are the targets, of course, of vendors, builders, investors, technologists, consultants, planners, and architects, all trying to sell their wares to buyers and clients. But they are increasingly part of the game, independent agents in the service of global exchange. They are conduits that enable small and medium-size enterprises to access global markets and overcome the multiple hurdles around exporting. They are part of intricate supply chains, with trading partners all across the world. They are vehicles for foreign investment, through both companies and investors. They are distinctive brands that not only attract visitors and investors but also buttress local products (for example, the price premium conferred by a "Made in New York City" label). Metropolitan areas are no longer just the stage set for the machinations of countries and corporations; they are protagonists in the new global drama. Globalization, in essence, is giving way to global urbanization.

For American metros, long cushioned by a large and diverse domestic economy, the imperative to trade and globally engage is a seismic shock. Kunming in China and Kanpur in India—metropolitan areas that few Americans have ever heard of—are both bigger than Buffalo, Charlotte, and Jacksonville combined.[1] The manufacturing powerhouse Shenzhen, China, now 11 million in population, was a small fishing village a mere thirty years ago.[2] In a world where the natural market for a metro's goods and services lies in a foreign metropolis 3,000 miles away rather than in a community within a two-hour drive, many U.S. mayors, local business leaders, philanthropy heads, and university presidents find the pace of global urbanization disorienting and the necessity of trading globally daunting.

These leaders are being compelled to design and execute their own trade and foreign policy rather than do what they have done for decades, focus on the size of the school or police budget or a zoning variance for a mixed-use development downtown. They are being confronted with the harsh reality that to succeed economically, they must engage globally. These leaders are being wrested from their domestic comfort zone and thrust out onto the global stage with little preparation, scarce training, and limited resources.

To be sure, some U.S. metros are investing in key assets that drive trade, enhancing their innovation platform in New York, retooling their manufacturing sector in Northeast Ohio, strengthening human capital in Houston, embracing sustainable development and mobility in Denver. Those interventions help them compete on the global stage, but, for the most part, they are not explicitly global.

The global future of the American metropolitan revolution is just beginning to take shape. In this early period, many U.S. metros continue to practice economic isolationism. But a small number of courageous communities are stepping forward, designing and implementing export and foreign investment strategies, creating structured, multilayered relationships with their trading partners abroad, and generally embracing the perspective of a trading culture. The end result could be something that the world has not seen since the medieval era: a new global network of trading metros engaged in the seamless and integrated exchange of people, goods, services, energy, capital, ideas, and culture.

THE GLOBAL METROPOLITAN ECONOMY UNLEASHED

Why engage globally, and why engage globally now? The answer is quite simple: that is where markets are rising today and where they will disproportionately rise tomorrow. The brave new metro world is one of large numbers.[3] Since the early 1980s, billions of people around the world, long sheltered by authoritarian regimes and protectionist policies, have sequentially come online.[4] The rapid progression of technology, the rise of multinational corporations, and the growth of Latin America and Asia have helped triple trade's share of global GDP since 1950.[5] The combined economies of Brazil, India, and China accounted for more than a fifth of global gross domestic product in 2009, surpassing the United States for the first time. Their share is expected to grow to more than 26 percent by 2015, while the United States' share shrinks to less than 18 percent.[6] Analysts predict further growth in global trade, powered by the budding industrial sectors in emerging markets, and increased demand from their middle-class consumers. The Carnegie Endowment projects that the share of trade from emerging markets will rise to about 70 percent by 2050, from less than one-third today.[7] Brookings's Homi Kharas and Geoffrey Gertz estimate that China and India, which currently account for only 5 percent of the world's middle-class consumption, could account for nearly half of that consumption by 2050.[8]

The rise of nations and the revolution in global growth and trade are fundamentally interwoven with the explosion of urbanization. People are on the move and metros are on the rise at a scale and speed unprecedented in human history. Since 1950 the world's metropolitan population has more than quadrupled to 3.6 billion; it is expected to exceed 5 billion sometime between 2030 and 2035.[9] In 2010 there were 457 metros with populations of more 1 million people, whereas a century ago there were only 16. In recent decades, the world has grown a network of megametros; there are now 23 metros with more than 10 million people.[10]

Rising nations are, in essence, becoming more like the United States: metropolitan nations where metros concentrate and agglomerate critical assets and sectors, punch above their weight economically, and drive national prosperity and macro-level trade patterns. As Emilia Istrate and Carey Anne Nadeau have found, "the world's 300 largest metro economies now contain approximately 19 percent of the global population but account for 48 percent of world GDP."[11] Metros magnify and amplify economic innovation and exchange; the cross-pollination between disparate cultures, different clusters, and distinct disciplines has synergistic and multiplier effects.

As cities and metros have filled with greater shares of the world's population, metro building has created immense market opportunities—urbanization means industrialization, innovation, and infrastructure.

Metros incubate entrepreneurs, deploy technologies, build middle classes, upgrade standards of living, and prompt the constant creation of public, private, and civic institutions of learning, business, and culture. As metros grow, they need infrastructure of all kinds—energy, transportation, telecommunications, housing, schools. At the same time, as metro residents' incomes grow and their aspirations rise, they spend more on daily necessities and sophisticated consumer products. Markets are increasingly metropolitan, and metropolitan areas are increasingly markets.

The world is still in the early phases of global urbanization. By 2030 the metro share of the world's population will surpass 60 percent.[12] The Boston Consulting Group projects that the total investment required in transportation, electricity, water, and other infrastructure to keep pace with population growth in emerging market cities in Asia and Latin America over the next twenty years will be $30–40 trillion—about 60–70 percent of the total global investment in infrastructure.[13] McKinsey & Company estimates that China's metros will add 350 million people by 2025, triggering an astronomical burst in demand: 5 billion square meters of roads to be paved; 170 mass transit systems to be built; 40 billion square meters of commercial and residential floor space; and 50,000 new skyscrapers—all told, roughly equivalent to building ten versions of New York City.[14]

These numbers suggest enormous market opportunities. It is not surprising that the globalists—multinational corporations and multilateral institutions—have gone urban. Iconic global brands like Caterpillar, Procter and Gamble, and Ford Motor Company are seeing larger and larger shares of their business come from emerging markets and their rising metros. In the past decade, major financial institutions (JPMorgan Chase, Deutsche Bank, Citigroup), manufacturing firms (General Electric, Siemens, Hitachi, Phillips Lighting), and technology firms (CISCO, IBM, Microsoft, Google) have announced high-profile city engagements. Business consultancies and think tanks such as McKinsey & Company, Boston Consulting Group, Brookings, the London School of Economics, and the Economist Intelligence Unit now routinely publish league tables on global cities, comparing progress on core economic, environmental, and social indicators. The United Nations, the World Bank, the Inter-American Development Bank, and a host of other multilateral institutions, long focused on rural poverty, have started major urban and metropolitan initiatives to keep pace with change on the ground.

Now the question: Will America's urbanists go global?

THE STRAITJACKET OF SELF-REFERENTIAL THINKING

The path of American metros to a true trading culture will not be an easy one. The United States is the largest economy in the world and has been since 1871.[15] In 2011 it made up only 5 percent of the global population but generated 19 percent of global output (at purchasing power parity rates).[16] Until recently, metro areas and their firms, situated within a large, diverse, and growing domestic economy, had far fewer incentives to internationalize because they were able to realize desired growth from domestic demand. For that reason, a relatively small portion of the U.S. economy is dedicated to exports. In 2011, according to the Economist Intelligence Unit, total exports made up only 14 percent of our GDP, compared with 31 percent in Canada, 29 percent in China, 25 percent in India, and 15 percent in Japan.[17] According to the U.S. Department of Commerce, fewer than 1 percent of American companies export. And of those, just over half export to more than one country.[18]

The relatively low level of exporting reflects and is reinforced by a striking cultural insularity. Americans don't get out much; only about 36 percent of Americans had a valid passport in 2012, far fewer than the 67 percent of Canadians in the same year.[19] Americans' knowledge of geography is limited; in a 2006 survey of eighteen- to twenty-four-year-olds conducted by the National Geographic Society, 63 percent could not find Iraq on a map, 70 percent did not know the location of Iran or Israel, and about 90 percent were unable to identify Afghanistan on a map of Asia.[20] The share of Americans who speak a second language is just 18 percent, significantly less than the share of Europeans (53 percent) and people from other parts of the world who are able to speak a second language—if not more.[21] Americans seem content to live in a continental cocoon separated from the world by oceans, culture, and a sense of exceptionalism.

This insularity makes the United States ill prepared to relate to emerging markets that are characterized by intense cultural diversity. As McKinsey & Company has noted,

> China has 56 different ethnic groups, who speak 292 distinct languages; India embraces about 20 official languages, hundreds of dialects, and four major religious traditions; Brazil's citizens are among the world's most ethnically and culturally diverse; the residents of Africa's 53 countries speak an estimated 2,000 different

languages and dialects. Even geographically proximate tier-one cities can be radically different. Consider Guangzhou and Shenzhen, two southern Chinese metropolitan centers of comparable size, separated by a distance of just 100 kilometers. In the former, the majority of consumers are locally born Cantonese speakers. In the latter, more than 80 percent are migrants who communicate in Mandarin and, reflecting their disparate regional origins, have far more diverse tastes in consumer electronics, fashion, and food.[22]

This insularity extends deep into the metropolitan leadership class. Most U.S. metropolitan leaders, even from the business community, would be hard pressed to estimate the share of their metropolitan economies that derives from trade, let alone their metro's top exports and trading partners. Thirty years' obsession with the idea of consumer cities and "Starbucks, stadiums, and stealing business" strategies have created confusion about what drives what in metropolitan economies. Many metropolitan leaders have forgotten the clear distillation of Jane Jacobs: "The economic foundation of cities is trade."[23] Her words echo in more recent analyses of global trade:

> Metro areas depend on trade for their own prosperity. The goods and services produced by a metro area's firms that are consumed elsewhere—its exports—inject income from outside the region into the local economy. In turn, that income supports the purchase of local goods and services, creating a "multiplier effect" which increases regional employment and income. Moreover, exporting—especially to international markets—entails high fixed costs and demands high firm productivity. As a result, exporting metro economies are overall more productive and wealthier.[24]

It is not unusual in public and private gatherings to hear metropolitan business leaders ask, Isn't it all the same to a metro whether it trades with Milwaukee or Mumbai? The answer is emphatically no. Milwaukee's metropolitan population is 1.5 million people; Mumbai's is 21 million. Milwaukee's nominal gross metropolitan product (at purchasing-power parity rates) was $80.9 billion in 2012 and grew 12 percent in real terms between 2000 and 2012; Mumbai's nominal GMP was $125 billion in 2012 but grew by 165 percent in real terms during the same period.[25] Milwaukee remains, like many midsize metropolitan economies in the United

States, an important market for U.S. metros. But Mumbai and Indian metros more broadly represent the future for those companies sharp, clever, and productive enough to crack the market. The McKinsey Global Institute predicts that nearly 590 million people will live in India's cities by 2030, including 91 million urban middle-class households—a significant increase from about 22 million similar households in 2010. In total, about 70 percent of the net new employment in India between 2010 and 2030 will be created in its urban areas.[26]

Many metro leaders in the United States have not flexed their communities' exporting muscle. As a result, the system for global engagement in most metros is either nonexistent or badly frayed. Most American metros have no baseline information on what—and with whom—they trade. Few resources are dedicated to exporting, foreign direct investment, and global exchange. In most metropolitan areas, the export services system is deeply fragmented, with no unified vision for global exchange, and small and medium-size companies (the ones that need government assistance) are often completely unaware of the services being offered to identify foreign opportunities, deal with complicated logistics, and comply with foreign regulations.[27] And local media and citizens are prone to criticize their local elected leaders for traveling abroad, assuming these trips are luxury vacations in disguise rather than necessary trade missions.

The absence of an exporting system in U.S. metros is replicated in the private sphere. Analysts have observed that American financial institutions, addicted to cookie-cutter loans in housing markets and credit card debt in consumer markets, have been slow to adapt products to the export sector. There is a "missing middle" in international trade that is not touched by government credit programs or private sector innovations in finance.[28]

The final challenge to internationalizing metropolitan economies lies outside the control of metropolitan leaders. The hard fact is that the federal government's approach to trade is anachronistic and fundamentally unrelated to the central driving role of metropolitan areas. The Obama administration, to its credit, has placed enormous emphasis on expanding exports and improving federal support for foreign direct investment. But it inherited a creaky, underfunded trade services infrastructure, which is outclassed by our major competitors. There is limited federal or state support for metropolitan trade and investment initiatives. The federal government's limited role on the ground and its inadequate support for data sharing, coordination, and resource allocation hurts the work at the local level. The existing system is largely reactive, focusing primarily on servicing the needs of current exporters rather than expanding the pool of export-ready firms.[29] Separate but related, the United States has no national freight strategy. Our competitors know better. As Brad McDearman, Greg Clark, and Joseph Parilla write, "The aggressive and well-funded trade and investment programs of China, Germany, Japan, and Korea prove indispensable in opening up doors globally for their respective metro areas. Hamburg's partial self-government has also facilitated a long history of economic re-positioning and investment in education and culture. When federal, state, and local agendas are in alignment, and distinct roles are clarified, the opportunities for success are dramatically increased."[30]

TRADING ASSETS HIDDEN IN PLAIN SIGHT

What American leaders have going for them are communities with rich, mostly hidden assets, ready to be leveraged and exploited for global purposes. In a country that watches Black Friday retail statistics like baseball scores and is convinced that it has a postindustrial economy that produces little, the real productive and innovative economy has surprising strengths. Those strengths, captured in earlier chapters, start with the tremendous innovative capacity in the United States, concentrated in metropolitan areas because of the special mix of firms, workers, and institutions that foster innovation. This metropolitan capacity to innovate constantly on products and services is the essential foundation for trade and exchange.

People typically think of exports as goods that are manufactured, boxed, and shipped to foreign markets. That is a big part of the story, and, contrary to popular opinion, the United States and its metros still manufacture a range of advanced goods that the rest of the world wants, including aircraft, spacecraft, automobiles, electrical machinery, precision surgical instruments, and high-quality pharmaceutical products. The United States remains the world's third-largest exporter of manufactured goods, behind only China and Germany, having exported $944 billion in 2010. The United States is also the world's largest exporter of services, with a trade surplus in commercial services of $160 billion in 2010.[31] When a U.S. firm designs a building in Shanghai or Mumbai or São Paulo, that design is a service export. When a foreign student pays tuition at the University of Southern California, Carnegie Mellon University in Pittsburgh, or the New School in New York City, that tuition payment is also a service export. Service exports can include a tourist from abroad paying to see the sights in New York or New Orleans, Las Vegas or Los Angeles, or a physically ill patient from a foreign country coming to see a doctor at the Cleveland Clinic, the Kleinert Kurtz Hand Care Center in Louisville, or the Methodist Debakey Heart Center in Houston.

The importance of trade and the latent export potential of U.S. metropolitan economies were especially clear during the postrecession period. An incredible 37 percent of the economic recovery to date has come from the export sector.[32] Manufacturing, battered during the first decade of this century, is staging a slight resurgence, buoyed by rising wages in China, the shale-gas revolution at home, and the growing realization that the production and innovation economies are inextricably linked. The growth in export services at home has also brought many Americans face to face with the rising middle class from Asia and Latin America. International tourism in the United States has grown steadily in recent years, from 49 million international visitors in 2005 to 62 million in 2011, with continued strong growth projected for at least the next several years.[33] The U.S. Department of Commerce's International Trade Administration reports that by 2016 "the number of travelers from Brazil, China, and India is expected to increase by 274 percent, 135 percent, and 50 percent respectively."[34] The number of international students studying in the United States almost doubled between 1990 and 2010, from 387,000 to 764,000. In that same period, students from China increased by a factor of five; students from India by a factor of nearly four.[35]

These numbers indicate a rapidly diversifying population in metro America. In contrast to Europe, Japan, and even China, the United States is on a path of sustained population growth, fueled by immigration. In the past forty years, the United States has grown by 105 million and is slated to grow by another 112 million by 2060.[36] Immigration accounts for more than 29 percent of the overall population surge over the past forty years.[37] Some 40 million of residents today were born outside the United States. That is 13 percent of the population, the highest share since 1920.[38] If insularity was America's prime characteristic before the Great Recession, diversity may be its prime asset in the recession's aftermath.

Chapter 5 explored the social impact of this growing diversification and the efforts by innovators like Neighborhood Centers in Houston to integrate immigrants into the American mainstream. Immigration has another supersize implication; it helps ease the path to further internationalization of the U.S. economy. Part of that results from the behavior of people who migrate. As Robert Guest explains this dynamic in his book *Borderless Economics:*

> Another big difference between migrants and less mobile folk is that migrants are more likely to form cross border networks. These networks serve two critical functions. First, they speed the flow of information. Second, diaspora networks foster a high level of trust. The world's most flexible and resilient trading networks—the Chinese in Southeast Asia, the Indians in East Africa and the Lebanese in Latin America—are based on diasporas. Traders whose global networks were already in place were in a perfect position to profit from this boom.[39]

The potential impact of immigration on global trade is rising because more and more immigrants are highly educated. In 1980 only 19 percent of working-age immigrants had a bachelor's degree, but by 2010 that number had risen to 30 percent. Similarly, nearly 40 percent of working-age immigrants had not received a high school diploma in 1980, but that share had fallen to about 28 percent by 2010.[40] Educated immigrants have played an important role in dynamic parts of the U.S. economy, such as manufacturing, information technology, Internet commerce, and clean energy.

The importance of America's continued attraction for international talent cannot be diminished. As James Fallows writes in an article in *The Atlantic* titled "How America Can Rise Again,"

> The American culture's particular strengths could conceivably be about to assume new importance and give our economy new pep. International networks will matter more with each passing year. As the one truly universal nation, the United States continually refreshes its connections with the rest of the world—through languages, family, education, business—in a way no other nation does, or will. The countries that are comparably open—Canada, Australia—aren't nearly as large; those whose economies are comparably large—Japan, unified Europe, eventually China or India—aren't nearly as open. The simplest measure of whether a culture is dominant is whether outsiders want to be part of it. At the height of the British Empire, colonial subjects from the Raj to Malaya to the Caribbean modeled themselves in part on Englishmen; Nehru

and Lew Kuan Yew went to Cambridge, Gandhi to University College, London. Ho Chi Minh wrote in French for magazines in Paris. These days the world is full of businesspeople, bureaucrats, and scientists who have trained in the United States.[41]

The United States is not only a magnet for immigrants; it is also a preferred destination for foreign direct investment of immense scale. After prerecession highs of $320 billion in 2000 and $310 billion in 2008, foreign investment in the United States is rebounding, with $234 billion invested in U.S. firms and real estate by foreign entities in 2011. At the end of that year, the aggregate stock of foreign investment on a historical-cost basis had increased to roughly $2.55 trillion, with the United Kingdom, Japan, the Netherlands, Germany, Switzerland, Canada, and France having the largest holdings.[42]

The manufacturing sector accounts for more than $838 billion of the total $2.55 trillion in foreign direct investment stock in the United States.[43] Foreign investment in U.S. manufacturing encompasses a wide range of activities, from a Toyota auto production plant in Mississippi or Kentucky to a Samsung semiconductor plant in Austin, and it is a major source of jobs and economic activity in the United States. The Manufacturing Institute estimates that "about 1.68 million Americans are directly employed by foreign-owned manufacturing firms."[44]

Foreign equity investment is also a critical source of capital for large-scale redevelopment projects. Throughout the country, there are numerous examples of significant investments in urban regeneration in cities and metropolitan areas by sovereign wealth funds. In Washington, D.C., for instance, the Qatari Investment Authority announced in 2011 its plan to invest $700 million in the redevelopment of a ten-acre mixed-use project on the site of the former downtown convention center. The CenterCityDC project is estimated to create as many as 1,700 construction jobs in the near term and an additional 3,700 permanent jobs on completion.[45]

As the world urbanizes, the United States has one other asset: U.S. metros and their leaders are singularly positioned to leverage the economic opportunities presented by global urbanization in ways that treat rising cities not just as markets but as partners grappling with supersize challenges. It takes a metropolis to know a metropolis. As Beijing, Shenzhen, and other Chinese metros have learned, the pace of urbanization and the harsh reality of environmental degradation and climate change have

placed a high premium on designing spatially efficient metros and constructing sustainable infrastructure and buildings that can lower energy
use, reduce greenhouse gas emissions, and ensure clean, breathable air.[46]
As Mumbai, Bangalore, and other Indian metros have learned, the pace
of urbanization and the concomitant explosion of urban poverty require
interventions that promote more inclusive growth in the way metros are
designed, transit is built, education is provided, and employment opportunities are extended.[47] U.S. metro leaders know that global metros and
their residents do not just need to buy more stuff; they need basic help
in shaping metropolitan areas that marry high growth, low carbon emissions, and great opportunity. Metropolitan leaders are mindful of both
the pitfalls of rapid growth and its opportunities. This means that U.S.
metros that invent sustainable and inclusive ways of growth through new
products, processes, and modes of delivery to resolve challenges at home
are also creating the base to export that knowledge (and those goods and
services) abroad.

EXPORTING FROM HOME: PORTLAND

The cumulative lesson of these large economic and demographic forces is
clear. There is now an imperative to trade and engage globally, given the
trajectory of growth abroad and the continued fallout from the prerecession consumption binge at home. And there is also the *potential* to trade
and engage due to the current and future export base of U.S. metropolitan
areas, the global orientation of our foreign-born population, our attrac-
tiveness for foreign investors, and the natural insights that metropolitan
areas have about the needs of other metropolitan areas. Now comes the
doing. How does a domestic metropolitan revolution go global?

Portland, Oregon, a prosperous metropolis of 2.2 million people,
offers an early glimpse of what is possible.[48] Portland has one of the most
recognizable brands in the United States. It regularly makes popular top-
ten lists for most green or eco-friendly cities, and for good reason. The
metropolis runs a comprehensive system of light-rail, suburban commuter
rail, buses, and bike lanes, and residents recycle more than half their
waste.[49] In the 1970s Republican governor Tom McCall pushed through
an urban growth boundary law aimed at curbing sprawl at the periphery
and promoting reinvestment in the city.[50] Governor McCall and others
also initiated a successful effort to tear down a 1950s freeway along the

Willamette River in downtown Portland and replace it with a waterfront park.[51] Liberated from concrete, the downtown houses microbreweries and cutting-edge restaurants and has become a magnet for aspiring musicians, artists, and techies. A recent hit TV comedy called *Portlandia* embraces the "weird and crunchy" character of the city.

Yet Portland is also one of America's most export-oriented and globally integrated economies. More than 18 percent of its gross metropolitan product comes from exports, the third-highest export intensity among the top 100 metros in the United States. Between 2003 and 2010, Portland increased its export volume by 109.3 percent, making it the second-fastest-growing export market among the major metros.[52] Weird and crunchy Portland, it turns out, is also the home of Silicon Forest, a robust cluster of computer and electronics firms. Silicon Forest was initially planted in 1946, when four returning war veterans started Tektronix to invent and manufacture oscilloscopes.[53] Tektronix grew to be one of the top manufacturers of test and measurement instruments and, over time, spun off dozens of start-up companies.

In 1976 the semiconductor maker Intel started up in Silicon Valley. Portland was conveniently close to Silicon Valley, with a lower cost of living and inexpensive raw materials for manufacturing (like water and electricity). Soon thereafter, Intel moved a cadre of engineers to Portland, and a Portland-based team developed the company's signature Pentium chip. Intel did not spur as many spin-offs in the region as Tektronix had, but it did attract a group of specialized suppliers, who sought to be near a major customer. Soon, Intel's competitors came to Portland to take advantage of the network of expert support and supply companies and the trained and talented workers who might be willing to leave Intel for another employer.[54] Portland's computer and electronics manufacturing cluster now employs 33,200 people, and it is the region's top international export industry, thanks in large part to TriQuint (a Tektronix spin-off) and Intel. This sector represents 57 percent of the region's total exports and 63 percent of export growth between 2003 and 2010.[55]

In his 2010 State of the Union address, President Obama issued a challenge to the country: "We need to export more of our goods. Because the more products we make and sell to other countries, the more jobs we support right here in America. So, tonight, we set a new goal: We will double our exports over the next five years, an increase that will support two million jobs in America."[56]

The Portland leadership community rose to the challenge. The metropolis had been hit hard by the Great Recession, shedding 80,000 jobs and seeing unemployment rise to over 11 percent.[57] With an initiative initially led by Portland mayor Sam Adams and the Portland Development Commission, a team of business and civic leaders sorted out how to double the region's exports. They dug deep into the data, deconstructing the metro's economy and distilling its economic performance and profile, its export strengths and weaknesses, its prominent clusters and industries, and its key trade partners. They conducted surveys and interviews with local firms and export service providers to gain further market insights.

From this intense assessment emerged the Greater Portland Export Plan, which outlined several strategies to leverage the region's dual strengths: its leading global position in computers and electronic products manufacturing and its global edge in sustainability. To further boost the exports from its computers and electronics sector, the plan focuses on maintaining and protecting the location advantages that initially brought the cluster to the region, strengthening supply chain relationships within the industry, and providing early-stage incentives to industry spin-offs that have the potential for significant export growth. To build on the region's strengths in sustainability, the plan has launched a major marketing campaign called We Build Green Cities to promote the region's clean-tech companies and products as solutions for global clean-economy challenges.[58]

Portland's export plan reflects a core understanding that looking abroad for growth is critical to the future of the metropolis. As Tom Hughes, the president of Portland's Metro Council, says, "It's not just us selling each other microbrews. What you really need is a culture where manufacturers or entrepreneurs begin to include foreign markets as part of their business strategy."[59] Hughes now cochairs the export plan's implementation strategy with Jill Eiland, Northwest corporate affairs manager for Intel, and the entire effort is given added heft by being based at Greater Portland, Inc., a new regional economic development partnership.

Green cities and sustainable growth might seem an unusual sector for export growth. But as the magazine *Grist* noted in a November 2012 profile of Susan Anderson, Portland's sustainability director, "Being the sustainability director of Portland is a bit like being the oil minister of Saudi Arabia. You don't exactly run the place, but you do have the region's chief export on tap." Anderson echoes that assessment: "There's money to be made, to be crass. There are hundreds and hundreds of companies in Portland that are manufacturing or offering services that are sustainable technologies or products or services. They are selling them to the rest of the world now."[60]

Rising metros in emerging markets increasingly demand products and services that enable development that is economically supportive and environmentally sensitive. Portland is betting on the notion that those products and services will disproportionately emerge from firms located in metros that are first movers on sustainable development. And they seem to be right. Interface Engineering, a Portland-based company that provides sustainable building services, is leading a five-year, $5.5 billion redevelopment project in Doha, Qatar. Interface Engineering's specialization in developing water and energy conservation strategies and LEED-certified buildings is a critical component of constructing the new mixed-use "eco-district" in Doha. LRS Architects, a leading Portland architecture firm with a second office in Shanghai, is currently working on a major sustainable development within Shanghai's Zhangjiang Hi-Tech Park. The 2.28 billion square-foot commercial building project aims to become one of China's first LEED Platinum-certified developments. SSI Shredding Systems, in the suburb of Wilsonville, has customers for its industrial shredders for solid waste recycling in fifty-one countries worldwide, including the Singapore Ministry of Environment, industrial manufacturers such as Komatsu Limited in Japan and Samsung in Korea, and tire-recycling facilities such as a PCC Group in China and a Bridgestone plant in Brazil.[61]

Portland companies have primarily looked east to Asia for their markets. But there is also enormous potential and need in our hemisphere. After a trip to Brazil, Mayor Sam Adams established a formal relationship with Sustainable Hub, a São Paulo–based clean-tech consulting firm, to help Portland firms crack the Brazilian market and vice versa.[62]

Portland is not the only U.S. city attempting to organize for trade. Los Angeles and Syracuse are implementing purposeful export strategies that leverage their distinctive trading position. Miami, Savannah, and Norfolk have made transformative investments in their seaports and related logistics infrastructure to accommodate the larger ships that will move goods after the expansion of the Panama Canal. Technology centers like Silicon Valley and Austin are scrambling to import talented workers; university hubs like Chicago and Boston are actively recruiting qualified students. Global destination metros as disparate as New York and New Orleans, Las Vegas and Orlando, are devising focused tourism strategies, and advanced health care metros like Baltimore, Houston, and Cleveland are doing the same with so-called health tourism.

The common thread through all these efforts is differentiation. Following the recession, U.S. metros seem to be rediscovering what makes them special, the distinctiveness of what they make or provide and sell to the world, rather than what makes them the same, the ubiquitous design and offerings of sports stadiums, big-box retail, and restaurant chains. And so it is abroad. Metropolitan areas, whether located in mature economies like Germany or Japan or in rising nations like Brazil, India, and China, do not exist in the aggregate but in the specific.

The focus on differentiation is essential to sorting out where a particular metro fits in the new global order. Twenty years ago, pathbreaking work by Saskia Sassen made "global cities" part of the popular lexicon.[63] Her initial definition was intentionally narrow, focused on a relatively few metropolitan areas that acted as command-and-control centers for global finance and advanced services. Sassen's work, which had enormous influence on market analysis and business investment, put heavy emphasis not only on traditional financial hubs like New York, London, Frankfurt, Zurich, Hong Kong, and Tokyo but eventually on emerging ones like Shanghai, São Paulo, Buenos Aires, Seoul, and Singapore.

Today, as Portland demonstrates, notions of globalization (including new important work by Sassen) are more expansive, recognizing that all cities are fueled, to different degrees, by global investment and connected, in distinctive ways, through global commerce and exchange, global product and labor supply chains.[64] Peter Marcuse and Ronald Van Kempen use the term *globalizing cities* to reflect that relationship, noting that "(almost) all cities are touched by the process of globalization and . . . involvement in that process is not a matter of being either at the top or the bottom of it, but rather of the nature and extent of influence of the process."[65]

This observation has practical consequences. The global economy is essentially operating as a network of globalizing metros that trade with one another because of natural links between their major companies and universities, driving economic clusters and financial and migration flows. Portland shares a common focus on sustainable development (and an emerging cluster of like-minded firms) with Copenhagen, Stockholm, Curitiba, and Singapore.[66] Madrid, Hong Kong, and Dubai are media hubs. Nagoya, Stuttgart, and Detroit are globally significant manufacturing hubs. The Hague, Brussels, Washington, New York, Geneva, and

Nairobi are centers of global decision making. Boston, Cambridge, and Nanjing are important nodes in the global academic network.[67] In short, a new global map is being drawn in the world, not of nation-to-nation trade but of metro-to-metro exchange based on distinctive clusters, specialized expertise, and cultural affinity.

THE NEW SILK ROAD: MIAMI AND SÃO PAULO

It is a small, measured step from organizing within to relating without, and that's what U.S. metros are slowly starting to do, constructing deliberate partnerships with global counterparts with whom they trade. That's precisely what Portland is doing in its outreach to São Paulo in the sustainable development space. Structured links, of course, have always existed between firms and ports that do business with each other. And sister-city cultural and educational relationships between local governments have grown since their inception at President Eisenhower's 1956 White House conference on citizen diplomacy.[68] In recent years, however, bilateral relationships are occurring between a much broader array of institutions, including economic development organizations and business associations that help companies up their trading game, universities that have research and student exchanges, and cultural institutions that help set the international image for cities and metros. The cumulative impact of these institutional relationships will be not only more trade but trade that is iterative and innovative, starting with one set of products and services and then, through synergistic effects, graduating to another. To better understand the promising nature of metro-to-metro relationships, it is helpful to first understand the distinct rise of two major hubs of the Americas.

Since 1513, when Ponce de León left Puerto Rico in search of gold and happened on what are now Florida's southeastern shores, Miami's economic, political, and cultural life has been shaped by actors and events in Latin America and the Caribbean. In the 1960s and 1970s an influx of mostly wealthy Cuban immigrants fundamentally altered the city's communities, politics, and leadership circles.[69] Waves of immigrants and visitors from other Latin American countries followed throughout the rest of the century. The result is a region (encompassing Miami, Fort Lauderdale, and Pompano Beach) that ranks first among the top 100 U.S. metros in its share of foreign residents (39 percent).[70] In a period in which some U.S. regions put up the No Vacancy sign to the rest of the world,

Miami marked itself with an indelible cultural signpost that welcomed and assimilated new migrants. Miami has leveraged that ethos to become the country's "gateway to Latin America and the Caribbean," serving as the Americas' shared hub for international tourism, arts and culture, global business, and trade and investment.[71]

If Miami represents one city-pole for the Americas, then São Paulo is the other. Having lived in Rio de Janeiro's shadow throughout the nineteenth century, São Paulo was the locus of much of Brazil's economic growth during the country's coffee boom and rapid industrialization in the twentieth century.[72] As noted earlier, the economic rise of emerging markets has much to do with the economic gains that are associated with urbanization. It is not surprising, then, that Brazil's two-decade-long economic ascendance reflects the economic dynamism of its largest metropolis. With a population (of 20 million) near that of Australia and an economy ($473 billion) larger than Sweden's, metro São Paulo houses 10 percent of Brazil's population but generates 20 percent of its GDP.[73]

São Paulo and Miami have historically had a robust trade relationship. Both are logistics hubs for their respective nations and anchor the $74 billion goods trade between the United States and Brazil.[74] São Paulo's macro-metropolis contains the Port of Santos, South America's busiest container port, and the São Paulo–Guarulhos International Airport, Brazil's busiest airport.[75] The Miami metropolis, for its part, moves the most seaborne and aviation freight value of any Florida metro area and is the gateway for one-third of all trade between the United States and Latin America.[76] In 2011 two-way movement of goods between Brazil and the Miami customs district totaled more than $15 billion, representing more than 20 percent of total U.S. goods trade with Brazil.[77]

São Paulo and Miami are also global financial hubs. As Saskia Sassen argues, the most important nodes in the global economy remain those cities that concentrate and dispense the world's financial services and capital.[78] São Paulo has nineteen of the top twenty-five international banks and the world's third-largest financial exchange.[79] Miami, for its part, harbors the second-largest concentration of foreign banks in the United States.[80] Brazil's two top banks, Banco do Brasil and Banco Itaú, have had offices in Miami since the 1970s.[81]

But there is more to this city-to-city relationship than logistics and finance. After all, investments by firms in São Paulo flow through New York and London, and Brazilian goods travel to ports in Houston and

Singapore—so what makes Miami special to São Paulo? The answer lies, in part, in the historic role Miami has played in the hemisphere. First Cubans, then Nicaraguans, Colombians, Panamanians, and Peruvians arrived in Miami seeking political stability and economic opportunity. Yet as Latin America stabilized politically and entered into an unprecedented period of prosperity and growth, Miami's role in the region changed. As the geographer Jan Nijman explains, Latin Americans "come to Miami to shop for luxury goods, send their children to attend the University of Miami, or purchase a second home in one of the city's affluent neighborhoods. To Latin Americans, Miami is a central point of reference on the road to a successful future."[82]

Brazilians have certainly discovered Miami. Denerson Mota, the CEO of a São Paulo–based investment firm, calls Miami the "U.S. version of Rio de Janeiro," only with more efficient urban mobility, safer streets, and cheaper shopping. And Miami's de facto dual citizenship within the hemisphere matters for business as well. Mota notes that Miami

> is also a city that is more comfortable for Brazilian entrepreneurs to do business since there are many of their own countrymen and other Latinos to contact, more cultural flexibility, and English is not as "mandatory" as it is in most other locations, which gives the place an additional edge. And this combination of elements, in the end, translates into lots of economic opportunities for both Brazilians and Americans and a view that Miami can easily be a nice platform for both business deals and personal life.[83]

For these reasons, Brazilian visitors and investors are remaking the city yet again. The Miami International Airport, for example, was the twelfth busiest in the United States in terms of total passengers in 2011, second busiest for international passengers. But when it comes to international passengers from São Paulo in that same year, the Miami International Airport ranked first in the nation.[84] When Brazilians visit, they spend. In 2010 more than 500,000 Brazilians visited Miami-Dade County (nearly half of total Brazilian visitors to the United States), generating an estimated economic impact of $1 billion.[85]

Brazilians' affinity for Miami's shopping, beaches, and cultural amenities has had tremendous knock-on effects on the real estate market. Like many other Sunbelt metros during the early years of this century, real estate speculation fueled a housing bubble in Miami. When the bubble burst in 2008, foreclosures, plummeting housing prices, and job losses in construction sent the region spiraling into recession. Low prices, the strength of the Brazilian real relative to the American dollar, and frequent visits to Miami made real estate investment in the city an obvious choice for many wealthy Brazilians.[86] These purchases, like all foreign direct investment, matter greatly to a metropolitan economy. Foreign direct investment helps create jobs and growth in the short term, establishes international connections that catalyze further growth in the long term, and helps cities hedge against domestic downturns in demand.

The visitor economy of Brazilian tourists and the real estate economy of Brazilian investors have also yielded a growing number of entrepreneurs who seek to capitalize on extended ties between the linked metros. In a profile by NBC's *Rock Center* news program, Cristiano Piquet, a native Brazilian and the founder of Miami-based Piquet Realty, said, "I was trying to help the Brazilians because I knew how it was to come to the United States, trying to do something. There's nobody that speaks Portuguese, nobody that could give us good service. So I said, 'You know what? I'll do this myself.'"[87]

Piquet saw a high-demand niche and then leveraged his cross-border network to build a client list and launch a business. Millions of individual decisions like these by people and firms constitute the market forces that dictate the flows of goods, services, people, capital, and ideas between cities like São Paulo and Miami. In this way, trade and commerce both shape and are shaped by a growing web of institutional, professional, and personal relationships. Robust movement of goods between the two regions has nurtured a working dialogue between the Port of Santos and its counterparts at the Port of Miami and Port Everglades. Multinational corporations with presence in both metros have developed their own dynamic of internal operations and external networks. São Paulo and Miami-Dade County have been official sister cities since 1988, strengthening linkages between the two governments.

Yet relationships are now growing among a broader set of business, civic, academic, and cultural institutions. Manny Mencia, a senior vice president at Enterprise Florida, the Miami-based trade and investment organization for the state of Florida, has called Brazil "Florida's China," with Miami and São Paulo being the epicenters for trade and exchange. As a result, the region's global strategy has centered on São Paulo, where Enterprise Florida opened an office in 2011 to help Miami businesses crack a complex Brazilian market. Both Enterprise Florida and the Greater Miami Chamber of Commerce have taken local business and political leaders on trade missions to São Paulo, where they are welcomed by InvesteSP, the state of São Paulo's investment promotion agency. In turn, APEX-Brasil, Enterprise Florida's Brazilian counterpart, has its only U.S. location in Miami's free trade zone. There it designs and executes special projects, such as providing clean and renewable fuels (Brazil specializes in ethanol produced from sugarcane) to IndyCar, the American-based auto-racing body.[88]

Universities are also cementing city-to-city links. Both Florida International University and the Miami Ad School have partnerships with ESPM, a São Paulo–based university particularly known for advertising and communications. Students at ESPM's business school are eligible to transfer to the Certificate in International Business program at Florida International University for a minimum of two consecutive semesters.[89]

Finally, cultural affinities continue to bind the two regions. The most recent example: Art Basel, the largest series of art events in the world, staged its eleventh art show in Miami in December 2012. The event showcased 260 galleries from across five continents. Miami's exhibit had fourteen Brazilian galleries (eleven from São Paulo); at the June 2012 show in Basel, Switzerland, by contrast, only four Brazilian galleries were represented.[90] These shared tastes, behaviors, languages, and amenities attract well-traveled visitors from São Paulo and can curb the fear of the unknown for a São Paulo business eyeing the U.S. market or a Miami entrepreneur hoping to expand in Brazil.

Similar multilayered trade links exist between New York and London, Silicon Valley and Bangalore, Tijuana and San Diego, and San Francisco and Shanghai. Each of these pairings illustrates the evolution of organic, networked globalism that grows sector by sector, institution by institution. Relationships run separate and parallel, intersecting at key points because of interlocking boards, unanticipated consequences of trade visits, or the chance serendipity of human interaction.

For American metros, the lessons from the São Paulo–Miami relationship are clear: Rethink your mental map of who your trading partners are, given what you trade. As McKinsey & Company advises corporations, "Do not try to achieve blanket coverage of an entire country or chase growth in scattered individual cities."[91] Draw your map based on clusters and culture rather than on physical proximity. Engage your global partners across multiple domains of business, government, philanthropy, education, and culture. Establish partnerships based on mutual respect and notions of mutual benefit. Grow together by linking together.

The Portland and São Paulo–Miami stories give a sense of how metros evolve up the ladder of trade and investment. Metros organize for trade, building off their distinctive strengths. They structure bilateral, multilayered relationships with other metros with whom they trade. In both cases, they see the benefits of trade, which inspires them to bolster support for export-oriented activity and to deepen and expand the focus on building and maintaining relationships. None of this is easy or, as yet, common. But global dynamics are so strong that this is the inevitable wave of the future.

Organizing for trade and structuring bilateral relations could merely be the opening act to the main show in the twenty-first century. Cities and metropolitan areas, as these stories show, are networks of people, institutions, universities, firms, and governments coproducing economies and cogoverning places. The global economy is similarly emerging as networks of metropolitan economies that link and trade together. The end result might be a structured multilateral network of global trading cities that realizes the full potential of metros around the world to trade and engage.

LOOKING TO THE PAST TO SHAPE OUR FUTURE

We have seen such a global network of trading cities before. In 1241 Lübeck and Hamburg concluded a "treaty of friendship and free trade."[92] The cities were natural allies, united by strategic location, complementary economies, and mercantilist orientation. Lübeck, located on the Trave River, a tributary to the Baltic Sea, was a major exporter of herring, thanks to its position near the rich spawning grounds of the prized fish in Scania. Hamburg, located on the River Elbe, which flows into the North Sea, had close access to salt mines, the key ingredient in preserving fish.[93]

The marriage between these two river cities and their merchants (the Hansa) altered the economic geography and evolution of northern Europe. The proximity of the rivers (the Trave runs inland, ending thirty-two miles from the Elbe) allowed an alternative trade route between the Baltic and North Seas.[94] Merchants were able to circumvent the dangerous passage around Denmark and provide more security for the shipment of goods.

The growth of trade spurred demand for more infrastructure (for example, the opening of the Stecknitz canal between the Elbe and Trave rivers in 1398),[95] other products (such as barrels for shipping the salted fish), and supportive services (taverns, shoes, clothing). As one historian recounts, "We might expect that during the busy period when thousands of men were hard at work fishing, salting, packing the herring, beer should have been drunk in large quantities, but the amount consumed almost passes belief. This was entirely supplied by the Hanseatic cities."[96]

Commerce yielded technological innovation. In the early thirteenth century, ships used to transport goods in the Baltic and North Seas were typically low-quality fishing boats that were small, vulnerable in bad weather, and hard to navigate. As trade grew and became more secure, a new type of ship, the Hanseatic cog, was invented, "which was larger, could better protect the cargo and was also more navigable than local vessels."[97]

As Lübeck and Hamburg extended trade with other cities, the alliance's membership and structure became larger and more formal. Cologne, with its close trading links to London, became a key member. In 1280 Lübeck allied with Visby to ensure safe passage of goods along trade routes to Gotland, Sweden, and Novgorod, Russia. Shortly thereafter Riga and Tallinn, two Baltic trading cities, joined as well. Thus was opened a gateway for Russian goods, crops, and materials needed for ship building.[98]

Scholars give different dates for the formalization of this network of trading cities into the Hanseatic League, but by the fourteenth century, a "powerful compact of cities" had emerged, "with far reaching trade agreements and almost total control of North European trade."[99] As Jennifer Mills recounts, "Since there were no navies to protect their cargoes, no international bodies to regulate tariffs and trade and few ports had regulatory authorities to manage their use, the merchants banded together to establish tariff agreements, provide for common defense and to make sure ports were safely maintained."[100]

A semiformal governance structure, the Hanseatic Diet, was established, which met every twenty-five to thirty years to discuss league policy.[101] With economic power came political influence. The Holy Roman Empire granted five cities—Lübeck, Rome, Venice, Pisa, and Florence—the ducal rank, affording them membership in the emperor's council. In 1375 the emperor himself, Charles IV, visited Lübeck, indicating the power not only of the city but of the league as well.[102] The Hanseatic

League remained a powerful force in northern Europe for centuries, until nation-states took the place of collaborative networks.

Lübeck and Hamburg illustrate the origins of trade and globalization. Before there were nations, there were cities. Before there were unions of nations or the United Nations, there were networks of cities. These medieval communities also suggest some ageless economic truths: Places that collaborate to compete thrive and prosper. Trading clusters that complement one another lead to unanticipated innovation. The brewing of beer, in other words, is rooted in salt and fish.

A TWENTY-FIRST-CENTURY NETWORK OF TRADING CITIES

The Hanseatic League is not a dusty relic of a bygone age. In a metropolitan century, when urbanization is the unifying thread across the globe, the league is living history, telegraphing not what the metropolitan revolution is but what it could become.

This century's network of trading cities, of course, will not be a carbon copy of the Hanseatic League. The global trading system has become an intricate, sophisticated matrix, grounded in global trading rules enforced by global institutions, embellished by bilateral and regional treaties between nation-states and blocs of nations, driven by the actions of multinational firms, amplified by the activities of nongovernmental organizations like universities, museums, advocacy groups, and philanthropies. Cities are no longer expected to define or police the system, as they were in medieval times; rather, they leverage the infrastructure of their existing nations and build on their distinctive sectors and competitive advantages.

What would a twenty-first-century network of trading cities look like? The climate arena might provide some insight into what could transpire. In 2005 groups of local leaders, frustrated with the slow pace of national and global action on climate change, formed the C20 (now C40) Cities Climate Leadership Group, "a network of the world's megacities taking action to reduce greenhouse gas emissions." Now led by New York City mayor Michael Bloomberg, the coalition is helping individual cities forge "innovative solutions to common sources of greenhouse gas emissions" to "provide proven models that other cities and national governments can adopt." In 2007 New York City, for example, pioneered PlaNYC 2030, a comprehensive plan for the green growth of the city; in 2012 Copenhagen made an ambitious commitment to turn itself carbon neutral by 2025 through shifts to clean energy sources and extensive deployment of energy efficiency techniques and technology. Since 2008 Philadelphia, under the leadership of Mayor Michael Nutter, has pursued a Greenworks initiative to marry sustainable development to job creation. The C40 group has aligned with former U.S. president Bill Clinton's Clinton Climate Initiative to form "one of the preeminent climate action organizations in the world."[103] Metros are beginning to find their collective voice on the continental and international stage, binding together and advocating, if not demanding, that nations and multilateral institutions act on urgent matters like climate change.

One can imagine a trade network—a T40—similarly being formed to help metros around the world innovate on trade and investment, link with trading partners, and collectively engage on altering national and global rules of the game. Like C40, this would be an effort driven by evidence and clear-eyed objective assessments of what cities and metros can actually do, across multiple sectors, to boost global engagement. It could be an educational tool, to help make "global fluency," a term first applied to cities by former Chicago mayor Richard M. Daley, a core part of the metropolitan leadership curriculum in the United States. It could be an advocacy tool, to identify key parts of national and global trading regimes that inhibit exchange across metropolitan areas. And it could be a market-shaping tool, to identify financing and other barriers to trade and challenge market actors to compete to invent and apply new investment and lending vehicles.

An expansive network of trading cities would be a welcome departure from the current global circuit: the showy, exclusive globalism of the annual World Economic Forum at Davos or the political, conflict-oriented theater of the G20 or world trade summits. This network of metros could be formal or informal, enabled by innovative technologies, supported by still-to-be-invented modes of communication. Advanced universities in the United States and elsewhere are now experimenting with teaching tens of thousands of students at a time through the Internet. There is absolutely no reason that these techniques cannot be applied to advancing global trade and exchange, perhaps through structured links between leaders in networks of global metropolitan areas that share common economic and cultural ties.

Unlike the C40, a T40 could go beyond local elected officials to inform and catalyze action by an intricate web of private, civic, and cultural institutions, extending well beyond the ties naturally drawn between municipal governments or the subunits of multinational corporations. It could capture and buttress an inclusive, ever-shifting confederation, engaging multinational corporations, metropolitan business associations, economic development entities, ports, airports, universities, museums and other cultural institutions, think tanks, advocacy organizations, ethnic and religious groups, and crossnational organizations of every stripe.

This would be pragmatic globalism reflective of the metropolitan ethic: dedication to solving problems, advancing and sharing innovation, making deals, collaborating rather than competing. This is the future of the metropolitan revolution: global in design, in reach, in impact.

8

METROS AS THE NEW SOVEREIGN

The people of this country ... [must] establish good government from reflection and choice ... [or be] forever destined to depend for their political constitutions on accident and force.
—ALEXANDER HAMILTON, *Federalist Papers No. 1*

With talk of revolution in the air, the impulse at this point in the book might be to call on metropolitan revolutionaries to use their talents and energies to realize the full potential of their communities, leaving behind the dysfunctional federal and uneven state governments. Sometimes, metro leaders act on that impulse, stating boldly that they can get stuff done themselves, without any help from higher powers. But it's not that simple.

Cities and metropolitan areas constitute the engines of the national economy and our centers of trade and investment. They deliver and help finance the public goods in our country, whether transport infrastructure or education or workforce training or services for new immigrants. They influence, through myriad powers, the shape of our built environment, the physical space of our communities, and, hence, the way individuals negotiate their personal and professional lives on a daily basis. Economic stagnation, disruptive global dynamics, fiscal turmoil, and federal gridlock are sparking a fundamental rethinking of the metropolitan role. Responsibilities once left to federal and state policymakers are now the remit of city and metropolitan leaders.

Yet cities and metropolitan areas cannot go it alone. Their efforts depend on the support of federal and state governments—maddening, meddling, and domineering as they may be. State and federal governments are, through mandatory entitlements, tax incentives, and spending programs, the largest single investors in cities and metropolitan areas, their infrastructure, their residents (particularly disadvantaged residents), and their leading-edge institutions. They set the regulatory rules of the game by which cities and metros (and their companies and core institutions) grow advanced industries, attract global talent, and compete on the world stage. It is impossible to ignore these higher levels of government, even as we condemn their inaction and unreliability or decry their prescriptive and intrusive tendencies.

The fact is that state and federal governments have played an important if mostly hidden role in each of the stories told in this book. The Applied Sciences initiative in New York City rests on a foundation of hundreds of millions of federal research dollars that has made Cornell University the world-class research institution it is. The Youngstown, Ohio, National Manufacturing Innovation Institute (focusing on 3-D printing) depends on a significant federal grant, and the intermediaries and manufacturing firms in Northeast Ohio routinely receive grants, loans, tax incentives, and strategic advice from federal agencies as disparate as the Department of Commerce, the Small Business Administration, and the Export Import Bank of the United States as well as the state of Ohio's Third Frontier Fund. In Houston, Neighborhood Centers helps families, largely immigrants, access federal resources they are entitled to (like the earned-income tax credit or the refundable child credit), runs federally backed Head Start programs for young children, and uses state resources to provide elementary education through a charter school. The market momentum behind the innovation district in Detroit is likely to accelerate, given the governor's recent appointment of an emergency financial manager for the city. The stories we have told here about Denver, Portland, and Miami are similarly based on some combination of state and federal rules, investments, and permissions.

Throughout the past century, states and the federal government—at different times, at different levels, for different purposes—have been large, shared investors in both the economic infrastructure (for example, institutions of higher learning, advanced research institutions, vast health care complexes), physical infrastructure (roads, transit, water and sewer), and social infrastructure (schools, supportive services) of cities and metropolitan areas. It is impossible to imagine the late twentieth-century rise of "cities of knowledge" in Silicon Valley or the Research Triangle or the Boston megalopolis without recognizing the foundational role played by federal investments in basic and applied science and state investments in public universities.[1] It is similarly dangerous to underestimate the positive impact that a national safety net has had on the economic evolution of cities and metropolitan areas. There has been a hidden, virtuous intersection of people-oriented and place-oriented policies. Federal and state support for the elderly and the very poor, for education, and for health care has mitigated the fiscal burden of supplementing income and providing services that cities and metropolitan areas—and their private and civic charities— must bear. At the same time, federal and state support has helped provide a strong base for both hyperlocal economies (for example, neighborhoods where poverty is concentrated) and key sectors (for example, health care) of broader economies.

At the same time, there have been some negative effects and unintended consequences of state and federal action in cities. As early as 1969, Professor Daniel Patrick Moynihan (later urban affairs adviser to President Nixon and eventually a powerful U.S. senator) explained,

> There is hardly a department or agency of the national government whose programs do not in some way have important consequences for the life of cities, and those who live in them. Frequently—one is tempted to say normally!—the political appointees and career executives concerned do not seem themselves as involved with, much less responsible for the urban consequences of their programs and policies. They are, to their minds, simply building highways, guaranteeing mortgages, advancing agriculture, or whatever. No one has made clear to them they are simultaneously redistributing employment opportunities, segregating or desegregating neighborhoods, depopulating the countryside and filling up the slums, etc: all these things as second and third consequences of nominally unrelated programs.[2]

Moynihan was describing the way that federal and state governments have organized themselves as a collection of balkanized executive agencies overseen by separate legislative committees. These agencies have looked at challenges through narrow lenses, confining the reach of solutions to the powers and resources at hand. Specialization has been complicated by random accretion. As the economist Herbert Stein writes, the federal government is largely a "machine constantly generating new programs and expansions of old ones."[3] Like hoarders, it has tended to collect rather than discard, aggregate rather than streamline and rationalize. The result has been sprawling, byzantine government, and cities and metropolitan leaders have to navigate incoherent and inconsistent programs and policies played out side by side.

The rise of the bureaucratic state has not only exacerbated balkanization but has also limited local discretion and impeded metropolitan problem solving. Federal agencies have promulgated highly prescriptive rules intended more to prevent hypothetical wrongdoing ("don't screw up") than stimulate innovation ("surprise us"). As Gerald Frug and David Barron show in their superb book *City Bound,* states are even guiltier of constraining local autonomy.[4] Despite their reputation as laboratories of democracy, states have often constricted their metros, fiscally, programmatically, and governmentally. States have used their power not only to define and limit the power and geography of cities and municipalities but also to create a dizzying, often comical array of special-purpose entities: school districts, fire districts, library districts, sewer districts, mosquito districts, public benefit corporations, industrial development authorities, transportation authorities, port authorities, workforce investment boards, redevelopment authorities, control boards, and emergency financial managers.[5] Fundamentally, cities and metropolitan areas have either been places acted on or the backdrops and locations where state and federal interventions have been made, whether for ill or good. They have been treated like one more constituency group to be ignored (or occasionally placated) rather than an integral part of economy shaping in their own right.

It is time to recognize that cities and metropolitan areas are actors, not subjects. We know how to talk about the relationship between the federal government and states—we call it federalism. We perhaps dimly remember from high school civics class that federalism is an arrangement in which the states cede some powers to the federal government but retain others, so that the different tiers of government act as dual sovereigns. But metros have been conspicuously missing from that construct. They do not have a place in the U.S. Constitution and are absent from state law, which recognizes municipalities, villages, cities, townships, and counties, but not the metropolitan areas of which they are a part. Metros are not governed by a single executive but rather are loosely knit together by overlapping networks of business, civic, philanthropic, nonprofit, and elected leaders. We need to think again about federalism and remake it in a way that accounts for the economic power, networked structure, and irreducible diversity of America's metros.

WHERE FEDERALISM HAS BEEN

Federalism has always been an evolving practice, a dynamic rather than static arrangement.[6] The U.S. Constitution created a multilayered government in which federal and state bodies shared the authority to govern as dual sovereigns with separate lines of responsibilities. Unlike the unworkable Articles of Confederation, the Constitution reordered the American polity around a more robust central government with express delegations of power. Article 1, section 8 explicitly gives Congress the power to fund its activities by collecting taxes and borrowing money, to regulate commerce with foreign nations and among the states, to declare war and raise and support armies and navies, and to choose all means "necessary and proper" to carry the expressly listed powers into effect. These express delegations leave a vast number of subjects uncovered, such as public education, commerce within the individual states, and the regulation of public welfare and safety below the level of national defense. The responsibility for those tasks is reserved to the states and citizens by the Tenth Amendment, which states that "the powers not delegated to the United States by the Constitution, nor prohibited by it to the States, are reserved to the States respectively, or to the people."

In the first century and a half of our nation's existence, the federal government was a bit player in economic growth.[7] States and ultimately their cities and private capital led the nation's expansion and literally built the country and its infrastructure during the nineteenth century. First, states and cities developed a canal system to move goods and people along the inland waterways of the northeastern and mid-Atlantic states. This system, significantly, was not a federal project; James Madison, in his last act as president in 1817, vetoed federal legislation to create a system of "internal improvements" that included an interstate road and canal system, believing that it fell outside Congress's power to regulate "interstate commerce" and to spend for the "general welfare" under article 1, section 8. State and local government bonds, which had facilitated the development of the canal system, were not sufficient to create the system of railroads that drove the nation's westward expansion, so states responded by passing laws that allowed early corporations to sell stock, raise money, and build railroads. Federal regulatory activity during this period was minimal. The economic historian John Joseph Wallis notes that the deepest regulatory and financial activities of this time, continuing until the turn of the century, were undertaken by states, followed by local governments, which pursued infrastructure and municipal development using funds raised through property taxes.[8]

The federal government enters the picture as a heavyweight in economic growth and development only in the twentieth century, as a response to the upheavals brought about by rapid industrialization and growing corporate consolidation at the turn of the century and then the collapse caused by the Great Depression.[9] In the 1930s the federal government quickly made up for its previous absence and started a dramatic shift of power to Washington that rolled on for decades: the enactment of entitlements like Social Security during the 1930s and Medicare and Medicaid during the 1960s; the authorization of real estate–shaping institutions like the Federal Housing Administration and then Fannie Mae and Freddie Mac; the deployment of massive infrastructure investments like the 1949 Housing Act's urban slum clearance program and the 1956 Highway Act's interstate highway system; and the expansion of an advanced-technology, engineering-innovating economy through Cold War–era institutions like the National Science Foundation, the National Aeronautics and Space Administration, and the Defense Advanced Research Projects Agency.

The growth of Washington bureaucracy fundamentally altered the nature of the relationship between the states and the federal government. To receive funding during the New Deal and afterward, states basically had to align with the federal government, creating mirror image agencies and administrative processes. Now these two sovereigns, rather than separate, had overlapping and conjoined responsibilities. States found themselves operating as essentially the frontline administrators for federal programs. Federal power reached its apex in the 1960s, when Senator

Everett Dirksen of Illinois warned that soon "the only people interested in state boundaries will be Rand-McNally."[10]

On August 8, 1969, President Richard Nixon gave an hour-long televised address on what came to be called the New Federalism. Nixon called for a reversal of the trend toward more centralization of power: "After a third of a century of power flowing from the people and the States to Washington it is time for a New Federalism in which power, funds, and responsibility will flow from Washington to the States and to the people."[11] (The Nixon address on federalism is a fascinating artifact of history. It is virtually impossible to imagine a president in the current era delivering an hour-long address on the topic of federalism or, for that matter, anyone watching such an address.)

The impulse to devolve was given new force with the election of President Reagan. As Alice Rivlin recounts in her insightful book *Reviving the American Dream,* "By the beginning of the 1980s, the drive for centralization had peaked, and power began shifting back to state capitals. No new concept emerged of how responsibilities should be divided. The current era has been called a period of 'competitive federalism,' meaning the federal government and the states are competing with each other for leadership in domestic policy."[12]

Thus began a period of state experimentation, supported by subsequent presidents with a bevy of executive orders, all pledging support for federalism.[13] States acted as the proving ground for policies that, if successful, were replicated at the federal level or by other states. For example, governors from both parties experimented with welfare reform in the 1980s and school reform in the 1990s, paving the way for federal advances in successive decades. States as disparate as Ohio, California, North Carolina, New Jersey, and Texas went to the ballot box to raise dedicated resources for economic development, advanced research, and higher education.[14] More recently, health care reform was law in Massachusetts years before the passage of the federal Affordable Care Act in 2010.

RETHINKING FEDERALISM

History has shown that federalism is an economic arrangement as well as a political one. The division of power affects how the economy is shaped—the kinds of investments made, the amount of money spent, and the different legal and financial tools put in place. Throughout history, there have been shifts in the level of government that promulgates the predictable rules and supplies the public goods—such as infrastructure, education, or advanced research—that the economy and individual firms need to thrive and prosper. Thus rethinking federalism is imperative given the changing realities of the economy and the fiscal storm that is brewing in both Washington and state capitals. We are on the cusp of what appears to be another historic shift in federalism, this time, however, not between the states and the federal government but between these dual sovereigns and their subjects, cities and metropolitan areas.

Some readers may object to this idea, because metros are not governments—they are aggregations, networks, and economic rather than political entities. But we are not suggesting a constitutional amendment. Instead, we are considering the division of powers from an economic standpoint, and we find the concept of federalism essential as we reimagine relationships between the federal government, states, and metros when it comes to shaping the country's economy. We are trying to advance a theory of federalism that asks how federal and state sovereigns, and other partners and networks in governance, should interact to coproduce the economy. The metropolitan revolution is, at its core, an economic revolution, and every economic era requires a division of power among governments and other actors that is aligned with and attuned to the distinctive ways things work. As Mark Muro writes,

> The rise of the large factory-based industrial economy in the 1890s, for example, brought about wide-scale municipal and state government reform, as well as the increased federal role of the Progressive Era. These reforms balanced and channeled the new scale and power of corporations with anti-trust oversight, financial-system reform and consumer protections designed to stabilize capitalism in a time of uncertainty.
>
> Likewise, the enlargement of the mass production corporate economy engendered the New Deal and Great Society paradigms that relied on the "top-down" "managerial" state and "big government" to manage society. This government configuration also proved for a time effective, and gained legitimacy by winning World War II, building the Interstate Highway System, and sending a man to the moon.[15]

We are now in a different economic epoch. The favored production system is now flexible and distributed rather than standardized and concentrated. The key factors of production are now innovation and knowledge rather than capital and labor. The modus operandi between firms and their broader ecosystem is now collaboration rather than isolation.[16] Waves of economic change have put cities and metros at the forefront of developing nimble, customized responses to the new fundamentals: knowledge exchange, networks of innovators, the rising importance of collaboration, and the centrality of local mediating institutions and platforms, including metros themselves. As Muro concludes, "Neither the mid 20th century model of 'made in Washington' nor the late 20th century model of 'get it out of Washington' appear well suited for the exigencies of the dawning Metropolitan Age."[17] Overhauling the self-referential mindset that pervades Washington and state capitals will not be easy—it's hard to convince anyone to cede power. But just as an economic crisis forced people in New York, Northeast Ohio, and Greater Denver to change, a fiscal crisis (the offshoot of the Great Recession) is likely to drive change, like it or not, throughout federal and state governments.

At the federal level, four consecutive years of deficits in excess of $1 trillion have sharpened budget consciousness. The Congressional Budget Office projected in February 2013 that by the end of 2013, total federal debt will rise to its highest level as a share of U.S. GDP since 1950.[18] And the situation will only get worse with the ballooning cost of entitlement programs—by 2023, the estimates are that net interest on the debt will join Social Security and major health care programs like Medicare and Medicaid as the largest spending categories in the federal budget.[19] Similarly, total discretionary spending is expected to grow by about $139 billion, from $1.29 trillion in fiscal year 2012 to $1.42 trillion in fiscal year 2023, while mandatory spending will increase by more than $1.6 trillion during this time, from $2.03 trillion to $3.69 trillion.[20] Given the comparatively small growth in discretionary spending levels, both defense and nondefense discretionary spending as a share of GDP will actually decline over the next decade, with nondefense discretionary spending falling to its lowest level as a share of GDP since at least the 1960s, affecting almost all programs critical to city and metropolitan economies, from housing to infrastructure to education to research and development.[21]

Unfortunately, states will step in only partially (and unevenly) where the federal government is likely to withdraw. Several years of using gimmicks and rainy-day funds to close large budget gaps resulting from the recession have left many states in a precarious fiscal position. A 2012 report by the State Budget Crisis Task Force outlines the years ahead: an expanding gap between state tax revenue and growing Medicaid costs; increasing state and local unfunded pension liabilities; and declining state revenue.[22] Federal cuts will worsen things further still, as 32 percent of state revenue, on average, has come from federal grants.[23] The same 2012 report details what this might look like: "Replacing the annual $60 billion that states would lose from, for example, a 10 percent cut in federal grants would be hard—equivalent to more than doubling the corporate income tax, cutting police and fire spending almost in half, or eliminating all spending on libraries, parks, and recreation."[24]

The writing—or rather, the equation—is on the wall. The fiscal crisis will trigger hard choices about which level of government takes primary responsibility for the financing of which public goods, alone or in conjunction with private or civic actors. This is particularly true given the country's projected population growth and demographic transformation, which will continue to put added pressures on infrastructure, education, and other services just as federal and state spending is constrained.[25] Cities and metropolitan areas—somehow, some way—will need to compensate for the mismatch between business and citizen demands and fiscal realities. So a new kind of federalism will emerge from necessity.[26]

TOWARD COLLABORATIVE FEDERALISM

The federalism that best serves the cities and metros that drive economic development in the twenty-first century is not the traditional "dual sovereignty" that splits power between federal and state governments according to subject matter[27]—but a form of collaborative federalism put in the service of cities and metros that set priorities and lead implementation.[28] This requires a re-sorting of the roles and responsibilities of government that focuses on how the constitutional sovereigns—the state and federal governments—interact with their city and metro partners across the private and public sectors to coproduce the public good.

Central governments, both federal and state, have an important role to play in the collaborative federalism that the metropolitan revolution demands. As one scholar puts it, federalism "is barely possible without a semblance of a center." We therefore identify the core things that federal and state governments should be doing to prime their metropolitan engines. Yet how federal and state governments do these things—whether they are prescriptive or flexible, output or outcome oriented—is often as important as what they do. By that token, the same scholar notes, "without independence, that is, without noncentralization, a federal system can hardly be said to exist."[29] Independence allows cities and metros the critical freedom to experiment in what Justice Louis Brandeis famously described as "laboratories for experimentation."[30]

Every metropolitan area and its leadership network could easily start hosting sessions several times a year with the people who represent that metro in the U.S. Congress and state legislature. These "metropolitan caucuses" could be a bipartisan, business-like vehicle for keeping track of metro-generated visions and initiatives and the federal and state policies and investments that could be put to work in service of same. The meetings should be roll-up-your-sleeves work sessions, providing a federalist equivalent to the problem-solving process that city and metro leaders follow on the ground level. Some federal delegations from large cities like New York do have a tradition of meeting as a caucus. We suggest that these caucus meetings be metro led and include both the state (or states) and the federal delegation so that the dual sovereigns can tackle issues together, along with their network of public and private partners at the city and metropolitan level.

Beyond this regular interaction and collaboration, what metropolitan areas need most from federal and state governments is fairly straightforward, if rarely discussed.[31] First, metropolitan leaders need federal and state governments to set a strong safety net for the nation's frail and disadvantaged citizens and a progressive tax system. That means strengthening entitlement programs like Social Security, Medicare, and Medicaid (with improvements and efficiencies) as the country grows and ages. That also means, given broader wage dynamics, making work pay by investing smartly at both the federal and state levels in the earned-income tax credit and the refundable child credit. But smartly investing in people is not enough. The tax code must be fair so that poor citizens do not bear an undue burden for financing government services, for example, through regressive state sales taxes.[32]

Second, metros need both states and the federal government to support the kind of economy they are trying to build. A panoply of business, university, and philanthropic leaders have consistently argued for the government to further invest in innovation, infrastructure, and education and skills training to enhance American competitiveness in the twentieth-century global economy. The President's Council on Jobs and Competitiveness—which is chaired by Jeff Immelt, the CEO of General Electric—has recommended that public and private R&D investment increase to the level of at least 3 percent of U.S. GDP by 2020 in order for America to maintain its position as a global leader in innovation.[33] Respected business leaders such as Felix Rohaytn have been consistent champions of a national infrastructure bank that would use public resources to leverage private sector capital for a wide range of needed investments.[34] Andrew Liveris, the CEO of Dow Chemical, has called for significant investment in STEM (science, technology, engineering, and mathematics) education and improved skills-training programs at community colleges so that workers can learn the skills necessary for high-paying advanced manufacturing jobs in the United States.[35]

Indeed, the common thread through all the stories captured in these pages is the virtuous cycle between idea generation, the commercialization of innovation, the iterative evolution of tech-driven advanced industries, the improvement of work skills to staff these productive sectors, and the export of our competitive products and services to the rest of the world. This kind of economy does not arise in a vacuum or because of the isolated actions of exceptional entrepreneurs. As our brief history of federalism shows, smart investment in the right kinds of public goods fuels the growth of advanced industry clusters and, by extension, the rest of the economy.

In many respects, the question is not what to invest in, but how. In a fiscally constrained environment, where will the resources come from? One answer is to cut to invest.[36] The federal tax code is replete with provisions that subsidize excessive consumption rather than production and wasteful rather than sustainable growth. The worst offender, the federal mortgage-interest deduction, is scheduled to grow steadily over the next five fiscal years. By the Obama administration's estimate, the single act of limiting the income tax rate at which taxpayers can deduct certain itemized deductions and exclusions like the mortgage interest deduction to 28 percent would save $580 billion for the federal government between fiscal years 2013 and 2022.[37] This would raise more than enough revenue to contribute to deficit reduction and finance every market-shaping solution mentioned above. Others have identified programs such as subsidies for farms and fossil fuels and tax deductions for dining and entertainment as targets for cuts that could free up money for productive investment.[38] Beyond shifting resources from ineffective spending to innovative investment, there is ample room to make programs less rigid and prescriptive. Just imagine if metropolitan leaders were included in conversations about deficit reduction. Treated as peers and creative leaders, they might be able to say, "We can make do with fewer dollars, if you give us some more flexibility—and rules changes come cheap."[39]

In the absence of federal leadership, some states are picking up the advanced industry baton. New York and Connecticut have recently established green banks to accelerate clean energy innovation, and Virginia, Florida, and California have invested in infrastructure banks. Connecticut, Florida, and Virginia have created research institutes focused on breakthroughs in manufacturing technology based on a successful German model.[40] North Carolina and Ohio have tied community college curriculums directly to their distinctive advanced industries. Colorado and Tennessee are explicitly promoting advanced industry clusters in the space and automotive sector, respectively. In the next half decade, it is highly likely that these state innovations will continue, with funding coming either from specific voter-approved tax increases or bond issues or from cuts in unproductive state spending.[41]

The federal government has one other critical task. To help metropolitan leaders such as those in Portland and Miami further internationalize the American economy, Congress and the president need to act on immigration reform, favorable trade agreements, and a new openness to foreign investment, including from China. America's simultaneous diversity and insularity sets us apart from every other nation on earth. Our metropolitan areas have enormous potential to participate in and benefit from the seamless exchange of goods, services, ideas, capital, and people. But Los Angeles does not set the rules on immigration, nor does Portland determine the framework for trade and investment, nor does Miami determine the antitrust laws that condition business competition. These decisions must be taken at the national or state level to create common markets and common rules, or chaos will ensue at the metropolitan scale. Metropolitan power does not absolve the federal and state governments of taking strong, clear action on enhancing America's economic position in the world. The consequence of inaction is to further constrict metropolitan globalism and stunt metropolitan performance. If U.S. metros are to be fully globally fluent, their co-sovereigns need to lay down a path for global engagement.[42]

All the things mentioned here fall outside the traditional bounds of urban policy. And that's the way it should be. The federal government does not have a "state" policy. Confining what matters to states to small offshoots and corners of the federal government would be absurd, given the multidimensional nature of modern challenges and the multilayered, intertwined nature of the engagements between the federal and state governments. But that is what the United States has done with cities and metropolitan areas. We have had a federal Department of Housing and Urban Development since 1965, even though the policies with the greatest impact on cities and metros (and housing, for that matter) are hatched somewhere else in the government. Recall the ways that the federal government (and states) engaged with the big, game-changing initiatives described in earlier chapters: policies and dollars related to immigration, research, and development, Head Start, and the National Science Foundation. Nobody would call these "urban" policies. They aren't taking up a little tiny speck of the federal budget, like community development block grants or other typical "urban" programs. Urban policy can no longer contain, if it ever did, the power of cities and metropolitan areas.

THE RISE OF A NEW ECONOMIC SOVEREIGN

Now that we've established what metros most need from the federal and state governments, let's think bigger. The nation needs metro sovereignty (or co-sovereignty), a recognition that cities and metropolitan areas exist in the real world as coequal economic sovereigns and that their health and vitality is as critical to the nation as that of federal and state governments. Being coequal sovereigns doesn't mean that each sovereign does the same thing; the republic was initially founded on the separation of responsibilities. It does mean, however, that each sovereign recognizes the value the others bring and defers where appropriate given special expertise or competence. In this construct, there is no such thing as urban or metropolitan policy. Rather, federal and state governments act as partners with their cities and metropolitan areas around common issues of national significance. In some cases, cities and metros lead and states and the federal government follow. In other cases, it is the reverse. But in either case, mutual respect and comity hold.

What would this new arrangement look like? It might look like what happened in Los Angeles, when the city's need for a modernized transportation system and an economic boost drove a significant shift in federal law. In the November 2008 election, voters in Los Angeles County passed Measure R, a ballot initiative requiring a two-thirds majority to raise county sales taxes by one-half cent for thirty years to pay for major transportation projects and improvements (similar to what voters in Denver approved to pay for FasTracks). With projected revenues of $40 billion, the referendum provided sufficient funds for a state-of-the-art rail and bus rapid transit network as well as improvements like new carpool lanes for the area's overstressed highways. These projects were fit to L.A.'s form and scale. (Although derided as the sprawl capital of the world, the Los Angeles metropolitan area is actually quite dense.)[43]

The passage of Measure R coincided with the collapse of the U.S. economy. In this crisis environment, Mayor Antonio Villaraigosa thought that the city needed to implement Measure R faster than scheduled, to get a boost from the construction jobs the massive public works project would bring. Villaraigosa and his team wanted to use the anticipated sales tax revenue from Measure R as collateral for long-term bonds and a low-interest federal loan so that construction on twelve important transportation infrastructure projects could be completed in ten years, not thirty, as was initially planned.[44] So they embarked on a new initiative, dubbed Los Angeles 30/10, to compress the building timelines for Measure R projects from three decades to one and generate 160,000 jobs in a metro where 765,000 people were unemployed. But the size and complexity of these projects made it impossible to secure enough funds from the private capital market to accelerate the work.

Next, the city pursued a low-interest loan from an innovative program within the U.S. Department of Transportation known as TIFIA (Transportation Infrastructure Finance and Innovation Act). The problem was that L.A.'s proposal—including the whole package of projects approved under Measure R—did not exactly meet TIFIA's requirements, which were crafted to finance individual investments. So in 2010 Mayor Villaraigosa and a broad-based coalition of political, environmental, union, and business leaders from Los Angeles made a push for TIFIA reforms to back a group of projects. But the proposal fell afoul of growing congressional opposition to any action resembling an earmark or favored treatment for one particular community.

Stymied by Washington rules and attitudes, Mayor Villaraigosa turned to his peers for help. If a host of metropolitan leaders asked for the kind of flexibility and reform that Los Angeles needed, the change could be promoted as better policy, not special treatment. Mayor Villaraigosa built and led a national coalition of local elected officials and business and labor leaders to secure federal support for a legislative reform they called America Fast Forward, a way for the federal government to reward regions that help themselves by providing flexible, low-cost credit assistance backed by a dedicated revenue stream, such as sales tax revenue, for any region that met the new requirements.

The cross-metro coalition succeeded. The federal transportation reauthorization bill that passed in June 2012 with bipartisan support included major changes to the TIFIA program. In October Los Angeles received a TIFIA loan under the new criteria, $545.9 million for investments in the Crenshaw-LAX Transit Corridor.

The L.A. story at once exemplifies the problems that metros face in their dealings with the federal government and the essence of the metropolitan revolution. On one hand, the city's leadership spent two years battling Washington for reforms that most people recognized were valuable and necessary—two years during which people could have been put to work building the transit system. On the other hand, L.A.'s experience shows that metro leaders can innovate in areas like infrastructure and find new ways, in essence, to deliver and finance old goods that state and federal governments used to fund. This alters the nature and scale of the resources and incentives that the federal and state governments must offer.

There are other examples in the United States of higher levels of government responding to metropolitan direction rather than the other way around. Greater Miami is America's gateway to Latin America. To capitalize on the coming expansion of the Panama Canal and the growth of Latin American and Caribbean economies, the Port of Miami needed to make more than $1 billion in improvements to increase freight capacity, including a new tunnel to increase freight flow capacity by bypassing downtown streets. Officials from the Miami-Dade county–owned port turned to the state for help in paying for this massive project. Florida leaders responded by kicking in half of the $663 million total cost, which will support a public-private partnership between the state, city and county, and a private firm, which is handling the design, building, finance, operation, and maintenance of the tunnel. Building on smart investments at the Port of Miami, Governor Rick Scott created a new agency, the Office of Freight Logistics and Passenger Operations, in 2012, to direct and align the state's strategic infrastructure investments with regional assets and strengths.[45]

Other governors are also coming to understand that, as New York governor Andrew Cuomo put it in a 2011 speech, "The state can set the stage, but there is no single New York state economy. There's a Long Island economy, a Western New York economy, a North Country economy. They're all on the same framework because they're all within the state's boundaries, so state policies affect all regions. But the growth is going to come from a regional development strategy."[46] Governor Cuomo devised a plan whereby New York's ten regions (which are, in most cases, anchored by one metropolitan area) compete for state grants to support the development of their particular regional strategies, based on their distinct advantages.[47]

In the Central New York region, anchored by the Syracuse metro, for example, leaders wanted to build on the region's strengths in industries like clean energy and biosciences, increase the global orientation and competitiveness of businesses in the region, and revitalize urban cores. State leaders and outside experts found their ideas so compelling that they awarded the region $103.7 million in 2011 and $93.8 million in 2012 to move things forward.[48] The money could come from as many as twelve state agencies, and a consolidated funding application helps local and metropolitan actors navigate myriad state programs, which had, in the past, been an impediment to receiving state support. Some of the funds have gone to urban regeneration and housing projects, but additional money will go to increase the region's innovative capacity by investing in improvements at the Syracuse University Center of Excellence R&D facilities, assisting in the expansion of manufacturing facilities, and developing a sustainability plan to lower the region's carbon footprint.

METRO DEALS

To liberate metros across the country from the strict oversight and regulations that accompany federal and state support, the United States might borrow an idea from the United Kingdom. In 2011 the British government instituted City Deals to empower cities and their metropolitan areas to drive local economic development. Cities make bids to pursue their own development plans in their own way, and the central government grants them exceptions to normal oversight and restrictions. Cities can receive control of central government funds for transportation, housing, and apprenticeships that are normally dispersed by specialized agencies for projects designed at the national level. Greater Manchester, for example, finalized a City Deal in March 2012 that included an infrastructure fund that "earned back" revenue from increases in gross value added taxes, an investment framework to align economic development funds, apprenticeship skills, low carbon, and business growth hubs, and a housing investment fund. Power over these funds is exercised by the Greater Manchester Combined Authority, joining ten local governing authorities in a corporate structure, with assistance and input from a group of business leaders called the Local Enterprise Partnership.

In the case of low carbon, for instance, the Greater Manchester Combined Authority agreed to establish a low-carbon hub that will devise a regional strategy to achieve a 48 percent reduction in carbon emissions in Greater Manchester by 2020. In return, the central government in London agreed to give the metro "consideration" in the development of national policies and initiatives, to support the region's applications for funding from the European Union, and to commit national funds from the U.K. green investment bank to a new joint green venture fund called Greater Manchester Green Developments Ltd.[49] As the City Deal outlines, the Greater Manchester Green Developments fund will have the authority and flexibility to develop an investment portfolio in areas like retrofits to public buildings and houses to help meet the overall carbon reduction target.[50] In October 2012 the Greater Manchester Combined Authority and the U.K. Department for Energy and Climate Change signed a memorandum of understanding that outlined goals and division of responsibilities between the metro and the central government for implementing the low-carbon hub and realizing the region's ambitious carbon reduction goal.[51]

In the United States, the concept would translate into Metro Deals, with the premise that metropolitan areas, because of their unique assets, goals, funding schemes, and resources, sometimes need special treatment, or special deals, from state or federal governments. Los Angeles needed an adjustment to a federal loan program. If Houston leaders sought changes to make the work of Neighborhood Centers easier, they would ask for waivers to facilitate the weaving together of funding flows for immigrants, children, and families that come from separate agencies, encrusted with separate rules and reporting requirements, but that have more impact when joined together than when pulled apart. But the fundamental premise of the Metro Deal is that metro leaders are trustworthy partners—not children or miscreants who are likely to squander federal money or make foolish choices unless they are blanketed in rules and regulations. This is where the ideas of federalism come in. Metro Deals are deals between economic co-sovereigns, not sovereigns and subjects.

The shift to Metro Deals could be particularly valuable as the federal government (and many state governments) continues to scale back existing programs and investments. By offering tangible ways that higher-level governments could cut and reform, metros could be given greater flexibility in the administration of programs like transportation, housing, and skills training, enabling them to better align these investments with distinct metropolitan realities and essentially do more with less. In dealing with the states and the federal government, in other words, metros might take a line from the 1996 film *Jerry Maguire:* "Help me, help you."

Metro Deals also accept that reinventing entire systems—mired in statutory, regulatory, and legalistic complexity and constituent politics—is tilting at windmills, a Don Quixote exercise of the first order. The perfect is the enemy of the good. Reinventing for the deal, however, sows the seeds for broader reform while getting stuff done in the interim.

A final benefit of Metro Deals is that they can help the federal and state governments begin to behave more like successful metropolitan networks. The current dynamic is that these governments talk (a lot) and talk at people. They tell them all the rules and requirements and regulations and are glacially slow in responding to new challenges or to critiques that their systems are not working. By contrast, cutting-edge metro networks take the opposite approach. They get things done because they listen to the people who are closest to the challenge or the opportunity and then they organize themselves so that they can respond effectively, flexibly, and reasonably quickly. The ability to listen and integrate responses is the hallmark of metropolitan behavior and should be of the other sovereigns as well.

A FATEFUL CHOICE

The Constitution of the United States and the principles of federalism that it enshrines seem preordained and inevitable, but they weren't. They represented a huge change from the loose affiliation under the Articles of Confederation. Some of the most powerful former colonies, such as New York, whose territory, population, and banking and industrial centers made it almost entirely self-sufficient, opposed the new constitution's change to the status quo. After all, it looked like they would be losers under the deal—what did they need a strong federal government for anyway?

But New Yorker Alexander Hamilton was convinced—as Benjamin Franklin had been before the American Revolution, and Abraham Lincoln would be during the Civil War—that a weak association of states without central authority over critical national matters would be the downfall of the new nation. Already, protectionist tariffs between the former colonies were impeding the growth of a national economy, and there was serious risk of being retaken by the imperial powers (the British marched on Washington and destroyed the White House as late as 1814).

So Hamilton, with the help of Virginian James Madison and fellow New Yorker John Jay, wrote a series of pseudonymous essays defending the need for a stronger, more centrally governed federal republic. Alexander Hamilton warned that the Articles of Confederation had produced "a crisis at which we are arrived" and asserted that his was an "era in which that decision is to be made" about good governance.[52] He urged New York to adopt the viewpoint of a "sincere and disinterested advocate for good government" and, from that perspective, to discern its deeper and lasting interests.[53] He advised New York that its patriotic obligation was to leaven its self-interest with public interest and cede some of its power to the national government by ratifying the proposed constitution. He asked New York to realistically assess how well it, and its public, would fare in a vast territory with no central military and no national currency and to turn its efforts to what it did best within its own borders.

Hamilton's broadest and most central point in the Federalist Papers was that Americans must reflect on and choose how they are governed— and not simply accept what happens by the accident of history. In 1788 he urged "the people of this country . . . to decide the important question, whether societies of men are really capable or not of establishing good government from reflection and choice, or whether they are forever destined to depend for their political constitutions on accident and force."[54] Today, we are living in another such era in which we must decide what constitutes good governance for our collective future.

The American political experiment rests on an idea of shared power among coequal sovereigns, requiring give-and-take between the national and state governments. The examples in this book and the broader dynamics unleashed in this country and across the globe have illustrated that power must shift, as it has done many times in our national past. The shift now moves away from both the states and the federal governments and toward new economic sovereigns, metropolitan areas. On a practical level, this shift is already happening, accelerated by market forces, enabled by technology, furthered by the entrepreneurial, collaborative, problem-solving spirit that permeates the nation. And this reality forces our federal and state leaders to assess how well the Union will fare if our metropolitan engines are not fully respected, supported, leveraged, and unleashed. Like New York in 1787, will federal and state leaders recognize the inevitable and align themselves with the affirmative forces of history?

9

A REVOLUTION REALIZED

What we want to bring into the world is revolution. Revolution has values. Revolution has purpose. Revolution has direction. Revolution has leaders. . . . What I encourage you to do today is to pick a movement, pick a revolution and join it.

—JACK DORSEY, COFOUNDER, *Twitter*

What would a true metropolitan revolution look like? Imagine if metros pursued their own revolutions—stepping up, setting ambitious goals, making distinctive bets, and acting with deliberation, purpose, and conviction. They could unleash their economies. They could reshape their places. They could expand opportunities. They could instill an infectious sense of confidence. They could become, in short, the best twenty-first-century version of themselves.

Imagine, for example, if every metropolis had a friendly competition over the scope and ambition of innovation districts. Metros would become test beds for addressing some of society's toughest challenges: how to create low-carbon or even no-carbon communities to grapple with climate change; how to develop products, services, and living environments that served the needs of our aging and retired populations; how to reintroduce manufacturing into the urban fabric by taking advantage of new digital technologies; how to grow in inclusive ways that created opportunities not just for highly educated workers but for the vast numbers of low-skilled urban residents who often do not realize the benefits of growth.

Imagine further if innovation in one metropolis spread quickly to others, building on the natural tendency of metro leaders to observe their peers and to learn, tailor, and adapt new solutions to their own conditions and culture. Soon we would experience a snowball effect of metropolitan transformation, collecting speed, energy, and adherents as it moves through the country (and the world), altering one metropolis after another.

Imagine still further if metros collectively used their economic power to shape markets, alter business and philanthropic practices, and catalyze new forms of innovative finance. As federal and state resources diminished, private and civic investment would increase, unlocking not only capital but expertise.

Imagine, finally, if metros aggregated their political power to bend state and federal policies and investments to their pragmatic, distinctive visions of advanced industries, global trade, transformative infrastructure, and skilled workers. States would compete not just over their tax or business climate but also over the extent to which they were fully supportive of their metropolitan engines. Metro Deals would proliferate throughout the country, substituting imaginative and productive solutions for legislative obstructionism and inaction. Representative democracy in the service of place and people rather than party or ideology would triumph.

This is the way the United States fixes its broken politics and renews its fragile economy, from the bottom up.

America circa 2013 can seem like a place defined by drift and dysfunction. The supposed adults in our constitutional system have, with some important exceptions, left the building. Yet below the surface, innovation is bubbling, common sense is pervasive, and a deep-seated commitment to place permeates American life. The metropolis is humanity's greatest collective act of invention and imagination.[1] Our cities and metropolitan areas—and the networks of individuals and institutions who lead them—are charting a new path forward and leading what is, in essence, an affirmative campaign for national renewal. Do you want a revolution with direction and purpose? A revolution with leaders? A revolution you can join wholeheartedly? You can make your metro not just great but revolutionary.

STARTING YOUR OWN REVOLUTION

If you are a mayor, the head of an economic development corporation or business association, a university president, a business executive, the head of a philanthropy or civic institution or local union, or any other kind of metropolitan leader, there are five essential steps you must take to bring the metropolitan revolution to life in your region: build your network; set your vision; find your game changer; bankroll the revolution; and sustain the gain. The metropolitan revolution is ambitious, but it is eminently doable.

These steps usually don't unfold in a linear fashion. Take New York City's Applied Sciences initiative. When the people at the New York City Economic Development Corporation first reached out to metropolitan leaders, asking the right questions of the right people, they were both building a network and setting a vision. The same was true in Northeast Ohio. You build a network, in part, by exchanging ideas about the vision; and you establish a vision, in part, by talking and listening to lots of people who may or may not end up in your network. Metropolitan innovations operate through a complicated iteration of purpose and serendipity, of intentionality and accident, of three steps forward and two steps back. Building a unique metro is an intricate, deliberate, and, at its best, exhilarating act of economy shaping and place making.

Build Your Network

Revolutions happen when a network of leaders dares to set out on a course of transformational change. The challenge for metropolitan areas is not whether they have leaders but whether those individuals work together in a concerted way to drive change.

Building a network in a modern city or metropolis, where no one person or entity is fully in charge of all the levers of change, can sound like a daunting task. Yet getting a network started does not have to be hard: Denver mayor Federico Peña demonstrated that when he crossed the county line to have steaks and beer with a county commissioner. Nor does it have to be expensive: in Northeast Ohio, metro leaders say that supplying doughnuts for group meetings is one of their best investments. Small, simple gestures matter. Sit down with your fellow metro leaders, within and outside of your sector. Tell them what you're thinking about. Solicit their ideas. Ask them whether they want to participate in a network focused on growing the economy, or integrating disparate communities, or developing cultural institutions. Ask them who else you should talk to, and what other kinds of organizations could be involved. The costs of building a network can be comically low compared with the potential return of transformative investments—as demonstrated by the success of a multibillion-dollar referendum in Denver and Los Angeles or a multibillion-dollar public-private partnership as in New York City and Detroit.

The informal power to convene is probably the least respected tool an elected official or recognized private or civic leader possesses but the most important one when addressing issues as multidimensional as the desired shape and structure of a metropolitan economy. Mayor Bloomberg understood this in responding to the Lehman Brothers collapse, when he and his administration reached out to dozens of corporate and civic leaders. So did philanthropic leaders in Northeast Ohio and Detroit as the "quiet crisis" of deindustrialization took full effect in the early years of this century. A metro, of course, does not need a crisis to build a network. Houston's Neighborhood Centers has been creating and stewarding networks throughout its 100-year history, accumulating trust and legitimacy in the process. Network building can be a useful technique in the early months of a new administration, the path chosen by Chicago mayor Rahm Emanuel in 2011, at the beginning of his term, when he deputized a group of business, civic, and community leaders to establish the city's Plan for Economic Growth and Jobs.

The health of a metro's networks is as important a gauge of metropolitan potential as traditional economic or social metrics. It is measured more by qualitative than quantitative means—"You know it when you see it," as Justice Potter Stewart famously said, in a different context, years ago.[2] We have devised a simple test to discern whether a metropolis is open or closed, collaborative or divisive: Spend fifteen minutes in conversation with elected officials or appointed leaders, such as the head of the business chamber or local philanthropy. If they talk about the networks they are organizing or participating in and talk up their fellow partners, you have entered an open, functioning metropolis. If they talk about what they themselves are doing and talk down other players in the community, you have entered a closed, competitive zone. You can predict in a quarter of an hour which metros are on a path to attract talent, crack hard problems, and make important choices. Leaders in any given metropolis know intuitively whether they pass the test we have posited. Knowing your starting point on the open-closed continuum is important to gauging how to proceed, whom to involve, and, frankly, whom to circumvent in the early stages of network building.

In the end, collaboration and network building are the most important foundations for transformative action in a city and metropolis. Everything that follows—vision, strategy, tactics, and impact—is derivative. Build and steward a strong network, and you have set a platform for generational change. Networks, in short, are the gift that keeps on giving.

Set Your Vision

All transformative innovations begin with a vision, often one bold enough to redefine the identity and image of the metropolis. Mayor Bloomberg and his team imagined New York City's economy powered by advanced technology and engineering. Sue Mosey and Dan Gilbert envisioned the core of Detroit bursting with energy and possibility. Mayor Antonio Villaraigosa saw Los Angeles as a metropolis at the vanguard of reinventing density and mobility.

Visions clarify. Visions inspire. Visions catalyze. Visions matter. Successful visions are grounded in evidence, developed through the accumulation of relevant data and information, accompanied by smart analysis, experience, and intuition. This is, in part, *Moneyball* for metros. *Moneyball*—Michael Lewis's popular book and a subsequent movie—documents the unique metrics developed by the Oakland Athletics' general manager Billy Beane and his staff to assess offensive talent in baseball. By using distinctive measures to assemble the right players, the low-revenue Oakland A's were able to successfully compete with free-spending teams like the New York Yankees and the Boston Red Sox.[3]

In other words, measure what matters. Portland's leaders did that when they took stock of their leading export-oriented clusters and firms and, by extension, their natural trading partners. Houston, through appreciative inquiry, measured the hidden assets of their low-income neighborhoods rather than the usual accumulation of deficits. Detroit revalued the market, creating potential in its anchor institutions, historic architecture, and low land values. In all cases, leaders rewarded and leveraged the distinct rather than celebrating the uniform.

Yet data are not enough. There is no super metropolitan computer that can take in information about every metropolis and mechanically spit out the right vision for each community. Once the data are gathered, leaders and stakeholders need to bring all their collective experience and intuition to bear in analyzing and assessing them. That is what leaders in Northeast Ohio did when they bet on their small and medium-size manufacturing firms, a prescient move, as firms now realize that they can make things again in the Unites States. There is no substitute for a network of leaders working the numbers and working through options, based on their metros' strengths and assets, both hidden and evident. Only then can leaders set a vision that fits the metropolitan legacy and culture. And the side benefit of operating this way? It sharpens the relationships between leaders, fosters common understanding about the true drivers of metropolitan economies, and builds a platform for long-term change.

Former president George H. W. Bush once admirably admitted that he struggled with the "vision thing," feeling more comfortable with strategies and tactics than with overarching narratives and aims. Most city and metropolitan leaders, if pushed, would probably admit that their education and experience had similarly led them to look down rather than lift up. But setting visions is a critical step in the metropolitan revolution and, like network building, a platform for everything that follows. It is also the most natural and organic act at the level of place and community, where there is a great sense of common experience and shared responsibility.

Find Your Game Changer

Settling on a vision naturally leads to the design and delivery of game-changing initiatives. Once a vision is set, specify and sharpen a conversation toward implementing it. Aim high. What intervention has the potential to alter the trajectory of an economy? What carries the promise of synergistic and multiplier effects, which enable, in the words of Henry Cisneros, the former U.S. secretary of the Department of Housing and Urban Development, "two plus two to equal five?"[4] What can generate the national and global buzz that burnishes a metro's brand as a cutting-edge community of global reach and power?

Each metropolitan innovation described in this book is a game changer, albeit in a distinctive way. Some innovations are game changers because of their topical focus: they embrace ideas and initiatives that were once largely seen as the prerogative of states or the federal government. Los Angeles and Denver are part of a growing number of metropolitan areas that are contributing higher and higher shares of the cost of building transit and innovating new financing mechanisms along the way. Portland is focused on leveraging its distinct niches in export-oriented trading sectors, an area conventionally seen as outside the purview of metropolitan economic development.

In other cases, the technique chosen—structural interventions rather than individual transactions—is what qualifies as the game changer. Consider Houston's Neighborhood Centers' effort to build an institution of scale that can operate with the efficiencies and discipline of market-tested corporations and at the scale of a metropolis and the pace of demographic transformation. Or Northeast Ohio's move to build an intricate ecosystem of strong intermediaries to serve the existing network of small and medium-size manufacturing companies. Or New York City's ingenious offer of strategic location and public improvements to attract a state-of-the-art applied sciences and engineering campus. This is a far cry from the modus operandi of conventional economic development—steal a business from an adjoining county with the allure of costly trinkets and subsidies.[5]

Whatever kind of game changer you choose, make sure that it is multidimensional, integrated, and holistic, just like your city and metropolis. As Angela Blanchard writes, "Real transformation comes from an integrated, focused approach to neighborhood transformation, not from an 'either/or' set of choices like housing or school, health or financial, infrastructure or immigration."[6] In that spirit, Northeast Ohio joins up workforce and economic development, public investment and private capital. Detroit's innovation district is the ultimate synthesis of economy shaping and placemaking activities. Bridging the divide between related but separate areas of specialization and technical expertise is as important for metropolitan areas as bridging partisan and ideological divides is for our national government and many state legislatures.

Here is a lesson some metropolitan leaders have learned the hard way: Moving a game-changing initiative often requires managing the politics of what does not get done. Game-changing initiatives always have opportunity costs (and community opposition), namely other worthy interventions that are not high priorities and must wait their turn. This is particularly true as time goes on, even if the initiative is perceived as wildly successful. Although supporters of game-changing initiatives may believe it is logical to "double down" on a successful intervention (either with more time and effort or with additional resources), others in the community may determine that it is time to look elsewhere, believing that signature initiatives have already received their fair share. Success, in short, does not obviate competition or alleviate tension. Politics is ever present.

Bankroll the Revolution

Every revolution needs to be bankrolled. Initiatives without financial resources (or clear organizational responsibility or competent management, for that matter), like visions without specific agendas, have no currency. The conventional wisdom today is that government is broke and the private and civic sectors are otherwise engaged. Neither is true.

In an era of public austerity and fiscal strain, some of the metropolitan innovations show that public funding can still be garnered for game-changing initiatives. Some initiatives, of course, are low cost but high impact. The costs of devising the Portland export plan or the Northeast Ohio manufacturing effort were, in the scheme of things, de minimis. In other cases, tough budget choices freed up the necessary resources; that was the path New York City used in its capital budget to fund the Applied Sciences initiative. For supersize investments, most cities and metropolitan areas have the option (with state approval) to go back to the voters and seek approval of targeted tax increases by public referendum. That is the path Denver and Los Angeles took with transit funding. They are not alone. In the past fifteen years, a growing number of metropolitan areas have either sought or approved ballot referendums to build, extend, or operate major public transit systems. Voters hate taxes in the abstract. But they will tax themselves if they believe the investment has merit, the delivery system is sound, and the returns are likely to be real and large.[7]

Other metropolitan innovations illustrate the rise of new forms of public-private partnerships to design, finance, deliver, and operate core elements of metropolitan infrastructure. In Detroit, the nation's poster child for fiscal distress, the Canadian government is financing a new bridge across the Detroit River, private sector investment is remaking the energy supply and distribution system in the core of the city, and private and civic investors are driving the construction of the M1 light-rail network. Pushed to the wall, metros have latent ability to innovate in areas like infrastructure and find new ways to deliver and finance old goods. Market mechanisms such as value capture, congestion pricing, or metric-driven financing (around home energy retrofits, for example) are proven ways of raising private capital for public goods. There is more than one way to skin a cat, in essence, or to finance a transit project, a bridge, a port-dredging or water modernization project, an innovation district, or a citywide energy makeover.

The initiatives highlighted in this book show the intricate interplay of public, private, and civic sector investments. Smart public sector investments create and enhance market value and catalyze and leverage private and civic investments. New York City's pledge has already enticed Cornell and Technion to commit to building a twelve-acre $2 billion campus, which, by conservative estimates, will stimulate another $23 billion in investment over the next thirty years.[8] The transit investments in Denver and Los Angeles, as elsewhere, will shape countless investment decisions by individuals and institutions, particularly around the real estate—residential, office, commercial, retail, and industrial—that is likely to be located near transit stops.

On the flip side, smart private and civic investments can drive the substantial allocation of public sector resources. A relatively small investment in the capacity of intermediary and provider institutions can ensure that much larger public funds can be joined together and made more efficient. That is the role Neighborhood Centers plays with streams of federal social funding and the role Northeast Ohio's Fund for Our Economic Future plays with federal economic development funding. In Detroit, the strategic targeting of private and civic investment to the downtown and midtown areas is already triggering additional public sector investment in the form of Federal Transit Administration grants, credit-enhanced loans from the Small Business Administration or Federal Housing Administration, and additional research grants from the National Institutes of Health and the Defense Advanced Research Projects Agency.[9]

This mixing of public, private, and civic resources—and the diversity of traditional financing vehicles and newer market mechanisms—reinforces the central themes of this book. Metropolitan areas are not governments but networks that prosper together when working together. The metropolitan revolution will come in multiple shapes and sizes, as befits an economy and society as variegated as ours. And, most important, cities and metropolitan areas have reemerged as coequal economic sovereigns, capable of acting with purpose and at scale to reshape their economic destinies.

Sustain the Gain

The full impact of transformative visions and game-changing initiatives is achieved only over time. Innovations generated in an applied sciences campus need to be commercialized and produced for mass markets.

Transit systems built in a Los Angeles or Denver metro need to be main-tained and their full potential for transit-oriented development realized. Manufacturing firms in Northeast Ohio and elsewhere grow by having constant and reliable access to advice and capital to retool their facilities and skilled workers to operate their plants. In communities like Houston there is a never-ending supply of immigrants to serve, children to teach, and communities (particularly suburban ones) to revive. In Detroit, the early signs of revival and regeneration in the downtown and midtown need to be multiplied.

The metropolitan revolution, therefore, does not operate by the same rules as traditional legislative accomplishments. The game is not over when the law is passed or the regulation promulgated. Success comes only with sustained attention, constant vigilance, and regular monitoring. This can be complicated, given the natural tendency of leaders to cycle in and cycle out. In many cities and municipalities, elected officials are term limited. There can also be constant churning in key leadership positions: heads of universities, hospitals, key employers, philanthropies, and busi-ness associations. Sustaining impact can be trying in a world where cities and metropolitan areas, like the broader corporate and consumer market, live by the next new thing. Attention deficit disorder permeates city and metropolitan economic development; leaders are deeply affected, and their decisions are often distorted by the latest "idea virus" that infects the field.

So how can you stick to your knitting in a world where leaders change and are easily distracted? It is essential to create and sustain strong, nim-ble, and entrepreneurial institutions. Some of the metropolitan innova-tions highlighted here benefited from being designed (and implemented or overseen) by venerable institutions that have maintained their edge through multiple economic, political, and philanthropic cycles, through boom and through bust. The New York City Economic Development Corporation, the lead agency behind the Applied Science initiative, has existed in one form or another since 1966 and the formation of the New York City Public Development Corporation.[10] Neighborhood Centers got its initial start in 1907 with the formation of the Houston Settlement Association.[11]

In other cases, such as Detroit and Northeast Ohio, new sets of insti-tutions have been created to inject new life into old conversations—the regeneration of the core in Detroit, the revival of the manufacturing sector in Northeast Ohio. The birth of the New Economy Initiative in Detroit and the Fund for Our Economic Future in Northeast Ohio shows that crisis can create a beneficial shake-up in the composition and focus of metropolitan institutions. Although the institutional mechanism selected was different in each community, the impetus was similar: business-as-usual giving by the philanthropic sector was no longer acceptable when the essential economic function of the city and metropolis was in question.

The key is not the age of the institution but its creativity and its persistence. A single game changer, no matter how transformative or creative, does not an economy reshape. Sustaining the gain means engaging in a continuous process of inquiry and investigation, reinvention and renewal, in which one gain leads to another, and then another, and then another. Successful metros, in other words, never stop. They do not rest on their laurels, they build on their successes.

SPREADING THE REVOLUTION

Innovations in one metropolis—a transit extension here, a manufacturing or export initiative there, an innovation district someplace else, a network of leaders throughout—do not stay bounded by geography for long. Cities and metropolitan leaders in the United States are an impatient, insatiable lot, ever hungry for new perspectives and approaches, particularly during periods (like the present one) of market disruption, political volatility, and fiscal strain. The demand among metropolitan leaders for pragmatic solutions that can be rapidly deployed could not be higher.

This is the new circuitry of innovation in the United States. One metropolis cracks the code on a tough challenge or new opportunity. The community (naturally) promotes its innovation and early success. A curious reporter or blogger or think tank distills the innovation, which then spreads to other cities and metropolitan areas that adapt and tailor it to their own circumstances and culture. This new circuitry is perfectly aligned with how innovators operate in the twenty-first century—through transparent disclosure of information and nimble market adoption rather than laborious legislation or rule-making processes—and with how they learn—by observing breakthroughs of peer companies or institutions or cities in similar situations. The metropolitan world is one of action and application rather than legislation and regulation.

It is often said that imitation is the highest form of flattery. In the same vein, replication is the quickest path to a metropolitan revolution.

This is a revolution of speed and agility, and there is every reason to believe that the pace of the revolution will accelerate in the coming decade. The simplest reason: crisis begets innovation. The popular saying "Insanity is doing the same thing over and over again and expecting different results" applies to metros. A decade of jobs deficits and opportunity gaps, of global rise and domestic drift, has prompted a radical shift in thought and action. Cities and metros cannot declare a recession over and retreat to the comfort of their legislative chambers and executive agencies when the reality on the street sends a different, disturbing signal. Ten years ago, few metropolitan areas were self-financing large infrastructure systems. Five years ago, no metropolis in the United States had a comprehensive approach to climate change or the clean economy. Three years ago, no city in the United States had a deliberate export or trade strategy. A year ago, *innovation district* was not even in the professional lexicon of city builders and economy shapers.

Spreading the revolution has been propelled by the rise of new media. The identification and dissemination of metropolitan innovation are at an unprecedented level. At a time when traditional regional media are stressed and stretched, the cadre of metropolitan rapporteurs is growing in number and sophistication. Specialty metropolitan media venues like *The Atlantic Cities, Next City,* and *Planetizen* and blogs like the *Urbanophile* command growing numbers of followers, and Twitter has become the town square by which they communicate. The segmentation of the media has actually helped fuel metropolitan innovation by giving millions of people interested in, intrigued by, obsessed with city and metropolitan areas a streamlined way to obtain information about the latest metropolitan product, service, research, or idea.

Technology obviously enables the rapid diffusion of information and the concomitant rise in game-changing initiatives. The Internet and the emergence of sophisticated purveyors and users have radically shortened the cycle of metropolitan invention, implementation, observation, distillation, and replication from years to months. Cities and metropolitan areas now fish for innovations in a larger global pond. German metros like Munich and Stuttgart offer relevant lessons on how to build and maintain centers of advanced manufacturing and production by integrated interventions on applied research, the commercialization and coproduction of innovation, and upgrading workforce skills.[12] Scandinavian metros like Copenhagen are becoming magnets for companies that are innovating on sustainable goods and services by embracing the environmental imperative of low carbon growth.[13] Asian cities like Songdo and Singapore are experimenting with the application of smart technologies to manage congestion and lower energy use.[14] Latin American cities like Bogotá and Curitiba have perfected the use of low-cost and flexible bus rapid transit.[15] And metros across the globe like Singapore (again), Stockholm, and London have designed and implemented congestion pricing that not only reduces congestion and carbon emissions but also raises revenue for expansive transit systems.[16]

The means for spreading the revolution are getting simpler, sharper, and more powerful. Traditional metropolitan constituencies like the United States Conference of Mayors and the National Association of Counties, originally formed in the 1930s to focus on Washington decision-makers, now see their role as informing their membership of the newest innovation, the most promising breakthrough. The rise of Internet learning in higher education could become, within the decade, the prime vehicle by which networks of metropolitan leaders have access to the sharpest information about metropolitan practice and policies, domestically and globally.[17] There is absolutely no reason why every metropolitan leader in the United States—public, private, civic—could not go back to school and learn the mechanics and techniques by which revolutions can be initiated and forged. The growing market for metropolitan knowledge could be delivered by new institutions—private, civic, university, and think tank–based—or by traditional institutions that revise their modus operandi to do the same.

Advances in innovative finance will similarly expand the geographic reach of the revolution. Creating standardized assumptions and metrics has always been the key to unlocking immeasurable levels of private and civic capital. Think about the impact rating systems have had on the evolution of the municipal finance system, or how cities routinely raise private capital for local infrastructure by estimating the anticipated tax revenues from development, a mechanism called tax increment financing. As the metropolitan revolution unfolds, we can expect this process to accelerate either as leaders across cities and metropolitan areas jointly agree to common investment protocols (around the retrofit of water infrastructure, for example) or as private innovators do what private innovators routinely do: figure out how to recognize and unlock market value and proceed accordingly. The scale of private and civic engagement will range from major transformative investments in transit systems, bridges, innovation districts, or energy networks to smaller, crowd-funded investments to create new parks or retrofit a prized cultural facility or neighborhood library or fund residents' efforts to revitalize dilapidated city blocks or neighborhoods.

Technological innovation will fuel both the creation and stewarding of leadership networks. It will also affect the form and function of metropolitan areas. Groups like Techonomy and Code for America are already breaking down walls between urbanists and technologists.[18] With the explosion of social media, the way in which leadership networks communicate within and without—with one another and with the broader citizenry—will evolve and iterate at rapid speed. With demographic and business preferences for home, office, and facility location shifting, the physical form of cities and metropolitan areas will evolve, perhaps as a new pattern of multiuse, multilayered, highly connected innovation districts, a far cry from the spatially isolated and car-dependent technology parks and university campuses of decades past. And with deployment rather than invention the core issue, we now face the tantalizing prospect of cities and metropolitan areas employing technology to address a wide range of issues, from managing urban congestion to maximizing energy efficiency to enhancing public security to allocating scarce resources based on real-time evidence to providing education through remote learning and health care through remote diagnostic and prescription.[19]

The upshot is this: the metropolitan revolution—already robust—is going to spread at a speed and scale unprecedented in American history.

SCALING THE REVOLUTION

The promise of the metropolitan revolution, of course, is not just to catalyze problem solving across metropolitan areas or even to unlock market innovations, as critical as those advances are. It is to repair what ails the United States, a political system mired in ruinous partisanship and ideological division. It is a short, logical step from collaborating locally on affirmative, pragmatic solutions to advocating at the state and federal level for systemic and structural policy reforms. Collaborative action on the ground leads naturally to collective advocacy at the federal and state levels.

The core of metropolitan power lies in simple math. In forty-seven of the fifty states, the majority of the state's economy is generated by its metropolitan areas. That includes such "rural" states as Arkansas, Iowa, Kansas, and Nebraska.[20] In twenty-four of the fifty states, more than 75 percent of the population lives in metros, and more than 80 percent of the gross domestic product is generated by metropolitan areas.[21] Metropolitan power today is less than the sum of its parts, owing to the failure to organize the disparate parts in a concerted way as much as anything else. The path to metropolitan power, therefore, is partly a question of political organizing. Metros individually or collectively organized around a common purpose—innovative investment in infrastructure, perhaps, or a special ballot referendum on advanced research—are a difficult lobby to ignore. This is particularly true in states where political, business, university, labor, and civic networks intersect at the state and metropolitan scale.

This is not just the power of raw numbers coming to bear on state and federal legislatures. The notion of a metropolitan caucus naturally exploits the power of representative democracy. As the Los Angeles example illustrates, the act of serving the interests of one's district or state, bringing home the bacon, in colloquial terms, is a powerful impulse. In prior decades, that impulse was achieved through the earmark system, now much derided. With earmarks banned, innovative financing mechanisms like the Los Angeles 30/10 initiative may become the new way in which members of Congress can deliver for their states and districts in the service not of abstract national goals or ideological principles but real, tangible, economy-shaping projects. The Metro Deals suggested in chapter 8 would tap this vein of representation. For most members of state or federal legislatures, particularly those who would like to stay in office, parochialism trumps partisanship and ideology.

The bottom line is this: Federal and state legislators, executives, cabinet heads, and other leaders who want to stay relevant have to figure out how to align themselves with metropolitan leaders and get on board with the revolution. This goes far beyond the typical federal or state nonsolution solution of a new task force on cities and regions or a new intergovernmental commission. The revolution will not be contained in a committee meeting.

The focus of the metropolitan revolution is on getting stuff done. This reflects quintessential, deeply held American values of pragmatism and problem solving, entrepreneurialism and innovation. In the end, most members of Congress or state legislatures are elected to do things rather than keep things from getting done; this is particularly true during a period of economic insecurity and uncertainty. In the end, legislators run for reelection based not on what they stopped but on what they achieved. State and federal legislators who fail to act in the service of their district's or state's pragmatic efforts will not be state and federal legislators for long. Pragmatism practiced in enough places over a sustained period of time is infectious and is as likely to alter the political culture as any technical fix to campaign finance or internal rules of the legislature or legislative process.

THE AMERICAN (METROPOLITAN) REVOLUTION

Let us end by returning to the beginning—of the federal republic, that is. The origins of the American Revolution can be seen in the cities of the time, even though cities were relatively small compared with the population as a whole.[22] The American Revolution, for all intents and purposes, was an urban revolution.

Cities were the epicenter of the succession of crises that rocked the colonies in the 1760s and 1770s. The contraction of credit by London banks after the French and Indian War largely affected merchants in the major cities, Boston in particular.[23] The recession of 1763 was followed by a series of acts by the English Parliament that also primarily hit urban populations by prohibiting them from doing business with other European powers and their colonies (such as the French Indies), restricting the use of paper currency, and imposing taxes on newspapers, diplomas, and other printed documents (the infamous Stamp Act).[24] Urban newspapers negatively affected by taxation encouraged protests in cities across the colonies, organized by networks of leaders of the social networks of the period, the local fire brigades. Benjamin Franklin founded Philadelphia's first fire brigade; John Adams once wrote that he would be lucky to "get admitted to a good one."[25] Many of these fire brigades ultimately became chapters of the Sons of Liberty (the prime mover behind the boycott of English goods) and then became brigades of the Continental Army when war broke out. With each successive crisis, the Townsend Act of 1767, the Boston Massacre of 1770, the Tea Act of 1773, networks of leaders within and across cities began to grow and gain traction. As one scholar writes, "Through waterfront networks and shared ritual practices, urban waterfront dwellers throughout North America were achieving a unity of grievances, values and identity."[26] America's burgeoning cities and their networks of leaders helped solidify the case against the British monarchy and lead the way toward war.

Today's metropolitan revolutionaries, of course, are not aiming to tear down an old regime or displace a tired clique of rulers. They are, in practical American fashion, trying to build something positive that has lasting value for places and people. Yet that should not diminish the import or the reach of what is happening. The metropolitan revolution has emerged in a period of deep economic crisis and political dissatisfaction that has sparked a fundamental reassessment of roles and responsibilities in our twenty-first-century system. It is being led by networks of individuals who share a deep commitment to their communities and a sense of common purpose and vision. It is amplified by regular exposure to innovations in sister metros by means never dreamed of 250 years ago. And it is a revolution with deep and profound consequences for the shape and structure of our society and our governmental institutions.

Power, in short, is shifting again in our country. We are, in the end, not a nation beholden to the 537 elected officials in the federal government, no matter how high the office. Nor are we a nation in thrall to almost 8,000 elected officials in state governments.[27] Rather, we are a powerful, growing nation of 315 million people, with tens of thousands, if not hundreds of thousands, of individuals playing active, participatory leadership roles in their communities and metropolitan areas.

America is a metropolitan nation. In this century, starting in this decade, we will finally and fully start acting like one.

NOTES

This book rests on a foundation of research and interviews with the people who are driving the Metropolitan Revolution in their communities. Unless otherwise indicated, the people quoted in this book were interviewed by Bruce Katz and Jennifer Bradley at the times and places indicated below. We are grateful for their willingness to share their stories with us.

David Abbott, conducted by Jennifer Bradley, August 6, 2012, Cleveland.

Adonias Arevalo, conducted by Jennifer Bradley, January 15, 2013, via telephone.

Rebecca Bagley, conducted by Jennifer Bradley, August 9, 2012, Washington, D.C.

Angela Blanchard, conducted by Jennifer Bradley, August 20, 2012, Houston. Follow-up interview with Blanchard conducted by Jennifer Bradley, January 17, 2013, via telephone.

Tom Clark, conducted by Jennifer Bradley, March 14, 2012, via telephone.

Mayor Michael Hancock, conducted by Jennifer Bradley, March 13, 2013, via telephone.

Governor John Hickenlooper, conducted by Jennifer Bradley, December 19, 2012, Denver.

Bob Jaquay, conducted by Jennifer Bradley, October 29, 2012, via telephone.

Peter Kenney, conducted by Jennifer Bradley, December 12, 2012, via telephone.

Steve Koonin, conducted by Jennifer Bradley, December 12, 2012, via telephone.

Roberta Leal, conducted by Jennifer Bradley, January 17, 2013, via telephone.

Neighborhood Centers staff members, conducted by Jennifer Bradley, August 20, 2012, Houston.

Cathy Noon, conducted by Jennifer Bradley, December 17, 2012, via telephone.

Secretary Federico Peña, conducted by Jennifer Bradley, January 9, 2013, via telephone.

Randy Pye, conducted by Jennifer Bradley, February 10, 2012, via telephone.

Kevin Ryan, conducted by Jennifer Bradley, December 13, 2012, via telephone.

Baiju Shah, conducted by Jennifer Bradley, November 2, 2012, via telephone.

Deputy Mayor Robert Steel, NYCEDC Director Seth Pinsky, and NYCEDC staff members, conducted by Bruce Katz and Jennifer Bradley, June 12, 2012, New York City. Follow-up interview with Steel and Pinsky conducted by Bruce Katz and Jennifer Bradley, June 15, 2012, via telephone.

Chris Thompson, conducted by Jennifer Bradley, October 26, 2012, via telephone.

Bill Van Meter and Mike Turner, conducted by Jennifer Bradley, February 21, 2013, via telephone.

Charles Vest, conducted by Jennifer Bradley, December 12, 2012, via telephone.

Brad Whitehead, conducted by Jennifer Bradley, August 6, 2012, Cleveland.

Kathryn Wylde, conducted by Jennifer Bradley, September 28, 2012, via telephone.

CHAPTER 1

The Rahm Emanuel quote appears in John Schwartz, "$7 Billion Public-Private Plan in Chicago Aims to Fix Transit, Schools, and Parks," *New York Times*, March 29, 2012.

1. Michael Bloomberg, "State of the Economy Four Years after Onset of the Financial Crisis," speech delivered to the Economic Club of Washington, D.C., September 12, 2012 (www.mikebloomberg.com/index.cfm?objectid=bba256ed-c29c-7ca2-f3d73c891fc64d80).

2. John Hofmeister, remarks at the symposium Tipping the Scale: Houston and the Next Economy, sponsored by Neighborhood Centers, Inc., and the Brookings Institution, May 16, 2012, Rice University.

3. Estimation by Brookings of top metropolitan areas based on information provided by metros on their long-term planning.

4. "Dolly Parton Quotes," GoodReads, 2013 (www.goodreads.com/author/quotes/144067.Dolly_Parton).

CHAPTER 2

The quotation at the beginning of this chapter is from Paul M. Romer, "Implementing a National Technology Strategy with Self-Organizing Industry Investment Boards," *BPEA*, no. 2 (1993), p. 345.

1. International Monetary Fund, "World Economic Outlook: Rebalancing Growth," April 2010 (www.imf.org/external/pubs/ft/weo/2010/01/pdf/text.pdf), p. xiv. See also Brian Knowlton, "Global Economy Called Worst since 1945," *New York Times*, April 22, 2009. Advanced economies were particularly hard hit, experiencing a decline in output by more than 3 percent in 2009, with the Euro-Zone countries of Germany, France, Italy, and Spain experiencing a combined 4.1 percent drop in output during the year. In the United States, the labor market was

particularly hard hit as a result of the crisis. International Monetary Fund, "World Economic Outlook: Rebalancing Growth," p. 45.

2. Fiscal Policy Institute, "The State of Working New York City: 2011," July 20, 2011 (www.fiscalpolicy.org/FPI_NewYorkCityUnemployment_20110720.pdf), p. 4.

3. New York City, Department of Housing Preservation and Development, "Mayor Bloomberg Announces 18 Initiatives to Help New Yorkers Face Current Economic Challenges," press release, 2008 (www.nyc.gov/html/hpd/html/pr2008/pr-10-31-08.shtml).

4. New York City, Office of the Mayor, "Mayor Bloomberg Outlines 11 Initiatives to Support New York City's Financial Services Sector and Encourage Entrepreneurship," press release, February 18, 2009 (www.nyc.gov/html/om/html/2009a/pr082-09.html).

5. See, for example, Jonathan Bowles and Joel Kotkin, "Engine Failure," Center for an Urban Future, 2003 (www.nycfuture.org/content/articles/article_view.cfm?article_id=1085&article_type=0). The Lehman collapse provided a powerful sense of urgency and accelerated and focused city leaders' efforts.

6. Jeffery Immelt, "An American Renewal," remarks to the Detroit Economic Club, June 26, 2009 (www.econclub.org/Multimedia/Transcripts/An%20American%20Renewal%206-26%20final.pdf), p. 10.

7. Lawrence H. Summers, "Rescuing and Rebuilding the U.S. Economy: A Progress Report," remarks to the Peterson Institute, July 17, 2009 (www.whitehouse.gov/the_press_office/Excerpts-from-Remarks-by-Lawrence-H-Summers-to-the-Peterson-Institute/).

8. Robert Atkinson and Howard Wial, "Boosting Productivity, Innovation, and Growth through a National Innovation Foundation" (Brookings, 2008), p. 6.

9. William J. Baumol, Melissa A. Schilling, and Edward N. Wolff, "The Superstar Inventors and Entrepreneurs: How Were They Educated?" *Journal of Economic and Management Strategy* 18 (Fall 2009), p. 725.

10. Jim O'Grady and Jonathan Bowles, "Building New York City's Innovation Economy" (New York: Center for an Urban Future, 2009), p. 4. See also Baumol, Schilling, and Wolff, "The Superstar Inventors and Entrepreneurs," p. 9.

11. Ibid.

12. Ibid., p. 16.

13. Jim O'Grady and Jonathan Bowles, "2009 Index of the New York City Innovation Economy," Center for an Urban Future, 2009 (www.nycfuture.org/images_pdfs/pdfs/InnovationIndex.pdf), p. 33.

14. "Engineering a Tech Sector," Center for an Urban Future, 2007 (www.nycfuture.org/images_pdfs/pdfs/Engineering_A_Tech_Sector.pdf).

15. Edward B. Roberts and Charles Eesley, "Entrepreneurial Impact: The Role of MIT" (Cambridge, Mass.: MIT Sloan School of Management and the Kauffman Foundation, 2009), p. 5.

16. Edward L. Glaeser, *The Triumph of the City: How Our Greatest Invention Makes Us Richer, Smarter, Greener, Healthier, Happier* (New York: Penguin Press, 2011), p. 36.

17. Mark Muro and Bruce Katz, "The New 'Cluster Moment': How Regional Innovation Clusters Can Foster the Next Economy" (Brookings, 2010), p. 10.

18. Rui Baptista and Peter Swann, "Do Firms in Clusters Innovate More?" *Research Policy* 27 (September 1998), p. 538. See also Barak S. Aharonson, Joel A.

C. Baum, and Maryann P. Feldman, "Industrial Clustering and the Returns to Inventive Activity: Canadian Biotechnology Firms, 1991–2000," Working Paper 04-03 (Toronto, Ont.: Rotman School of Management, University of Toronto, 2004), p. 1.

19. Muro and Katz, "The New 'Cluster Moment,'" p. 5.

20. Enrico Moretti, *The New Geography of Jobs* (Boston, Mass.: Houghton Mifflin Harcourt, 2012), p. 197. See also Margaret Pugh O'Mara, *Cities of Knowledge: Cold War Science and the Search for the Next Silicon Valley* (Princeton University Press, 2005).

21. See Muro and Katz, "The New 'Cluster Moment,'" pp. 25–30. See also Mercedes Delgado, Michael E. Porter, and Scott Stern, "Clusters, Convergence, and Economic Performance," Working Paper 18250 (Cambridge, Mass.: National Bureau of Economic Research, July 2012), p. 32.

22. Jonathan Rothwell and others, "Patenting Prosperity: Invention and Economic Performance in the United States and Its Metropolitan Areas" (Brookings, 2013), p. 12.

23. Joshua L. Rosenbloom, "The Geography of Innovation Commercialization in the United States during the 1990s," *Economic Development Quarterly* 21 no. 3 (2007), p. 4.

24. Peter Applebome, "Despite Long Slide by Kodak, Company Town Avoids Decay," *New York Times*, January 17, 2012.

25. New York City, Office of the Mayor, "Mayor Bloomberg Announces City Received 18 Submissions from 27 Academic Institutions for New Applied Sciences Campus," press release, March 17, 2011.

26. Patrick McGeehan, "By Deadline, 7 Bids in Science School Contest," *New York Times*, October 31, 2011.

27. Daniel Massey, "The Race Is On," *Crain's New York Business*, August 1–7, 2011.

28. New York City Economic Development Corporation, "Applied Sciences Facility in New York City: Request for Expression of Interest," internal document, December 16, 2010.

29. New York City Economic Development Corporation, "Growing Applied Sciences: A Game Changer for NYC," internal presentation, February 9, 2011.

30. New York City, Office of the Mayor, "Mayor Bloomberg Delivers Keynote Speech on the City's Initiative to Persuade a Top-Tier University to Build or Expand an Engineering and Applied Sciences Campus in New York City," press release, July 19, 2011.

31. Quoted in John Farley, "A *MetroFocus* Special: Tech Campus NYC," WNET Public Media, December 22, 2011, video (www.thirteen.org/metrofocus/news/2011/12/a-metrofocus-special-tech-campus-nyc/).

32. Nancy Scola, "Tech and the City," *Next City*, September 3, 2012 (http://nextcity.org/forefront/view/Tech-and-the-city).

33. Anjali Athavaley, "Cornell Gets U.S. Hand," *Wall Street Journal*, October 2, 2012.

34. Joseph Walker, "Google Gives Cornell $10 Million in Free Office Space," *Digits* (blog), *Wall Street Journal*, May 21, 2012 (http://blogs.wsj.com/digits/2012/05/21/google-gives-cornell-10-million-in-free-office-space/).

35. New York City, Office of the Mayor, "Mayor Bloomberg, New York University President Sexton, and MTA Chairman Lhota Announce Historic Partnership to

Create New Applied Sciences Center in Downtown Brooklyn," press release, April 23, 2012.

36. Center for Urban Science Progress, "Educational Programs," New York University, 2012 (http://cusp.nyu.edu/ms-in-applied-urban-science-and-informatics/).

37. New York City Economic Development Corporation, "Mayor Bloomberg and Columbia President Bollinger Announce Agreement to Create New Institute for Data Sciences and Engineering," press release, July 30, 2012.

38. These include state renewable portfolio standards as well as national carbon-reduction strategies, such as those promulgated by the U.K. Department of Energy and Climate Change. See Barry Rabe, "Race to the Top: The Expanding Role of U.S. State Renewable Portfolio Standards," *Sustainable Development Law and Policy* 7 no. 3 (2007). See also "The U.K. Low Carbon Transition Plan: National Strategy for Climate and Energy," July 15, 2009 (www.official-documents.gov.uk/document/other/9780 108508394/9780108508394.asp); and Angel Gurría and James P. Leape, "Climate Change: The Biggest Threat to Economic Recovery," *OECD Observer* (www.oecd observer.org/news/fullstory.php/aid/3074/Climate_change:_the_biggest_threat_to_economic_recovery.html).

39. One statement of the reach of this change can be found in the definition of the new energy economy in "Platform for Creating and Retaining Midwestern Jobs in the New Energy Economy," prepared by the Midwestern Governors Association: "A new energy economy generates jobs, businesses and investments while expanding energy production; increasing energy efficiency; reducing carbon emissions, waste and pollution; and conserving natural resources." Midwestern Governors Association, "Platform for Creating and Retaining Midwestern Jobs in the New Energy Economy," 2009 (www.midwesterngovernors.org/Publications/JobsPlatform.pdf). See also Jeremy Rifkin, "Leading the Way to the Third Industrial Revolution and a New Distributed Social Vision for the World in the 21st Century," Foundation on Economic Trends (www.foet.org/packet/Global.pdf); U.K. Department of Transport, "Low Carbon Transport: A Greener Future," July 2009 (www.dft.gov.uk/pgr/sustainable/carbonreduction/).

40. Glaeser, *The Triumph of the City*, p. 222.

41. See Mark Muro, Jonathan Rothwell, and Devashree Saha, "Sizing the Clean Economy: A National and Regional Green Jobs Assessment" (Brookings, 2011), p. 11. See also "Global Cleantech 100," *The Guardian,* 2010 (www.guardian.co.uk/globalcleantech100/cleantech-100-2010-list?CMP=twt_gu); Jonathan Rothwell and Mark Muro, "Where the Cleantech Companies Are," *New Republic: The Avenue*, February 23, 2011; Jonathan Rothwell and Mark Muro, "Top of the Class: The Role of Leading Academic Programs in Cleantech Innovation," *New Republic: The Avenue*, February 24, 2011.

42. Ibid.

43. Applied Sciences NYC, "Investing in Innovation for a Stronger Economy," September 13, 2011 (http://nycedc.tumblr.com/post/10165992406/check-out-our-infographic-that-illustrates-how). See also New York City, Office of the Mayor, "Mayor Bloomberg Delivers Keynote Speech," press release, July 19, 2011.

44. Population Reference Bureau, "World Population Highlights 2007: Urbanization," 2007 (www.prb.org/Articles/2007/623Urbanization.aspx). See also World Health Organization, "Urban Population Growth," 2013 (www.who.int/gho/urban_health/situation_trends/urban_population_growth_text/en/).

45. McKinsey Global Institute, "Urban World: Cities and the Rise of the Consuming Class" (McKinsey & Company, 2012), p. 1.

46. International Trade Administration, "Exporting Is Good for Your Bottom Line" (www.trade.gov/cs/factsheet.asp).

47. For an explanation of base-multiplier analysis, see Masahisa Fujita, Paul Krugman, and Anthony J. Venabel, *The Spatial Economy: Cities, Regions, and International Trade* (MIT Press, 1999), pp. 27–33. The authors argue that this model is incomplete, but mostly because it fails to account for agglomerations, which is the thrust of their argument in this volume.

48. Emilia Istrate and Nicholas Marchio, "Export Nation 2012: How U.S. Metropolitan Areas Are Driving National Growth" (Brookings, 2012), p. 7. Unless otherwise noted, all the export information presented is from this source.

49. Moretti, *The New Geography of Jobs*, p. 60.

50. Ibid., p. 59.

51. Jane Jacobs, *The Economy of Cities* (New York: Random House, 1969), p. 48.

52. See, for example, ibid., p. 163.

53. Emilia Istrate and Nicholas Marchio, "Export Nation 2012: Metropolitan and State Profiles," Brookings, 2012 (www.brookings.edu/research/reports/2012/03/08-exports/profiles).

54. Paul Barter, "Parking Policy in Asian Cities" (Mandaluyong City, Philippines: Asian Development Bank, 2009), p. 1. Barter observed parking needs at various cities and found that richer cities (Hong Kong, Seoul, Singapore, Taipei City, and Tokyo) had lower parking needs than middle-income cities (Bangkok, Jakarta, Kuala Lumpur, and Manila). Ibid., p. 14.

55. Deborah Gordon and Daniel Sperling, "Surviving Two Billion Cars: China Must Lead the Way," *Yale Environment* 360 (March 5, 2009). See also Niharika Mandhana, "'Untamed Motorization' Wraps an Indian City in Smog," *New York Times*, December 26, 2012.

56. "No Parking," *The Economist*, March 24, 2012.

57. See Christopher H. Wheeler, "Cities and the Growth of Wages among Young Workers: Evidence from the NLSY," Working Paper 2005-055A (St. Louis, Mo.: Federal Reserve Bank, 2005). Edward Glaeser and David Maré discovered that workers in large metro areas eventually accrued a 33 percent wage premium, which stayed with them even after they left the metro, indicating that being in the metro mix with other skilled people makes individuals more productive. Edward L. Glaeser and David C. Maré, "Cities and Skills," *Journal of Labor Economics* 19 no. 2 (2001).

58. See Steven Johnson, *Where Good Ideas Come From: The Natural History of Innovation* (New York: Penguin Group, 2010), pp. 9–10.

59. "Our evidence thus reinforces the view that policy action should focus on building upon pre-existing comparative advantage." Delgado, Porter, and Stern, "Clusters, Convergence, and Economic Performance," p. 6.

60. Richard Pérez-Peña, "Two Top Suitors Are Emerging for New Graduate School of Engineering," *New York Times*, October 16, 2011.

61. Moretti, *The New Geography of Jobs*, pp. 196–97.

62. O'Grady and Bowles, "Building New York City's Innovation Economy," pp. 6–7.

63. Ibid., p. 6.

64. Ibid., p. 31. See also Jonathan Bowles and David Giles, "New Tech City" (New York: Center for Urban Future, May 2012), p. 6; NYTechMeetup, "History" (http://nytm.org/about/history).

65. Bowles and Giles, "New Tech City," pp. 6–7.

66. Johnson, *Where Good Ideas Come From*, p. 58.

67. "One trouble with brainstorming is that it is finite in both time and space: a group gathers for an hour in a room, or for a daylong corporate retreat, they toss out a bunch of crazy ideas, and then the meeting disperses. Sometimes a useful connection emerges, but too often the relevant hunches aren't in sync with one another. One employee has a promising hunch in one office, and two months later, another employee comes up with the missing piece that turns that hunch into a genuine insight. Brainstorming might bring those two fragments together, but the odds are against it." Ibid., p. 126.

68. Seth Pinsky, remark at the forum Tech and the City, sponsored by *NextCity* (formerly *Next American City*) and the Van Alen Institute, Monday, September 10, 2012 (http://vimeo.com/49483079).

69. Johnson, *Where Good Ideas Come From*, p. 28.

70. Thomas Bender, *The Unfinished City: New York and the Metropolitan Idea* (New York University Press, 2007), p. 83.

71. Paul Israel, *Edison: A Life of Invention* (New York: John Wiley and Sons, 2000), p. 50. See also Thomas Edison Center at Menlo Park, "Thomas Edison and Menlo Park," 2009 (www.menloparkmuseum.org/thomas-edison-and-menlo-park).

72. Bender, *The Unfinished City*, p. 83.

73. See Edison Center at Menlo Park, "Thomas Edison and Menlo Park." See also Bender, *The Unfinished City*, p. 87.

CHAPTER 3

1. Arthur M. Schlesinger, "The City in American History," *Mississippi Valley Historical Review* 27 (June 1940), p. 64.

2. Ibid., pp. 43–66.

3. According to Bill Van Meter, the assistant general manager of planning for the Regional Transportation District, and Mike Turner, the district's manager of planning and coordination, the expansion of the metro's light-rail and rapid bus system, known as FasTracks, is the largest in the country in terms of miles of rapid transit capacity.

4. Alan Berube and Carey Anne Nadeau, "Metropolitan Areas and the Next Economy: A 50-State Analysis," Brookings, 2011 (www.brookings.edu/~/media/research/files/papers/2011/2/24%20states%20berube%20nadeau/02_states_berube_nadeau.pdf).

5. Campbell Gibson and Kay Jung, "Historical Census Statistics on Population Totals by Race, 1790 to 1990, and by Hispanic Origin, 1970 to 1990, for Large Cities and Other Urban Places in the United States," Working Paper 76 (U.S. Census Bureau, 2005).

6. *Keyes* v. *School District No. 1 Denver Colorado*, 521 F.2d 465 (10th Cir. 1975) (http://openjurist.org/521/f2d/465/keyes-v-school-district-no-denver-colorado-citizens-association-for-neighborhood-schools).

7. Franklin J. James and Christopher B. Gerboth, "A Camp Divided: Annexation Battles, the Poundstone Amendment, and Their Impact on Metropolitan

Denver, 1941–1988," in *Colorado History* (Denver, Colo.: Colorado Historical Society, 2001), p. 149.

8. Ibid., pp. 149–50.

9. Ibid., p. 141.

10. Ibid., p. 137.

11. Ibid., pp. 131, 151, 154, 150.

12. According to James and Gerboth, the independent Denver Water Board at times facilitated and at times hindered the city of Denver's annexation plans. It also sometimes encouraged and sometimes frustrated the growth of surrounding communities. In the 1950s, for example, the water board established a de facto "blue line" beyond which it would not provide service, effectively choking off growth in those areas unless they agreed to annexation. In the 1960s the board liberalized its policies, and this encouraged suburban growth and decreased pressure to become part of the city of Denver (whose water supply was guaranteed by the board). But "despite its inconstant and unreliable support of Denver's annexation policies, the [Denver Water Board] was a powerful force in alienating suburban leadership and in starting the annexation battles which ultimately severely constrained Denver's annexation powers. Its policies, often viewed as 'high-handed' and unfair, contributed to the eventual wars over Denver annexation. High Denver water rates for suburban residents were a consistent source of friction between Denver and its suburbs. Moreover, the [water board's] policy of favoring city residents over suburban users exacerbated city-suburban tensions." James and Gerboth, "A Camp Divided," pp. 144–45.

13. Ibid., p. 158.

14. See Colorado Legislative Council, "History of Election Results for Ballot Issues: 1974," 2012 (www.leg.state.co.us/lcs/ballothistory.nsf/). See also James and Gerboth, "A Camp Divided," p. 160.

15. James and Gerboth, "A Camp Divided," p. 163.

16. Elizabeth Kneebone, "Job Sprawl Stalls: The Great Recession and Metropolitan Employment Location" (Brookings, 2013).

17. Ibid.

18. William H. Frey, "Melting Pot Cities and Suburbs: Racial and Ethnic Change in Metro America in the 2000s" (Brookings, 2011), p. 3.

19. See, for example, David Rusk, "Denver Divided: Sprawl, Race, and Poverty in Greater Denver" (Denver, Colo.: Gamaliel Foundation, 2003).

20. See Colorado Department of Education, "Pupil Membership for 2012," 2013 (www.cde.state.co.us/cdereval/pupilcurrentschool.htm).

21. Audrey Singer, "Immigrants in 2010 Metropolitan America: A Decade of Change," keynote presentation, National Immigrant Integration Conference, Seattle, October 24, 2011 (www.brookings.edu/research/speeches/2011/10/24-immigration-singer).

22. "State of Metropolitan America Indicator Map," Brookings, 2010 (www.brookings.edu/research/interactives/state-of-metropolitan-america-indicator-map#/?subject=7&ind=70&dist=0&data=Number&year=2010&geo=metro&zoom=0&x=0&y=0).

23. Ibid.

24. Elizabeth Kneebone, "The Changing Geography of Metropolitan Poverty," *The Atlantic Cities*, September 20, 2012 (www.theatlanticcities.com/politics/2012/09/changing-geography-metropolitan-poverty/3348/).

25. Jordan Rappaport, "The Shared Fortunes of Cities and Suburbs," in *Economic Review: Third Quarter 2005* (Federal Reserve Bank of Kansas City), pp. 41–43.

26. Stephanie Post and Robert Stein perform a unique analysis in which they control for the impact of the state economy on metropolitan areas and their suburbs and cities. They do "find a positive and significant relationship between the economies of central cities and their suburbs that is independent of the state economy. This finding demonstrates that the economic relationship between cities and their suburbs is in part fashioned by conditions indigenous to metropolitan areas." Stephanie Shirley Post and Robert M. Stein, "State Economies, Metropolitan Governance, and Urban-Suburban Economic Dependence," *Urban Affairs Review* 36 (September 2000), p. 56.

27. Jennifer Vey, "Restoring Prosperity: The State Role in Revitalizing America's Older Industrial Cities" (Brookings, 2008), p. 19. There are other indicators of the interrelationship between city and suburban economic and social health: central city decline and wide disparities between city and suburban prosperity are associated with slower regional income growth, and job gains in a central city have a positive effect on housing prices in the suburbs. See, for example, Richard P. Voith, "City and Suburban Growth: Substitutes or Complements?" *Business Review* (September–October 1992); Richard Voith, "Do Suburbs Need Cities?" *Journal of Regional Science* 38, no. 3 (1998), pp. 445–64; H. V. Savitch and others, "Ties That Bind: Central Cities, Suburbs, and the New Metropolitan Region," *Economic Development Quarterly* 7, no. 4 (1993), pp. 341–57; Larry Ledebur and William R. Barnes, *All in It Together: Cities, Suburbs, and Local Economic Regions* (Washington: National League of Cities, 1993); Richard Voith, "The Suburban Housing Market: The Effects of City and Suburban Job Growth," *Business Review* (November–December 1996).

28. Robin M. Leichenko, "Growth and Change in U.S. Cities and Suburbs," *Growth and Change* 32 (Summer 2001), pp. 347–48.

29. Wilson D. Kendall, "A Brief Economic History of Colorado" (Denver, Colo.: Center for Business and Economic Forecasting, 2002).

30. See Greater Austin Chamber of Commerce, "2005 InterCity Visit: Denver, Colorado," 2005 (www.austinchamber.com/public-policy/files/EDplans.pdf).

31. Allan Wallis, "Denver's International Airport: A Case Study in Large-Scale Infrastructure Development, Part 1," *Municipal Finance Journal* 13, no. 2 (1992), p. 63. For information about the Rocky Mountain Arsenal site, see U.S. Environmental Protection Agency, "Rocky Mountain Arsenal," 2013 (www.epa.gov/region8/super fund/co/rkymtnarsenal/). The airport site itself was later converted into a popular New Urbanism–style residential development. The developers did have to invest in cleaning up the former airport land, which was polluted by jet fuel and other contaminants.

32. The city of Denver had experience in running an airport, and according to one unpublished study of the Denver region, "there never seemed to be any question that the airport would be owned and operated by the city, perhaps because Stapleton had always been a municipal airport. The mayor's ability to keep [Denver International Airport] a municipal airport attests to the power of that office, as well as to Denver's dominance in Colorado politics." Richard C. Schragger, "City Powers Project: Denver Colorado," City Powers Project, internal document, April 2004, p. 64. See also Wallis, "Denver's International Airport, Part 1," p. 76. Adams County

officials had made it clear that they were resolutely opposed to the expansion of Stapleton. Opposition to the airport expansion from Adams County residents was evident from as early as 1968. See Paul Stephen Dempsey, Andrew R. Goetz, and Joseph S. Szyliowicz, *Denver International Airport: Lessons Learned* (New York: McGraw-Hill, 1997), p. 101.

33. Wallis, "Denver's International Airport, Part 1," p. 72.

34. Ibid., p. 79.

35. Dempsey, Goetz, and Szyliowicz, *Denver International Airport*, p. 106.

36. Wallis, "Denver's International Airport, Part 2," *Municipal Finance Journal* 13, no. 3 (1992), p. 72.

37. Ibid.

38. Dempsey, Goetz, and Szyliowicz, *Denver International Airport*, p. 116.

39. Ibid., p. 117.

40. Michael McCarthy, "A Short History of the Scientific and Cultural Facilities District," Scientific and Cultural Facilities District, internal document, 1993.

41. Ibid.

42. See Scientific and Cultural Facilities District, "Annual Report: 04&05" (http://scfd.org/graphics/uploads/Files/annual_report/SCFD_2004-05%20 Annual%20Report.pdf).

43. The convention center, which opened in downtown Denver in 1990, was paid for by narrowly targeted tax increases on hotels, prepared food, and car rentals.

44. Rappaport, "The Shared Fortunes of Cities and Suburbs," p. 45.

45. Ibid., pp. 45–46.

46. Public financing of major-league sports facilities has been widely criticized as a poor use of public funds. Often, predictions of economic benefits generated from stadium construction and operation vastly overestimate actual economic benefits, and many times stadium construction costs end up higher than initial estimates describe. See, for example, Adam M. Zaretsky, "Should Cities Pay for Sports Facilities?" *Regional Economist* (Federal Reserve Bank of St. Louis), April 2001, pp. 4–9. See also Judith Grant Long, "Full Count: The Real Cost of Public Funding for Major League Sports Facilities," *Journal of Sports Economics* 6 (May 2005); Robert A. Baade and Victor A. Matheson, "Financing Professional Sports Facilities" (Worcester, Mass.: College of the Holy Cross, Department of Economics, 2011).

47. Leave aside the fact that these companies both make dozens of kinds of beverages.

48. Gerald E. Frug and David J. Barron, *City Bound: How States Stifle Urban Innovation* (Cornell University Press, 2008), p. 206.

49. See Metro Denver, "About Metro Denver EDC," 2013 (www.metrodenver. org/about-metro-denver-edc/).

50. See American Rails, "Colorado Interurban and Streetcar Railroads," 2013 (www.american-rails.com/colorado-interurbans.html). An especially charming narrative of the role that the interurban cars played in the region's social life can be found on the application to list car No. 25 from the Denver and Intermountain Railroad Company (the Golden-to-Denver line) on the National Register of Historic places. See National Park Service, "National Register of Historic Places Registration Form: Denver and Intermountain Railroad Interurban No. 25," 2011 (www.nps. gov/nr/feature/weekly_features/2012/den-imt-rr_interurbanno25.pdf).

51. See Ciruli Associates, "RTD's Tax History," 2000 (www.ciruli.com/archives/oppose2.htm). See also Kathleen Osher, "On the Right Track," *Urban Land*, September 2006, p. 102.

52. Ciruli Associates, "Public Wants Transit, But Not at Any Price," 2000 (www.ciruli.com/archives/transit-price.htm).

53. See Regional Transportation District, "Southeast Corridor Light Rail Line," 2013 (www.rtd-denver.com/FF-SoutheastCorridor.shtml).

54. "Still another example of an increasing-benefits public good is a mass transit system. All else equal, as a mass transit system increases the area it serves, users can go to more places. A well-designed metrowide transit system should benefit both city and suburban residents. Such a system can save time and commuting costs, lessen automobile traffic, and reduce parking needs. It can also facilitate 'reverse commutes' to suburban jobs by low-income city residents for whom automobile ownership is prohibitively expensive." Rappaport, "The Shared Fortunes of Cities and Suburbs," p. 46.

55. "A Full FasTracks? We Think It Can, We Think It Can," editorial, *Denver Post*, April 29, 2012. The initial FasTracks proposal called for the project to be completed in a dozen years, with an end date of 2016. RTD FasTracks, "FasTracks Plan," April 22, 2004 (www.rtd-fastracks.com/media/uploads/main/FasTracks_PlanA.pdf).

CHAPTER 4

The quotation at the beginning of this chapter is from Manuel Castells, *The Rise of the Network Society* (Cambridge, Mass.: Blackwell Publishers, 1996), p. 168.

1. This comment has been widely attributed to Rahm Emanuel. Quoted in Gerald F. Seib, "In Crisis, Opportunity for Obama," *Wall Street Journal*, November 21, 2008 (http://online.wsj.com/article/SB122721278056345271.html).

2. See "A Defining Point in the Mahoning Valley's Timeline," Vindy.com, September 19, 2007 (www4.vindy.com/content/opinion/editorial/364133706324003.php).

3. See "Default," in *Encyclopedia of Cleveland History* (Cleveland, Ohio: Case Western Reserve University and the Western Reserve Historical Society, 1997) (http://ech.case.edu/cgi/article.pl?id=D2).

4. Edward W. Hill, "The Cleveland Economy: A Case Study of Economic Restructuring," in *Cleveland: A Metropolitan Reader*, edited by W. Dennis Keating, Norman Krumholz, and David C. Perry (Kent State University Press, 1995), p. 55.

5. Larry Ledebur and Jill Taylor, "A Restoring Prosperity Case Study: Akron, Ohio" (Brookings, 2008), p. 10.

6. Quoted in Iver Peterson, "'Mistake by the Lake' Wakes Up, Roaring," *New York Times*, September 10, 1995 (www.nytimes.com/1995/09/10/us/mistake-by-the-lake-wakes-up-roaring.html).

7. Ibid.

8. Brookings Analysis of Moody's Analytics.

9. John Russo and Sherry Lee Linkon, "Collateral Damage: Deindustrialization and the Uses of Youngstown," in *Beyond the Ruins: the Meanings of Deindustrialization*, edited by Jefferson Cowie and Joseph Heathcott (Cornell University Press, 2003), p. 208.

10. Ibid.

11. Lavea Brachman and Alan Mallach, "Ohio's Cities at a Turning Point: Finding the Way Forward" (Brookings, 2010), p. 13.

12. Bob Paynter and Marcia Pledger, "Comeback City Fights Old-Shoe Image," *Cleveland Plain Dealer*, October 14, 2001 (www.cleveland.com/quietcrisis/index.ssf?/quietcrisis/more/1003059000242700.html).

13. Sean Safford, *Why the Garden Club Couldn't Save Youngstown: The Transformation of the Rust Belt* (Harvard University Press, 2009).

14. See Doug Clifton, "Region's Needs Won't Wait Any Longer," *Cleveland Plain Dealer*, June 17, 2001 (www.cleveland.com/quietcrisis/index.ssf?/quietcrisis/more/99268383317275184.html).

15. Gross metropolitan product is a measure of the value of the goods and services produced by a particular metropolitan area. It is the metrowide version of the more familiar gross domestic product (GDP), which measures the value of the goods and services produced by the nation as a whole. See U.S. Bureau of Economic Analysis, "U.S. Economic Accounts," Department of Commerce, 2013 (www.bea.gov).

16. Joe Frolik, "Who'll Lead the Region Out of Its Crisis?" *Cleveland Plain Dealer*, February 3, 2002 (www.cleveland.com/quietcrisis/index.ssf?/quietcrisis/more/1012744501219030.html).

17. Steven Johnson, *Future Perfect: The Case for Progress in a Networked Age* (New York: Penguin Group, 2012), p. 19.

18. Safford, *Why the Garden Club Couldn't Save Youngstown*, ch. 6.

19. Fund for Our Economic Future, "Making Northeast Ohio Great Again: A Call to Arms to the Foundation Community," internal document, July 2004.

20. Ibid.

21. Voices and Choices, "Report on the Public's Priorities for Northeast Ohio's Future," America*Speaks*, November 2006 (http://americaspeaks.org/wp-content/uploads/2010/05/VC_FinalReport.pdf), p. 6.

22. FutureWorks, "Assessment of the Fund for Our Economic Future," internal document, January 31, 2012.

23. Ibid.

24. Mt. Auburn Associates, "Findings from External Stakeholder Interviews," internal document, prepared for Fund for Our Economic Future, December 20, 2006.

25. Walter W. Powell and Stine Grodal, "Networks of Innovators," in *The Oxford Handbook of Innovation*, edited by Jan Fagerberg, David C. Mowery, and Richard R. Nelson (Oxford University Press, 2005), p. 67.

26. Jim O'Grady and Jonathan Bowles, "Building New York City's Innovation Economy" (New York: Center for an Urban Future, September 2009), pp. 25–26.

27. Catherine Clifford, "Ohio Gets Strong on Flexible Electronics Entrepreneurs," *Entrepreneur*, December 17, 2012 (www.entrepreneur.com/article/225296).

28. Fund for Our Economic Future, "Grant Application Form, July 1, 2011–June 30, 2012," internal document, March 15, 2011.

29. "Print Me a Jet Engine," *Schumpeter* (blog), *The Economist*, November 22, 2012 (www.economist.com/blogs/schumpeter/2012/11/additive-manufacturing).

30. "Difference Engine: The PC All Over Again?" *Babbage* (blog), *The Economist*, September 9, 2012 (www.economist.com/blogs/babbage/2012/09/3d-printing).

31. "Print Me a Jet Engine." See also "Difference Engine: The PC All Over Again?";
Vivek Srinivasan and Jarrod Bassan, "Manufacturing the Future: 10 Trends to Come
in 3D Printing," *Forbes*, December 7, 2012 (www.forbes.com/sites/ciocentral/
2012/12/07/manufacturing-the-future-10-trends-to-come-in-3d-printing/).

32. Fay Hanleybrown, John Kania, and Mark Kramer, "Channeling Change:
Making Collective Impact Work," *Stanford Social Innovation Review*, January
26, 2012 (www.ssireview.org/blog/entry/channeling_change_making_collective_
impact_work?cpgn=WP%20DL%20-%20Channeling%20Change), p. 8.

33. Fund for Our Economic Future, "Phase 4 Strategic Plan: Greater Collaboration, Greater Experience, Greater Impact," internal document, October 4, 2012.

34. John Hagel III and John Seely Brown, "Creation Nets: Harnessing the Potential of Open Innovation," *Journal of Service Science* 1, no. 2 (2008), p. 29.

35. Margaret Pugh O'Mara, *Cities of Knowledge: Cold War Science and the
Search for the Next Silicon Valley* (Princeton University Press, 2005), ch. 3.

36. Quoted in Henry Chesbrough, "Open Innovation: A New Paradigm for
Understanding Industrial Innovation," in *Open Innovation: Researching a New
Paradigm*, edited by Henry Chesbrough, Wim Vanhaverbeke, and Joel West
(Oxford University Press, 2006), p. 5.

37. Ibid.

38. Ibid., p. 6.

39. John Hagedoorn, "Inter-firm R&D Partnerships: An Overview of Major
Trends and Patterns since 1960," *Research Policy* 31, no. 4 (2002), pp. 479–80.

40. Hagel and Brown, "Creation Nets: Harnessing the Potential of Open Innovation," pp. 31–32.

41. Zhenzhong Ma and Yender Lee, "Patent Application and Technological
Collaboration in Inventive Activities: 1980–2005," *Technovation* 28 (June 2008),
p. 383.

42. Powell and Grodal, "Networks of Innovators," p. 57.

43. Ibid., pp. 67–68. This trend has been documented by researchers across a
wide variety of disciplines. The sociologist Manuel Castells notes that "networks are
the fundamental stuff of which new organizations are and will be made. And they
are able to form and expand all over the main streets and back alleys of the global
economy because of their reliance on the information power provided by the new
technological paradigm." Castells, *The Rise of the Network Society* (Cambridge,
Mass.: Blackwell Publishers, 1996), p. 168; emphasis in the original. The legal
scholar Yochai Benkler cites several examples of networked production. Benkler,
The Wealth of Networks: How Social Production Transforms Markets and Freedom
(Yale University Press, 2006). Henry Chesbrough of the Harvard Business School
echoes Powell and Grodal, finding that interorganizational ties are an element that
enables firms to innovate by increasing patenting rates, improving existing products,
creating new products, and quickening the time to market of products. Chesbrough,
Vanhaverbeke, and West, *Open Innovation: Researching a New Paradigm*. And
Caroline Simard and Joel West write that "networks are especially well suited to
knowledge-intensive industries where joint problem-solving is paramount: networks
foster problem-solving and learning mechanisms." Simard and West, "Knowledge
Networks and the Geographic Locus of Innovation," in *Open Innovation*, edited
by Chesbrough, Vanhauerbeke, and West, p. 223.

44. See also Hagedoorn, who writes: "In the literature, the explanation for this overall growth pattern of newly made R&D partnerships is generally related to the motives that 'force' companies to collaborate on R&D. Major factors mentioned in that context are related to important industrial and technological changes in the 1980s and 1990s that have led to increased complexity of scientific and technological development, higher uncertainty surrounding R&D, increasing costs of R&D projects, and shortened innovation cycles that favor collaboration." Hagedoorn, "Inter-firm R&D Partnerships: An Overview of Major Trends and Patterns since 1960," p. 480.

45. Hagel and Brown, "Creation Nets: Harnessing the Potential of Open Innovation," p. 30.

46. "In fields where scientific or technological progress is developing rapidly, and the sources of knowledge are widely distributed, no single firm has all of the necessary skills to stay on top of all areas of progress and bring significant innovations to market. . . . In such settings, networks can become the locus of innovation, as the creation of knowledge is crucial to improving competitive position." Powell and Grodal, "Networks of Innovators," p. 59.

47. Siddharth Kulkarni and Mark Muro, "AI Definition 3.0," memorandum, Brookings, March 23, 2013. Other advanced industries include specialized industrial machinery manufacturing for industries, such as agriculture, construction, and mining, and manufacturing for motor vehicles, aerospace products and parts, and medical equipment and supplies. See Daniel Pacthod and Michael Park, "How Can the U.S. Advanced-Industries Sector Maintain Its Competitiveness?" *McKinsey Quarterly*, June 2012, pp. 1–3. See also Mark Muro and others, "Launch! Taking Colorado's Space Economy to the Next Level" (Brookings, 2013), p. 2.

48. Kulkarni and Muro, "AI Definition 3.0."

49. Pacthod and Park, "How Can the U.S. Advanced-Industries Sector Maintain Its Competitiveness?" p. 2.

50. Jason Paur, "Chevy Volt: King of (Software) Cars," *Wired*, November 5, 2010 (www.wired.com/autopia/2010/11/chevy-volt-king-of-software-cars/). See also Lindsay Brooke, "Computer Code an Increasingly Precious E.V. Commodity," *New York Times*, January 21, 2011 (www.nytimes.com/2011/01/23/automobiles/23SPIES.html?_r=0).

51. Pacthod and Park, "How Can the U.S. Advanced-Industries Sector Maintain Its Competitiveness?" p. 1.

52. Susan Helper, Timothy Krueger, and Howard Wial, "Why Does Manufacturing Matter? Which Manufacturing Matters? A Policy Framework" (Brookings, 2012), p. 8. See also Gregory Tassey, "Rationales and Mechanisms for Revitalizing U.S. Manufacturing R&D Strategies" (Gaithersburg, Md.: National Institute of Standards and Technology, 2009).

53. Helper, Krueger, and Wial, "Why Does Manufacturing Matter? Which Manufacturing Matters? A Policy Framework," p. 8. See also Mark Muro, "Amazon's Kindle: Symbol of American Decline?" *The Avenue* (blog), *New Republic*, February 24, 2010 (www.newrepublic.com/tags/freescale-semiconductor).

54. Stephen J. Ezell and Robert D. Atkinson, "The Case for a National Manufacturing Strategy" (Washington: Information Technology and Innovation Foundation, April 26, 2011), p. 15. For further discussion of the strong link between innovation and manufacturing capacity, see ibid. See also Tassey, "Rationales and Mechanisms

for Revitalizing U.S. Manufacturing R&D Strategies"; Gary P. Pisano and Willy C. Shih, "Restoring American Competitiveness," *Harvard Business Review,* July 2009.

55. Susan Helper and Howard Wial, "Strengthening American Manufacturing: A New Federal Approach" (Brookings, Metropolitan Policy Program, 2010), p. 5.

56. See "PRISM: Partnership for Regional Innovation Services to Manufacturers," MAGNET, 2013 (www.manufacturingsuccess.org/Programs/PRISM.aspx).

57. Several of our Brookings colleagues advised the Fund and others in Northeast Ohio as they were developing a business plan for the region, and PRISM is one of the elements of this business plan. "Investing in Transformation: A Prospectus for Growing Manufacturing in Northeast Ohio" (Brookings, Metropolitan Policy Program, 2011). For more information about the Brookings business plan process, which includes Minneapolis–St. Paul and the Puget Sound Region, see "Building the Next Economy from the Ground Up: Metropolitan Business Plans in U.S. Regions" Brookings, Rockefeller Project on State and Metropolitan Innovation, 2011 (www. brookings.edu/about/projects/state-metro-innovation/mbp).

58. Steven Johnson, *Where Good Ideas Come From: The Natural History of Innovation* (New York: Penguin Group, 2010), p. 57.

59. *New York Times,* national ed., November 18, 2012, front sec., p. 23.

60. Samuel Leiken and Randall Kempner, "Collaborate: Leading Regional Innovation Clusters" (Council on Competitiveness, 2010).

61. Networks are a fertile ground for metaphor. A Council on Competitiveness report on regional innovation clusters compares networks to pickup basketball teams that need a league, a scheduler, playoffs, and rule enforcement. Ibid., p. 6.

62. Reid Hoffman, "Be the Entrepreneur of Your Own Life," TED conference, Long Beach, California, February 29, 2012.

CHAPTER 5

The quotation at the beginning of the chapter is taken from Jane Addams, *Twenty Years at Hull House, with Autobiographical Notes* (New York: Macmillan, 1912), p. 116.

1. See, for example, the evocative description of Gulfton's rapid change in Susan Rogers, "A New Center on the Periphery: The Baker-Ripley Neighborhood Center for Gulfton, Sharpstown," *Cite* 80 (Winter 2009), p. 21.

2. Ibid., p. 23. See also Susan Rogers, "Superneighborhood 27: A Brief History of Change," *Places* 17, no. 2 (2005), p. 39.

3. Rogers, "Superneighborhood 27," p. 39.

4. Neighborhood Centers, Inc., "Gulfton Promise Neighborhood Project Narrative," internal document, pp. 55–56.

5. Neighborhood Centers, Inc., "Gulfton and Sharpstown: Houston, TX Community Profile," internal document, 2011, p. 4.

6. Neighborhood Centers, "Gulfton Promise Neighborhood Project Narrative," p. 8. See also U.S. Census Bureau, "Income, Poverty, and Health Insurance in the United States: 2011 Highlights," Department of Commerce, 2012 (www.census. gov/hhes/www/poverty/data/incpovhlth/2011/highlights.html).

7. Neighborhood Centers, "Gulfton Promise Neighborhood Project Narrative," p. 5.

8. Ibid., p. 8.

9. Ibid., p. 4.

10. Angela Blanchard, "People Transforming Communities. For Good," Investing in What Works for America's Communities (www.whatworksforamerica.org/ideas/people-transforming-communities/#.USZCoFKmGyF).

11. Neighborhood Centers, "Gulfton Promise Neighborhood Project Narrative," p. 8. See also Neighborhood Centers, Inc., "Unlocking the Strengths of Our Communities: A Step-by-Step Guide to Appreciative Community Building," 2010, p. 8.

12. Marilyn M. Sibley, "Houston Ship Channel," *Handbook of Texas Online*, Texas State Historical Association (www.tshaonline.org/handbook/online/articles/rhh11).

13. Neighborhood Centers, "Gulfton and Sharpstown: Houston, TX Community Profile."

14. William H. Frey, "The Census Projects Minority Surge," Brookings, 2008 (www.brookings.edu/research/opinions/2008/08/18-census-frey).

15. See William H. Frey, "America's Diverse Future: Initial Glimpses at the U.S. Child Population from the 2010 Census" (Brookings, 2011).

16. Audrey Singer, "Immigration," in "State of Metropolitan America: On the Front Lines of Demographic Transformation" (Brookings, 2010), p. 67.

17. Jeffery S. Passel, "Demography of Immigrant Youth: Past, Present, and Future," in "Immigrant Children," special issue, *The Future of Children* 21, no. 1 (2011), p. 21.

18. Michael Greenstone and Adam Looney, "Ten Economic Facts about Immigration" (Brookings, Hamilton Project, 2010), p. 11.

19. Partnership for a New American Economy, "The 'New American' Fortune 500," June 2011 (www.renewoureconomy.org/sites/all/themes/pnae/img/new-american-fortune-500-june-2011.pdf).

20. Giovanni Peri and Chad Sparber, "Task Specialization, Immigration, and Wages" (University of California at Davis, January 2009), p. 26.

21. Giovanni Peri and Chad Sparber, "Highly-Educated Immigrants and Native Occupational Choices," Working Paper 16 (Hamilton, N.Y.: Colgate University, September 2010), p. 13.

22. David Dyssegaard Kallick, "Immigrant Small Business Owners" (Fiscal Policy Institute, 2012), p. 1.

23. It should be noted that immigrants own businesses in every major industry. The largest shares of immigrant-owned businesses are in leisure and hospitality (28 percent of all small businesses are owned by immigrants), transportation and warehousing (26 percent), and retail trade (22 percent). So the examples mentioned here are meant to be suggestive but not representative of the entire range of immigrant businesses. See ibid., p. 9.

24. Audrey Singer, "Investing in the Human Capital of Immigrants, Strengthening Regional Economies" (Brookings, 2012), p. 2.

25. Audrey Singer, Robert Suro, and Jill H. Wilson, "Immigration and Poverty in America's Suburbs" (Brookings, 2011), p. 1.

26. See Enrico Moretti, *The New Geography of Jobs* (Boston: Houghton Mifflin Harcourt, 2012). See also Jonathan Rothwell, "Education, Job Openings, and Unemployment in Metropolitan America" (Brookings, 2012).

27. See "State of Metropolitan America Indicator Map," Brookings, 2010 (www.brookings.edu/research/interactives/state-of-metropolitan-america-indicator-map#/?

subject=7&ind=70&dist=0&data=Number&year=2010&geo=metro&zoom=0&x
=0&y=0).

28. Ibid.

29. George J. Borjas, "Poverty and Program Participation among Immigrant Children," in "Immigrant Children," special issue, *The Future of Children* 21, no. 1 (2011), p. 250.

30. Neighborhood Centers, Inc., "100 Years of Caring," internal document, 2007, p. 2. See also U.S. Census Bureau, "Census of Population and Housing: 1910 Census," Department of Commerce, 1913 (www2.census.gov/prod2/decennial/documents/36894832v3_TOC.pdf).

31. Neighborhood Centers, "100 Years of Caring," p. 6.

32. See Neighborhood Centers, Inc., "Financials: 2010 Operating Results," 2013 (www.neighborhood-centers.org/en-us/content/Financials.aspx).

33. Neighborhood Centers, Inc. "People Transforming Communities. For Good," internal presentation. See also Neighborhood Centers, Inc., "Community Based Initiatives [and] Choices in Education," internal map, 2010.

34. Head Start and Early Head Start are federal programs that prepare infants and children from low-income families for school and include a broad range of services, such as health and nutrition. See "About Head Start," Head Start, 2011 (http://eclkc.ohs.acf.hhs.gov/hslc/hs/about).

35. Neighborhood Centers, "Gulfton Promise Neighborhood Project Narrative," pp. 36–41.

36. United Way, "2011 United Way Year-End Report: Community Services Programs," internal document, 2011, p. 2.

37. David L. Cooperrider and Diana Whitney, *Appreciative Inquiry: A Positive Revolution in Change* (San Francisco, Calif.: Berrett-Koehler Publishers, 2005).

38. American Society for Training and Development, "David Cooperrider," *T+D*, February 2009 (www.astd.org/Publications/Magazines/TD/TD-Archive/2009/02/David-Cooperrider).

39. Sue Annis Hammond, *The Thin Book of Appreciative Inquiry* (Thin Book Publishing, 1998), pp. 6–7.

40. Singer, "Immigration," p. 65; William H. Frey, "Melting Pot Cities and Suburbs: Racial and Ethnic Change in Metro America in the 2000s" (Brookings, 2011), p. 1.

41. Elizabeth Kneebone and Emily Garr, "Income and Poverty," in "State of Metropolitan America: On the Front Lines of Demographic Transformation," p. 133. See also Elizabeth Kneebone and Alan Berube, *Confronting Suburban Poverty in America* (Brookings Press, 2013).

42. Singer, Suro, and Wilson, "Immigration and Poverty in America's Suburbs," p. 5.

43. Ibid.

44. U.S. Census Bureau, "Final Response Rates for Local and Tribal Governmental Entities," Department of Commerce, 2000 (www.census.gov/dmd/www/response/disp-fro.48.txt).

45. Neighborhood Centers, Inc., "2012 Proposal for Head Start Grantee," internal document, 2012, p. 98.

46. Neighborhood Centers, "Gulfton Promise Neighborhood Project Narrative," p. 65.

47. Jane Addams, *Twenty Years at Hull House, with Autobiographical Notes* (New York: Macmillan, 1912), p. 126.

48. "Poverty in America: Economic Research Shows Adverse Impacts on Health Status and Other Social Conditions as Well as the Economic Growth Rate" (U.S. Government Accountability Office, January 2007), p. 3.

49. Joseph E. Stiglitz, *The Price of Inequality: How Today's Divided Society Endangers Our Future* (New York: W. W. Norton, 2013), p. 117.

50. Moretti, *The New Geography of Jobs*, p. 119. Moretti is too quick to write off communities as beyond recovery. He himself notes that Seattle in the 1970s was a scarred postindustrial town, deemed a "city of despair" by *The Economist*. But in 1979, native sons Paul Allen and Bill Gates decided to bring their Albuquerque-based company back home, and then everything changed (ibid., pp. 73–120). It is the case, though, that the overall level of educational attainment in a metropolitan area is a good predictor of economic success and also can have stark effects on the well-being of metro residents.

51. Rothwell, "Education, Job Openings, and Unemployment in Metropolitan America," p. 22.

52. Borjas, "Poverty and Program Participation among Immigrant Children," p. 247.

53. Ibid., p. 261.

54. "Poverty in America," U.S. Government Accountability Office, p. 18.

55. Robert Crosnoe and Ruth N. López Turley, "K–12 Educational Outcomes of Immigrant Youth," in "Immigrant Children," p. 135.

56. Robert T. Teranishi, Carola Suárez-Orozco, and Marcelo Suárez-Orozco, "Immigrants in Community College," in "Immigrant Children," pp. 156–57.

57. Rothwell, "Education, Job Openings, and Unemployment in Metropolitan America," p. 19.

58. Ibid., p. 1.

59. Neighborhood Centers, "2012 Proposal for Head Start Grantee," pp. 66–68.

60. Neighborhood Centers, "People Transforming Communities. For Good," p. 15.

61. Ibid.

62. Neighborhood Centers, "Unlocking the Strengths of Our Communities," p. 26.

63. Kneebone and Berube, *Confronting Suburban Poverty in America*, ch. 6.

64. Alan Berube and Angela Blackwell, e-mail correspondence with Ray Chung of Neighborhood Centers, Inc., August 30, 2012.

65. Kneebone and Berube, *Confronting Suburban Poverty in America*, ch. 6.

66. As Angela Blanchard has written, "Passion is insufficient to the task, and all the knowledge about neighborhoods will not be a substitute for good fiscal management. . . . It is essential to address the old nonprofit dilemma of choosing between more investment in programs or more investment in overhead: *both* are necessary." Blanchard, "People Transforming Communities. For Good." See also Angela Blanchard, "A Hierarchy of Needs: For Organizations," 2012 (http://angelablanchard.com/BlanchardModelofOrganizationalDevelopment.pdf).

67. Joel Garreau, *Edge City: Life on the New Frontier* (New York: Doubleday, 1991), p. 214.

68. Angela Blanchard, "Being United around a City," presentation at the United Neighborhood Centers of America Neighborhood Revitalization Conference, Washington, D.C., July 2011 (www.youtube.com/watch?v=AjUCt07ZIBkO).

69. Angela Blanchard, "The First New Question?" presentation at TEDxHouston, 2011 (www.youtube.com/watch?v=XU_vVt298gw).

CHAPTER 6

The quotation at the beginning of the chapter comes from Jane Jacobs, *The Death and Life of Great American Cities* (New York: Vintage Books, 1992), pp. 220–21.

1. *Innovation district* is a relatively new term just beginning to gain currency among political, business, and civic leaders focused on innovation-led economic development in the relatively small geographies of their cities and metros. Barcelona and Boston deserve credit for popularizing the new term and new approach. This chapter presents a broad definition and typology and draws from academic literature that captures both underlying shifts in innovation and demographics and changing trends in city building. For more information, see "22@Barcelona: The Innovation District" (www.22barcelona.com/index.php) and "Boston Innovation District" (www.innovationdistrict.org); for a similar idea, see "New Century Cities," MIT Center for Real Estate (www.web.mit.edu/cre/research/ncc/ncc.html).

2. Mark Muro and Julie Wagner, "How Colleges Can Foster Development Zones," *The Atlantic Cities*, February 14, 2012 (www.theatlanticcities.com/jobs-and-economy/2012/02/how-colleges-can-foster-development-zones/1209/).

3. Andrew Altman, former chief executive of the London Olympic Park Legacy Company, personal communication with Bruce Katz, January 22, 2013.

4. Lydia DePillis, "Dinosaur Makeover: Can Research Triangle Park Pull Itself Out of the 1950s?" *New Republic*, October 12, 2012.

5. Mohammed Arzaghi and Vernon Henderson find that advertising agencies in Manhattan "trade off higher rent costs of being in bigger clusters closer to the 'centers of action,' against lower rent costs of operating on the 'fringes' away from high concentrations of other agencies." Furthermore, they find that the benefits of locating within a small geography of firms (such as information spillovers, abundant skilled workers), though large, "dissipate very quickly with distance for advertisers and are gone by 750 meters." Mohammed Arzaghi and J. Vernon Henderson, "Networking Off Madison Avenue" (Brown University, 2006), pp. 1, 29.

6. Walter W. Powell and Stine Grodal, "Networks of Innovators," In *The Oxford Handbook of Innovation*, edited by Jan Fagerberg, David Mowery, and Richard Nelson (Oxford University Press, 2006), p. 59.

7. Daniel Pacthod and Michael Park, "How Can the U.S. Advanced-Industries Sector Maintain Its Competitiveness?" *McKinsey Quarterly*, June 2012, p. 2.

8. Her Majesty's Treasury and the Office of the Deputy Prime Minister, "Devolving Decision Making: Meeting the Regional Economic Challenge; The Importance of Cities to Regional Growth" (London: Office of the Deputy Prime Minister, 2006), p. 17.

9. Gerald A. Carlino, "Knowledge Spillovers: Cities' Role in the New Economy," *Business Review*, Federal Reserve Bank of Philadelphia, April 2001 (www.phil.frb.org/files/br/brq401gc.pdf), pp. 17–24.

10. Stuart S. Rosenthal and William C. Strange, "Evidence on the Nature and Sources of Agglomeration Economies," in *Handbook of Urban and Regional Economics*, edited by J. V. Henderson and J. F. Thisse (New York: Elsevier, 2004), pp. 2119–72.

11. Stuart S. Rosenthal and William C. Strange, "Geography, Industrial Organization, and Agglomeration," Working Paper 107 (Center for Policy Research, 2003) (www.maxwell.syr.edu/uploadedFiles/cpr/publications/working_papers2/wp56.pdf), p. 20.

12. Kyungjoon Lee and others, "Does Collocation Inform the Impact of Collaboration?" *PLoS One* 5, no. 12 (2010) (www.plosone.org/article/info:doi/10.1371/journal.pone.0014279); Katie DuBoff, "Close Proximity Leads to Better Science," Harvard Medical School, December 15, 2010 (http://hms.harvard.edu/news/close-proximity-leads-to-better-science-12-15-10).

13. CEOs for Cities and Initiative for a Competitive Inner City, "Leveraging Colleges and Universities for Urban Revitalization: An Action Guide" (Boston: Initiative for a Competitive Inner City, 2002).

14. Coalition of Urban Serving Universities, "Urban Universities: Anchors Generating Prosperity for America's Cities" (Washington, 2010).

15. Joseph Cortright and Heike Mayer, "Signs of Life: The Growth of Biotechnology Centers in the United States" (Brookings, 2002).

16. Henry Chesbrough, "The Era of Open Innovation," *MIT Sloan Management Review*, April 15, 2003.

17. Peter Hall, *Cities in Civilization: Culture, Innovation, and Urban Order* (London: Phoenix Giant, 1999).

18. Owen Washburn, senior policy analyst at Brookings Metropolitan Policy Program, personal communication with Randy Howder, senior associate and workplace strategist at Gensler, February 20, 2013.

19. Quoted in Leigh Gallagher, "Tony Hsieh's New $350 Million Startup," *Fortune*, January 23, 2012.

20. Arthur C. Nelson, *Reshaping Metropolitan America: Development Trends and Opportunities to 2030* (Washington: Island Press, 2013), p. 49.

21. Paul Taylor and others, "Barely Half of U.S. Adults Are Married—A Record Low" (Washington: Pew Research Center, 2011), p. 2.

22. Alan Berube and others, "State of Metropolitan America: On the Front Lines of Demographic Transformation" (Brookings, 2010), p. 93.

23. According to Chris Nelson, "Between 2010 and 2030, households with children will account for about 13 percent of the total change in households; households without children will represent the rest." Arthur C. Nelson, *Reshaping Metropolitan America*, p. 27.

24. Richard Florida, *The Rise of the Creative Class and How It's Transforming Work, Leisure, and Everyday Life* (New York: Basic Books, 2002).

25. Joseph Cortright, "Young and Restless 2011" (Washington: CEOs for Cities, 2011).

26. Robert Puentes, "Have Americans Hit Peak Travel? A Discussion of the Changes in U.S. Driving Habits," Discussion Paper 14 (Washington: International Transport Forum, 2012).

27. Nelson, *Reshaping Metropolitan America*, p. 3.

28. Puentes, "Have Americans Hit Peak Travel?" p. 13.

29. Saskia Sassen, "Cityness in the Urban Age," *Urban Age Bulletin* 2 (Autumn 2005). See also Bruce Katz and Julie Wagner, "Transformative Investments: Remaking American Cities for a New Century," *ETHOS*, June 2008.

30. "Facts on Cambridge, MIT, and the Biotech Industry," MIT News Office, May 6, 2002. See also Michael Joroff and others, "New Century City Developments: Creating Extraordinary Value" (Massachusetts Institute of Technology, 2009).

31. "The Cambridge Phenomenon," *The Economist*, March 16, 1985, p. 89.

32. Susan Diesenhouse, "Grand Finale: Two Decades Later, the Controversial University Park at MIT Is Nearly Ready for Last of Residential Tenants to Move In," *Boston Globe*, March 9, 2005.

33. "Overview," Forest City Science and Technology Group, 2008 (www.forest cityscience.net/mit/).

34. Mike Hoban, "Cambridge, Hub Downplay Rivalry Reports over District," *Boston Business Journal*, August 5, 2011.

35. This section draws heavily on an article by Karen Weintraub about the development around MIT and Kendall Square in Cambridge. Karen Weintraub, "Biotech Players Lead Boom in Cambridge," *New York Times*, January 2, 2013.

36. Weintraub, "Biotech Players Lead Boom in Cambridge."

37. Ibid.

38. Michael B. Farrell, "Kendall Sq Boom Times Squeeze Out Start-Ups; As Rents Climb, Tenor Changes," *Boston Globe*, October 25, 2012.

39. Thomas Grillo, "Projects Promise After-Hours Life in Kendall Square," *Boston Business Journal*, November 2, 2012.

40. Jay Fitzgerald, "MIT Injecting Life into Kendall Square: School Will Spend $700m; Some Seek More Housing," *Boston Globe*, November 30, 2011.

41. Weintraub, "Biotech Players Lead Boom in Cambridge."

42. Mayor Thomas Menino, quoted in "The Innovation District," Boston's New Waterfront, 2013 (www.bostonsnewwaterfront.com/civic-pride/the-innovation-district/).

43. "The Strategy and Core Principles," Boston Innovation District, 2013 (www.innovationdistrict.org/about-2/the-strategy/).

44. Bruce Katz and Jennifer Bradley, "Michigan's Urban and Metropolitan Strategy" (Brookings, 2012).

45. Statistics from "2011 in the ID . . . What's New for 2012?" Boston Innovation District, December 27, 2012 (www.innovationdistrict.org/category/live/).

46. Patrick Rosso, "South Boston Waterfront Now Home to City's First Innovation Center," Boston.com, May 2, 2012 (www.boston.com/yourtown/news/south_boston/2012/05/south_boston_waterfront_now_ho.html).

47. Julie Wagner, Metropolitan Policy Program, internal memorandum, Brookings, 2011.

48. Ibid.

49. Mitch Weiss, chief of staff to Boston mayor Thomas Menino, personal communication with Julie Wagner, August 1, 2011. See also Katz and Bradley, "Michigan's Urban and Metropolitan Strategy."

50. Samantha Hammar, former economic initiatives staff member at Boston Redevelopment Authority, personal communication with Julie Wagner, August 5, 2011. See also Katz and Bradley, "Michigan's Urban and Metropolitan Strategy."

51. Wagner, internal memorandum, 2011.

52. "Mayor Menino Releases Results of Innovation District Jobs Report," City of Boston, press release (www.cityofboston.gov/news/default.aspx).

53. Wagner, internal memorandum, 2011.

54. "Babson College / MassChallenge Celebrate Babson Graduate Student Hatchery Space in Boston's Innovation District," Babson College, March 4, 2011 (www.babson.edu/News-Events/babson-news/Pages/110304-babson-college-and-masschallenge-celebrate-hatchery.aspx).

55. Michael B. Farrell, "Battery Ventures Plans to Move to Boston," *Boston Globe*, December 21, 2012.

56. Ellen Keiley, "The Innovation District: Boston's New Hot Destination," Boston.com, February 28, 2012 (www.boston.com/business/blogs/global-business-hub/2012/02/the_innovation.html).

57. "North Carolina History Project: Research Triangle Park" (www.northcaro-linahistory.org/commentary/342/entry).

58. Research Triangle Foundation of North Carolina, "Research Triangle Park: Master Plan" (Research Triangle Park, N.C., 2012).

59. "Board Wants New Master Plan for Research Triangle Park," *Triangle Business Journal*, August 30, 2010.

60. Research Triangle Foundation, "Research Triangle Park: Master Plan."

61. DePillis, "Dinosaur Makeover."

62. Michael B. Farrell, "Cambridge Innovation Center Branches Out: Kendall-Based Operation Looks beyond Massachusetts," Boston.com, February 17, 2013 (www.boston.com/business/innovation/2013/02/18/cambridge-innovation-center-branches-out/cZS4M9PWbSSJUSGsz8AgsO/story.html).

63. Pete Engardio, "Research Parks for the Knowledge Economy," *Bloomberg Businessweek*, June 1, 2009.

64. The information on 22@Barcelona draws from the 2011 internal memorandum prepared by Julie Wagner. See also Katz and Bradley, "Michigan's Urban and Metropolitan Strategy."

65. Urban Land Institute, "Value Capture Finance: Making Urban Development Pay Its Way" (2009).

66. "Map of the 22@ District," 22@Barcelona, 2006 (www.22barcelona.com/10x22barcelona/planol/?lang=en).

67. For the media cluster, 22@Barcelona has universities, such as the Pompeu Fabra University, the University of Barcelona, and the Open University of Catalonia; institutions, such as Barcelona TV and RNE; companies, such as Media Pro and Yahoo R&D; spaces, such as the Audio Visual Production Center; a technology center, such as Barcelona Media-Innovation Center; incubators, such as the Media-TRC Building; and residences, such as the Melon District. Information from Ajuntament de Barcelona, "22@Barcelona: The Innovation District" (August 2011).

68. Ajuntament de Barcelona, "Barcelona Activa: the Local Development Agency of the City of Barcelona" (2010).

69. Anna Molero, personal communication with Julie Wagner, June 6, 2011.

70. Katz and Wagner, "Transformative Investments."

71. Ibid.

72. Research Triangle Foundation, "Research Triangle Park: Master Plan," p. 11.

73. Katz and Wagner, "Transformative Investments."

74. Detroit Works Project Long-Term Planning Steering Committee, "Detroit Future City: Strategic Framework Plan" (2013), pp. 160, 210.

75. Ibid.

76. Elizabeth Kneebone, "Jobs Sprawl Stalls: The Great Recession and Metropolitan Employment Location" (Brookings, 2013).

77. "Detroit Future City," p. 42.

78. State of Michigan, Department of Treasury, "Report of the Detroit Financial Review Team," February 19, 2013 (www.freep.com/assets/freep/pdf/C4201116219.pdf).

79. Monica Davey, "Bankruptcy Lawyer Is Named to Manage an Ailing Detroit," *New York Times*, March 14, 2013.

80. Thomas J. Sugrue, *The Origins of the Urban Crisis: Race and Inequality in Postwar Detroit* (Princeton University Press, 1996), p. 3.

81. As of this writing, several different geographies for a Detroit Innovation District have been proposed. This book uses the 5.2 square-mile area that encompasses downtown, midtown, Eastern Market, and Rivertown. The larger, 7.2 square-mile greater downtown area, which includes the areas of Corktown, Woodbridge, and Lafayette Park in addition to downtown, midtown, Eastern Market, and Rivertown, has been used in other publications. See also "7.2 Square Miles: A Report on Greater Downtown Detroit" (Detroit: Hudson-Webber Foundation, 2013).

82. John Gallagher, "Dan Gilbert's Downtown Detroit Building Tally Rises to 15," *Detroit Free Press*, December 19, 2012.

83. Nate Berg, "Downtown Detroit's Big Booster," *The Atlantic Cities*, January 12, 2012.

84. Gallagher, "Dan Gilbert's Downtown Detroit Building Tally Rises to 15."

85. "Detroit Future City," p. 69.

86. Tom Walsh, "Blue Cross to Celebrate Moving 3,400 Workers to Downtown Detroit," *Detroit Free Press*, June 6, 2012.

87. Joann Muller, "Detroit's Fix-It Men: In Their Own Words," *Forbes*, June 29, 2011; brackets in original.

88. Sherri Welch, "Sue Mosey: Slow and Steady Approach Revitalizes Midtown," *Crain's Detroit Business*, January 15, 2012.

89. Louis Aguilar, "Investment Proposals Put Midtown on Course for Growth," *Detroit News*, April 6, 2010.

90. Jay Greene, "Henry Ford Lands First Tenant for Health Park in Midtown," *Crain's Detroit Business*, June 3, 2012; Jay Greene, "Henry Ford Aims to Sow Green Space into Upgrade," *Crain's Detroit Business*, July 1, 2012.

91. Patricia Anstett and John Gallagher, "Health Systems' Midtown Plan Takes Shape," *Detroit Free Press*, May 31, 2012; "MDI Programs & Current Incentives," Midtown Detroit, Inc. (www.midtowndetroitinc.org).

92. Jonathan Oosting, "Wayne State Looks to 'Revitalize City Block' with $93 Million Midtown Research Facility," *Mlive.com*, June 26, 2012; Matt Roush, "New Report Reveals TechTown's Economic Impact on Detroit," *CBS Detroit*, May 26, 2012.

93. College for Creative Studies (www.collegeforcreativestudies.edu); Dennis Archambault, "Time Is on Their Side: Shinola Manufactures Instant Vintage," *Model D Media*, January 29, 2013.

94. Mark Stryker, "Voters in 3 Counties Approve DIA Millage, Get Free Admission," *Detroit Free Press*, August 8, 2012.

95. Brookings/The Reinvestment Fund analysis of NETS Database (February 2013).

96. Susan Stellin, "New Thirst for Urban Living, and Few Detroit Rentals," *New York Times*, December 11, 2012.

97. Bill Shea, "After Gilbert-Marchionne Meeting, Chrysler Group Commits $3 Million to M1 Rail Project," *Crain's Detroit Business*, April 30, 2012.

98. Nathan Bomey, "Ray LaHood on M1 Rail: 'They've Done Everything We've Asked Them to Do,'" *Detroit Free Press*, January 14, 2013.

99. Julie Wagner, personal communication with Bruce Katz, February 2013.

100. Statistics provided by the New Economy Initiative for Southeast Michigan (January 2013) (http://neweconomyinitiative.cfsem.org/).

101. "About Us," Woodward Corridor Initiative website, 2011 (www.woodward corridorinitiative.org).

102. John Gallagher, "Kresge Foundation Pledges $150 Million toward Detroit Future City Plan," *Detroit Free Press*, January 9, 2013.

103. David Muller, "$10 Million Live Midtown and Live Downtown Program Gets 676th Applicant, Shows No Signs of Slowing," *Mlive.com,* September 21, 2012 (www.mlive.com/business/detroit/index.ssf/2012/09/10_million_live_midtown_and_li.html).

CHAPTER 7

The quotation at the beginning of this chapter is taken from Antonio Villaraigosa's presentation at the forum, Going Global: Boosting the Economic Future of Greater Los Angeles, Brookings Institution, March 21, 2012.

1. United Nations Human Settlements Program, *State of the World's Cities 2012/2013: Prosperity of Cities* (Nairobi: UN-Habitat, 2012).

2. See Emilia Istrate and Carey Nadeau, "Global MetroMonitor Interactive" (Shenzhen), Brookings, November 30, 2012 (www.brookings.edu/research/interactives/global-metro-monitor-3).

3. For a more detailed version of the summary provided here, see Alan Berube and Joseph Parilla, *Metro Trade: Cities Return to their Roots in the Global Economy* (Brookings Press, 2012).

4. Richard Freeman, "The Great Doubling: The Challenge of the New Global Labor Market," University of California at Berkley, Department of Economics, 2006 (http://emlab.berkeley.edu/users/webfac/eichengreen/e183_sp07/great_doub.pdf).

5. International Monetary Fund, "Changing Patterns of Global Trade" (Strategy, Policy, and Review Department, June 15, 2011).

6. Brookings analysis of Economist Intelligence Unit data.

7. Uri Dadush and William Shaw, *Juggernaut: How Emerging Markets Are Reshaping Globalization* (Washington: Carnegie Endowment for International Peace, 2011).

8. Homi Kharas and Geoffrey Gertz, "The New Global Middle Class: A Crossover from West to East" (Brookings, 2011).

9. United Nations, "World Population Prospects: The 2010 Revision" and "World Urbanization Prospects: The 2011 Revision" (Department of Economic and Social Affairs, Population Division, 2012).

10. United Nations, "World Urbanization Prospects: The 2011 Revision: Data on Cities and Urban Agglomerations" (Department of Economic and Social Affairs, Population Division, 2012).

11. Emilia Istrate and Carey Anne Nadeau, "Global MetroMonitor 2012: Slowdown, Recovery, and Interdependence" (Brookings, 2012).

12. United Nations, "World Urbanization Prospects: The 2011 Revision" (Department of Economic and Social Affairs, Population Division, 2012).

13. David Jin and others, "Winning in Emerging Market Cities: A Guide to the World's Largest Growth Opportunities" (Boston: Boston Consulting Group, 2010).

14. Jonathan Woetzel and others, "Preparing for China's Urban Billion" (McKinsey Global Institute, 2009).

15. "Who's Bigger?" *The Economist*, June 14, 2012 (www.economist.com/blogs/graphicdetail/2012/06/daily-chart-8).

16. Brookings analysis of Economist Intelligence Unit data.

17. Brookings analysis of Economist Intelligence Unit data.

18. Suresh Kumar, "Helping U.S. Manufacturers Expand Exports," U.S. Department of Commerce, *The Commerce Blog*, June 2011 (www.commerce.gov/blog/2011/06/27/helping-us-manufacturers-expand-exports).

19. U.S. Department of State, "Passport Statistics," 2012 (www.travel.state.gov/passport/ppi/stats/stats_890.html). See also Government of Canada, Passport Canada, "Annual Report for 2011–2012," 2012 (www.ppt.gc.ca/publications/ar_11.aspx).

20. John Roach, "Young Americans Geographically Illiterate, Survey Suggests," *National Geographic News*, May 2, 2006.

21. David Skorton and Glenn Altschuler, "America's Foreign Language Deficit," *Forbes*, August 27, 2012.

22. McKinsey and Company, "Winning the $30 Trillion Decathlon: Going for Gold in Emerging Markets" (2012), pp. 9–10.

23. Jane Jacobs, *The Death and Life of Great American Cities* (New York: Vintage Books, 1992), p. 340.

24. Berube and Parilla, *Metro Trade,* p. 2.

25. Istrate and Nadeau, "Global MetroMonitor Interative" (Milwaukee, Mumbai), Brookings.

26. Shirish Sankhe and others, "India's Urban Awakening: Building Inclusive Cities, Sustaining Economic Growth" (McKinsey Global Institute, 2010).

27. Brad McDearman and Amy Liu, "10 Steps to Delivering a Successful Metro Export Plan" (Brookings, 2012).

28. Kati Suominen, "Can Trade Save Obama?" *Foreign Policy*, November 1, 2011 (www.foreignpolicy.com/articles/2011/11/01/can_trade_save_obama).

29. Amy Liu, Brad McDearman, and Marek Gootman, "Establish a Regional Export Accelerator Challenge (REACH) Grant Program to Boost U.S. Exports and Trade Capacity" (Brookings, 2013).

30. Brad McDearman, Greg Clark, and Joseph Parilla, "10 Traits of Globally Fluent Metros" (Brookings, forthcoming).

31. Emilia Istrate and Nicholas Marchio, "Export Nation 2012: How U.S. Metropolitan Areas Are Driving National Growth" (Brookings, 2012).

32. Brookings analysis of U.S. Bureau of Economic Analysis data.

33. U.S. Department of Commerce, "U.S. to See Boost in International Tourism," *The Commerce Blog*, April 23, 2012 (www.commerce.gov/blog/2012/04/23/us-see-boost-international-tourism).

34. See U.S. Department of Commerce, International Trade Administration, "Record Year for Travel to the United States," February 22, 2013 (http://trade.gov/press/press-releases/2013/record-year-for-travel-to-the-united-states-022213.asp).

35. Brooking analysis of Institute for International Education data.

36. See U.S. Census Bureau, "U.S. Census Bureau Projections Show a Slower Growing, Older, More Diverse Nation a Half Century from Now," Department of Commerce, December 12, 2012 (www.census.gov/newsroom/releases/archives/population/cb12-243.html).

37. Brookings analysis of U.S. Census Bureau data.

38. Elizabeth M. Grieco and others, "The Foreign Born Population in the United States: 2010" (Department of Commerce, U.S. Census Bureau, 2012).

39. Robert Guest, *Borderless Economics* (New York: Palgrave Macmillan, 2011), p. 20.

40. Matthew Hall and others, "The Geography of Immigrant Skills: Educational Profiles of Metropolitan Areas" (Brookings, 2011).

41. James Fallows, "How America Can Rise Again," *The Atlantic* (January–February 2010).

42. James K. Jackson, "Foreign Direct Investment in the United States: An Economic Analysis" (Congressional Research Service, 2012).

43. Ibid.

44. National Association of Manufacturers, "Foreign Investment in U.S. Manufacturing Grows," Manufacturing Institute, 2013 (www.themanufacturinginstitute.org/Research/Facts-About-Manufacturing/Section-1-Benefits-of-Manufacturing/Trade-and-Investment/Foreign-Investment/Foreign-Investment.aspx).

45. Tom Howell Jr., "Qatari Money Funds D.C. City Center Project," *Washington Times*, April 4, 2011.

46. Woetzel and others, "Preparing for China's Urban Billion."

47. Sankhe and others, "India's Urban Awakening."

48. See Emilia Istrate and Carey Nadeau, "Global Metro Monitor Interactive: Portland," Brookings, November 30, 2012 (www.brookings.edu/research/interactives/global-metro-monitor-3).

49. See Oregon Department of Environmental Quality, "Waste Recovery and Composting," 2011 (www.deq.state.or.us/lq/sw/recovery/rates.htm#me).

50. See Oregon Metro, "Urban Growth Boundary," 2013 (www.oregonmetro.gov/index.cfm/go/by.web/id=277).

51. See Congress for the New Urbanism, "Portland's Harbor Drive," 2011 (www.cnu.org/highways/portland).

52. Istrate and Marchio, "Export Nation 2012"; "Greater Portland Export Plan: Metro Export Initiative" (Brookings, 2012).

53. The story of Tektronix and Intel is based on Heike Mayer, "Bootstrapping High-Tech: Evidence from Three Emerging High-Technology Metropolitan Areas" (Brookings, 2009).

54. Heike Mayer, "Taking Root in Silicon Forest," *Journal of the American Planning Association* 71, no. 3 (2005).

55. Susan Helper, Timothy Krueger, and Howard Wial, "Locating American Manufacturing: Trends in the Geography of Production" (Brookings, 2012); "Greater Portland Export Plan."

56. White House, "Remarks by the President in the State of the Union Address," Office of the Press Secretary, January 27, 2010 (www.whitehouse.gov/the-press-office/remarks-president-state-union-address).

57. "Greater Portland Export Plan."

58. Ibid.

59. Richard Read, "Portland-Area Plan: Double Exports in Five Years, Create 113,000 Jobs," *The Oregonian*, October 2, 2012. Metro is a regional government for three counties in Greater Portland, the only one in the United States whose council members are elected directly by the region's voters. "The Metro Council provides

leadership from a regional perspective, focusing on issues that cross local boundaries and require collaborative solutions." Oregon Metro, "About Metro," 2013 (www. oregonmetro.gov/index.cfm/go/by.web/id=24201).

60. Darby Minow Smith, "Breaking: Portland Sustainability Chief Admits 'Portlandia' Isn't Really a Parody," *Grist*, November 2, 2012.

61. Christina Williams, "Interface, GBS Tapped for Huge LEED Project in Qatar," *Sustainable Business Oregon*, September 20, 2011; "LEED (Leadership in Energy and Environmental Design) is a voluntary, consensus-based, market-driven program that provides third-party verification of green buildings." U.S. Green Building Council, "LEED," 2013 (www.usgbc.org/leed); LRS Architects, "Projects," 2013 (www.lrsarchitects.com/EE/); Shredding Systems, Inc. (www.ssiworld.com).

62. Christina Williams, "Portland Partners with Brazilian Firm on Cleantech," *Sustainable Business Oregon*, February 15, 2012.

63. Saskia Sassen, *The Global City: New York, London, Tokyo* (Princeton University Press, 1991).

64. Saskia Sassen, *Cities in a World Economy*, 4th ed. (Thousand Oaks, Calif.: Sage Publications, 2012).

65. Peter Marcuse and Ronald Van Kempen, "Conclusion: A Changed Spatial Order," in *Globalizing Cities: A New Spatial Order?* edited by Peter Marcuse and Ronald Van Kempen (Oxford, U.K.: Blackwell Publishing, 2000), p. 262.

66. See Siemens, "Green City Index," 2013 (www.siemens.com/entry/cc/en/greencityindex.htm).

67. Berube and Parilla, *Metro Trade*, p. 17. See, generally, Greg Clark, "The Business of Cities: City Indexes in 2011," 2011 (www.gregclark.com).

68. See Sister Cities International, "Missions and History," 2012 (www.sistercities.org/mission-and-history).

69. See, generally, Alejandro Portes and Alex Stepick, *City on the Edge: The Transformation of Miami* (University of California Press, 1993).

70. Brookings analysis of U.S. Census Bureau data.

71. Jan Nijman, "Place-Particularity and 'Deep Analogies': A Comparative Essay on Miami's Rise as a World City," *Urban Geography* 28, no. 1 (2007): 92–107.

72. Jill Wilson and Nicole Prchal Svajlenka, "Metro Brazil: An Overview of the Nation's Largest Metropolitan Economies" (Brookings, 2012).

73. Brookings analysis of Oxford Economics data.

74. See Office of the U.S. Trade Representative, "Brazil" (www.ustr.gov/countries-regions/americas/brazil).

75. World Shipping Council and Brookings analysis of INFRAERO aviation data. See also World Shipping Council, "Top 50 World Container Ports," 2012 (www.worldshipping.org/about-the-industry/global-trade/top-50-world-container-ports).

76. Global Cities Initiative, "The Role of Freight and Logistics in Boosting Miami's Economic Future," Brookings, June 18, 2012 (www.brookings.edu/~/media/events/2012/6/19%20global%20cities%20miami/goods%20movement%20summary%20memo%20global%20cities%20miami.pdf.).

77. Data from U.S. Census Bureau, Foreign Trade Division, provided by Enterprise Florida via WISER (www.wisertrade.org).

78. Sassen, *Cities in a World Economy*.

79. Rankings based on total assets data from *The Banker Database*, 2013 (www.thebankerdatabase.com/index.cfm?fuseaction=top50.default&page=1).

80. Sassen, *Cities in a World Economy*, p. 184.

81. See Banco de Brasil, "Miami" (www.bb.com.br/portalbb/home2,7577,7577, 22,0,2,8.bb). See also Banco Itaú Europa, Private Bank International, "Address" (www.itauprivatebank.com/About/WhereAre/Address/index.html#EstadosUnidos).

82. Nijman, "Place-Particularity and 'Deep Analogies,'" p. 97.

83. Denerson Mota, CEO, Global Brazilian Investments, e-mail correspondence with Joseph Parilla, senior policy and research assistant, Brookings, March 11, 2013.

84. Brookings analysis of U.S. Census Bureau and Sabre data.

85. Beacon Council, "Economic Quarterly: Special Report," 2011 (http://business. fiu.edu/emba-consortium/pdf/EconomicQuarterly.pdf)

86. John Gittelsohn and Jose Sergio Osse find that in the first six months of 2011, "as many as half the downtown condos [in Miami] that were sold to foreigners for more than $500,000 were purchased by Brazilians." Gittelsohn and Osse, "Brazilians Buy Miami Condos at Bargain Prices as Real Gains 45%," *Bloomberg News*, June 21, 2011(www.bloomberg.com/news/2011-06-21/brazilians-buy-miami-condos-at-bargain-prices-after-45-surge-in-currency.html).

87. Quoted in Michelle Balani and Mary Murphy, "Brazilians Snap Up South Florida Real Estate Sparking New Boom," *Rock Center*, June 14, 2012 (http:// rockcenter.nbcnews.com/_news/2012/06/14/12207356-brazilians-snap-up-south-florida-real-estate-sparking-new-boom?lite).

88. Associated Press, "Rick Scott Heads to Brazil for Seven-Day Trade Trip," *Tampa Bay Online*, October 19, 2011 (www2.tbo.com/news/politics/2011/oct/19/1/ rick-scott-heads-to-brazil-for-seven-day-trade-tri-ar-273069/); Enterprise Florida, "Enterprise Florida Re-Establishes Florida Office in Brazil," press release, January 24, 2011 (http://eflorida.com/PressDetail.aspx?id=8782); Enterprise Florida, "Team Florida Business Expo & Trade Mission: Brazil," internal document, 2011 (http:// eflorida.com/uploadedFiles/Events/Brazil_Apr28.pdf); "Apex-Brasil IndyCar Program," Experience Our Energy, 2010, video (www.experienceourenergy.com.br/).

89. Florida International University, College of Business, "Graduate Dual Degree," 2013 (http://business.fiu.edu/international_programs/ip_graduate_dual_ degree.cfm). See also Escola Superior de Propaganda e Marketing, "Dual Degree Requirements," 2013 (www.espm.br/Unidades/SaoPaulo/PosGraduacao/MBA Executivo/Documents/ESPMAppendix1MBA.pdf).

90. See Art Basel, "Miami Beach: 2012 Galleries," 2012 (www.artbasel.com/en/ Miami-Beach/About-the-Show/2012-Galleries).

91. McKinsey and Company, "Winning the $30 Trillion Decathlon," pp. 9–10.

92. Henri Pirenne, *Economic and Social History of Medieval Europe* (Abingdon, U.K.: Routledge, 2006), p. 150.

93. Mark Lardas, "The Heritage of the Hansa," *German Life* 2 (October–November 2004).

94. Ellen C. Semple, "The Development of the Hanse Towns in Relation to Their Geographical Environment," *Journal of the American Geographical Society of New York* 31, no. 3 (1899), p. 249.

95. Raimund Wolfert, "A History of German-Scandinavian Relations," Germany's Federal Institute for Research on Building, Urban Affairs and Spatial Development, 2009 (www.bbsr.bund.de/nn_23470/BBSR/DE/Veroeffentlichungen/ IzR/2009/8__9/Geschichte__engl,templateId=raw,property=publicationFile.pdf/ Geschichte_engl.pdf), p. 6.

96. Helen Zimmern, *The Hansa Towns* (New York: G. P. Putnam's Sons, 1889), p. 151.

97. Walter Zinn, "The Hanseatic League and the Intermodal Nature of Multinational Business," Michigan State University, p. 92.

98. Lardas, "The Heritage of the Hansa"; Jennifer Mills, "The Hanseatic League in the Eastern Baltic," University of Washington, May 1998 (www.conflicts.rem33.com/images/The%20Baltic%20States/hansa_ost.htm).

99. Mills, "The Hanseatic League in the Eastern Baltic."

100. Ibid.

101. Zinn, "The Hanseatic League and the Intermodal Nature of Multinational Business," p. 86.

102. Zimmern, *The Hansa Towns*, pp. 80–81.

103. "C40 Cities: Climate Leadership Group," 2013 (www.c40cities.org); New York City, "PlaNYC 2030" (www.nyc.gov/html/planyc2030/html/home/home.shtml); City of Copenhagen, "Global Challenges, Copenhagen Solutions" (www.subsite.kk.dk/sitecore/content/Subsites/CityOfCopenhagen/SubsiteFrontpage/Business/Growth_and_partnerships/Strategy.aspx); "Guide to Copenhagen 2025" (Copenhagen: Monday Morning and Green Growth Leaders, 2012); City of Philadelphia, Mayor's Office of Sustainability, "Greenworks Philadelphia" (www.phila.gov/green/greenworks/index.html); C40 Cities, "Our Partners and Funders," 2011 (www.c40cities.org/partnerships).

CHAPTER 8

1. The phrase "cities of knowledge" comes from Margaret Pugh O'Mara's excellent book of the same name. Her book is a careful exposition of the role of the federal government in creating Silicon Valley and of the efforts of other places to create their own comparable centers of knowledge and economic development. Margaret Pugh O'Mara, *Cities of Knowledge: Cold War Science and the Search for the Next Silicon Valley* (Princeton University Press, 2005).

2. Daniel P. Moynihan, "Toward a National Urban Policy," *The Public Interest* 17 (Fall 1969), p. 8. Over his long career, Moynihan remained intensely focused on the sprawl-inducing impact of federal housing and transportation policies and investments on the American metropolitan landscape. As chairman of the U.S. Senate Committee on Environment and Public Works, he was the major architect of the Intermodal Surface Transportation Efficiency Act of 1991, which gave metropolitan areas greater powers over the allocation of federal transportation funds. States have also tended to distort and distend metropolitan development through their interventions on governance, municipal taxation, school finance, land use, and zoning. See Richard F. Weingroff, "Creating a Landmark: The Intermodal Surface Transportation Act of 1991," *Public Roads* 65, no. 3 (2001) (www.fhwa.dot.gov/publications/publicroads/01novdec/istea.cfm). See also Myron Orfield, *Metropolitics* (Brookings Press, 1996); David Rusk, *Inside Game / Outside Game* (Brookings Press, 1999).

3. Herbert Stein, *The Fiscal Revolution in America: Policy in Pursuit of Reality*, 2nd ed. (Washington: AEI Press, 1996), p. 14.

4. Gerald E. Frug and David J. Barron, *City Bound: How States Stifle Urban Innovation* (Cornell University Press, 2008).

5. Bruce Katz, "The Metro Moment," *Wall Street Journal*, April 15, 2010.

6. Bruce Katz, "Remaking Federalism to Remake the Economy: The Next President Should Harness the Power of States and Metros," in *Campaign 2012: Twelve Independent Ideas for Improving American Public Policy*, edited by Benjamin Wittes (Brookings Press, 2012).

7. This discussion is based on the comprehensive work of the economic historian John Joseph Wallis, "American Government Finance in the Long Run: 1790 to 1990," *Journal of Economic Perspectives* 14 (Winter 2000), p. 62.

8. Ibid. See also John Joseph Wallis and Barry W. Weingast, "Equilibrium Impotence: Why the States and Not the American National Government Financed Economic Development in the Antebellum Era," Working Paper 11397 (Cambridge, Mass.: National Bureau of Economic Research, June 2005). For a specific example of state financing during this period, see John Joseph Wallis, "The Property Tax as a Coordinating Device: Financing Indiana's Mammoth Internal Improvement System, 1835 to 1842," Historical Working Paper 136 (Cambridge, Mass.: National Bureau of Economic Research, November 2001).

9. See, for example, Alice M. Rivlin, *Reviving the American Dream: The Economy, the States, and the Federal Government* (Brookings Press, 1992).

10. Jon C. Teaford, *The Rise of the States: Evolution of American State Government* (Johns Hopkins University Press, 2002), p. 1.

11. American Presidency Project, "Richard Nixon: Address to the Nation on Domestic Programs," August 8, 1969 (www.presidency.ucsb.edu/ws/index.php?pid=2191).

12. Rivlin, *Reviving the American Dream*, p. 83.

13. See, for example, "Executive Order 13132 of August 4, 1999: Federalism," *Federal Register* 64 (August 10, 1999) (www.gpo.gov/fdsys/pkg/FR-1999-08-10/pdf/99-20729.pdf). See also Bruce Katz, "Remaking Federalism to Remake the American Economy" (Brookings, 2012), p. 3.

14. See, for example, Jessica Lee, "Advancing Innovation in States and Metropolitan Areas: Using Ballot Measures as a Platform for the Next Economy" (Brookings, forthcoming).

15. Mark Muro and others, "MetroPolicy: Shaping a New Federal Partnership for a Metropolitan Nation" (Brookings, 2008), p. 55.

16. Ibid., p. 56. See also Robert Atkinson, *The Past and Future of America's Economy: Long Waves of Innovation That Power Cycles of Growth* (Northhampton, Mass.: Edward Elgar, 2004).

17. Muro and others, "MetroPolicy: Shaping a New Federal Partnership for a Metropolitan Nation," p. 71.

18. Congressional Budget Office, "The Budget and Economic Outlook: Fiscal Years 2013 to 2023" (U.S. Government Printing Office, February 2013), p. 9.

19. In February 2013 the Congressional Budget Office projected that total federal debt would be equal to 76 percent of U.S. GDP by the end of the year. With federal spending expected to remain at a constant share of about 22.1 percent of GDP throughout the next decade, discretionary spending as a share of GDP will decline from 4.0 percent in fiscal year 2012 to 2.7 percent in fiscal year 2023 for nondefense discretionary spending and from 4.3 percent in fiscal year 2012 to 2.8 percent in fiscal year 2023 for defense discretionary spending. Congressional Budget Office, "The Budget and Economic Outlook: Fiscal Years 2013 to 2023."

20. Ibid., p. 9.

21. Richard Kogan, "Congress Has Cut Discretionary Funding by $1.5 Trillion over Ten Years: First Stage of Deficit Reduction Is in Law" (Washington: Center on Budget and Policy Priorities, 2012).

22. State and local unfunded pension liabilities could be as high as $3 trillion, and sales tax revenue as a share of state GDP has fallen, on average, by 37 percent in the past forty years and will likely continue to decline. State Budget Crisis Task Force, "Report of the State Budget Crisis Task Force: Full Report," July 2012, p. 35. See also State Budget Crisis Task Force, "Report of the State Budget Crisis Task Force: Summary Report," July 2012, p. 16.

23. State Budget Crisis Task Force, "Report of the State Budget Crisis Task Force: Summary Report," p. 9.

24. Ibid., p. 10.

25. The U.S. population grew by nearly 105 million over the past forty years, and the U.S. Census Bureau projects that it will grow to 420.3 million by 2060. As the country grows, it will become more diverse. The bureau estimates that the United States will be a "majority minority" nation by 2043, with the total nonwhite population more than doubling, from 116.2 million to 241.3 million, between 2012 and 2060. During this time, the number of people over the age of sixty-five will also more than double, from 43.1 million to 92.0 million. Given these trends, keeping federal and state discretionary program funding levels constant (or even adjusting for inflation) will drastically erode the spending power of these programs. U.S. Census Bureau, "U.S. Census Bureau Projections Show a Slower Growing, Older, More Diverse Nation a Half Century from Now," Department of Commerce, December 12, 2012 (www.census.gov/newsroom/releases/archives/population/cb12-243.html).

26. Alice Rivlin's compelling book *Reviving the American Dream* argues that the economic and fiscal challenges of the early 1990s required a re-sorting of responsibilities between the federal and state governments. "Washington not only has too much to do, it has taken on domestic responsibilities that would be handled better by the states. Revitalizing the economy may depend on restoring a cleaner division of responsibility between the states and the national government" (p. 31). "The states, not the federal government [should] take charge of accomplishing a 'productivity agenda' of reforms designed to revitalize the economy and raise incomes. These reforms would address needs such as education and skills training, child care, housing, infrastructure, and economic development" (p. 118). "These are functions of government that require experimentation, adaptation to local conditions, accountability of on-the-scene officials, and community participation and support" (p. 179). We believe that a resort will occur, but de facto rather than de jure and between the federal and state governments and metropolitan networks, rather than just between the "dual sovereigns."

27. In the Federalist Papers, James Madison describes the American republic as comprising separate spheres of government, each assigned a distinct role defined by the subject matter to which it attends: "In the compound republic of America, the power surrendered by the people is first divided between two distinct governments, and then the portion allotted to each subdivided among distinct and separate departments." James Madison, "The Federalist No. 51," in *The Federalist Papers: Alexander Hamilton, James Madison, John Jay,* edited by Clinton Lawrence Rossiter (New York: Mentor, 1999), p. 291. On this model, the Constitution's first article indicates specific functions to be performed by Congress, leaving all other

functions to the states (and localities, which go unmentioned)—an idea that became known as "dual" federalism. U.S. Constitution, art. 1, sec. 8, and Amendment X. The resurgence of interest in federalism during the 1970s and 1980s hewed closely to the dual federalism model, differing from what we propose here.

28. This definition has been described as "conceived not merely as a division of legal responsibility for governmental functions but as the diverse organizational elements of modern pluralist democracy (pluralism standing for a combination of organizational forms)." Aaron Wildavsky, "E Pluribus Unum: Plurality, Diversity, Variety and Modesty," in *The Costs of Federalism,* edited by Robert T. Golembiewski and Aaron Wildavsky (New Brunswick, N.J.: Transaction Books, 1984), p. 4.

29. Ibid., 6, 14.

30. *New State Ice Co.* v. *Liebmann,* 285 U.S. 262 (1932).

31. We are intentionally setting aside the intricacies of federal and state rule making (for example, environmental and banking regulation) in order to focus on the role the states and federal government play as investors in the domestic economy.

32. See Katherine Newman, "In the South and West, a Tax on Being Poor," *New York Times,* March 9, 2013.

33. See Council on Jobs and Competitiveness, "Foster a Climate That Lets Innovation Thrive" (www.jobs-council.com/recommendations/foster-a-climate-that-lets-innovation-thrive/).

34. Felix Rohaytn, "Time for a U.S. Infrastructure Bank," *Politico,* July 12, 2011 (www.politico.com/news/stories/0711/58786.html).

35. Andrew Liveris, *Make It in America: The Case for Re-Inventing the Economy* (Hoboken, N.J.: John Wiley and Sons, 2011).

36. Along with our colleagues and others, we have published a series of reform ideas to streamline federal programs in the face of budget cuts. See lead essay, Bruce Katz and Mark Muro, "Remaking Federalism / Renewing the Economy: Resetting Federal Policy to Recharge the Economy, Stabilize the Budget, and Unleash State and Metropolitan Innovation," Brookings, 2012 (www.brookings.edu/about/programs/metro/remaking-federalism).

37. Bruce Katz, "Reform the Mortgage Interest Deduction to Invest in Innovation and Advanced Industries" (Brookings, 2012).

38. Paul Weinstein Jr., "Cut to Invest: Establish a 'Cut-to-Invest Commission' to Reduce Low-Priority Spending, Consolidate Duplicative Programs, and Increase High-Priority Investments," Brookings, 2012 (www.brookings.edu/~/media/research/files/papers/2012/11/13%20federalism/13%20investments%20spending.pdf).

39. Bruce Katz and Peter Hamp, "Create a 'Race to the Shop' Competition for Advanced Manufacturing" (Brookings, 2012).

40. Anne Kim, "Three Ways to Bring Manufacturing Back to America," *Washington Monthly,* March–April 2013.

41. Lee, "Advancing Innovation in States and Metropolitan Areas." See also Robert Puentes and Jennifer Thompson, "Banking on Infrastructure: Enhancing State Revolving Funds for Transportation" (Brookings, 2012); Mark Muro and Devashree Saha, "Banking on Green Growth in Connecticut," *The Avenue: Rethinking Metropolitan America* (blog), Brookings, June 28, 2011 (www.brookings.edu/blogs/the-avenue/posts/2011/06/28-green-connecticut-muro); Devashree Saha and Mark Muro, "Cut to Invest: Create a Nationwide Network of Advanced Industries Innovation Hubs" (Brookings, 2013); Mark Muro, "Advancing Advanced Industries," *UpFront* (blog), Brookings, February 5, 2013 (www.brookings.edu/blogs/

up-front/posts/2013/02/05-advancing-advanced-industries-colorado-muro); Louise Story, "United States of Subsidies," *New York Times,* December 2012.

42. Mireya Solis and Justin Vaïsse, "Free Trade Game Changer," in *Big Bets and Black Swans: A Presidential Briefing Book,* edited by Martin Indyk, Tanvi Madan, and Thomas Wright (Brookings Press, 2012). See also David Ignatius, "A Free-Trade Agreement with Europe?" *Washington Post,* December 5, 2012; "The Transatlantic Partnership: A Statesman's Forum with Secretary of State Hillary Clinton," transcript, Brookings, November, 29, 2012; Doug Palmer, "U.S., Japan Agree on Approach to Trans-Pacific Partnership Talks," Reuters, February 22, 2013; "Obama's 2013 State of the Union Address," *New York Times,* February 12, 2013.

43. Southern California Studies Center and Brookings Center on Urban and Metropolitan Policy, *Sprawl Hits the Wall: Confronting the Realities of Metropolitan Los Angeles* (2001). See also William Fulton and others, *Who Sprawls Most? How Growth Patterns Differ Across the U.S.* (Brookings Press, 2001).

44. Ken Orski, "A Cutting-Edge Fiscal Policy Innovation," *National Journal,* July 20, 2010.

45. We write about the Miami Port improvements and Florida's Office of Freight Logistics and Passenger Operations in our 2013 "Innovations to Watch" report. See Bruce Katz and Owen Washburn, "Innovations to Watch," Brookings, 2013 (www.brookings.edu/research/interactives/2013/innovationstowatch#Exports).

46. Andrew Cuomo, governor of New York, speech at the Regional Council Awards Event, December 8, 2011 (www.livestream.com/newyorkstateofficeofthegovernor/video?clipId=flv_27189a8a-6ed8-4762-8f00-62e4ceb844a7).

47. Metros anchor nine of the ten key New York regions: Albany in the Capital Region, Syracuse in Central New York, Rochester in the Finger Lakes, Poughkeepsie in the Mid-Hudson region, Utica in the Mohawk Valley, Binghamton in the Southern Tier, Buffalo in Western New York, and the New York City metro, which is shared by the New York City, Long Island, and the Mid-Hudson regions. The North Country region does not contain a metropolitan area.

48. Bruce Katz was one of the judges of the first year's regional strategies, along with four other experts on national and state economic development and urban planning with experience in the public, private, and academic sectors: Cesar Perales, secretary, New York Department of State; Joan McDonald, commissioner, New York State Department of Transportation; Walter D. Broadnax, professor of public administration at the Maxwell School of Syracuse University; and Dall W. Forsythe, senior fellow at the Wagner School of Public Service, New York University.

49. Greater Manchester Combined Authority, "Greater Manchester City Deal," 2012 (www.dpm.cabinetoffice.gov.uk/sites/default/files_dpm/resources/Greater-Manchester-City-Deal-final_0.pdf).

50. Ibid.

51. Greater Manchester Combined Authority and the Department for Energy and Climate Change, "Memorandum of Understanding: Pathfinder Agreement Relating to Greater Manchester Low Carbon Hub," 2012 (www.agma.gov.uk/cms_media/files/full_mou_and_action_plan_21091211.pdf).

52. Alexander Hamilton, "The Federalist No. 1," in *The Federalist Papers,* edited by Rossiter, p. 1.

53. Ibid.; Alexander Hamilton, "The Federalist No. 36," in *Federalist Papers,* edited by Rossiter, p. 192; Hamilton, "Federalist No. 1," p. lix.

54. Hamilton, "Federalist No. 1," p. 1.

CHAPTER 9

The Jack Dorsey quote at the beginning of the chapter is taken from Laurie Segall, "Square CEO Jack Dorsey: I Never Wanted to Be an Entrepreneur," *CNN Money,* September 10, 2012 (www.money.cann.com/2012/09/10/technology/startups/jack-dorsey-techcrunch-disrupt/index.html).

1. The historian Lewis Mumford writes, "The city, as one finds it in history, is the point of maximum concentration for the power and culture of a community. . . . The city is the form and symbol of an integrated social relationship: it is the seat of the temple, the market, the hall of justice, the academy of learning. Here in the city the goods of civilization are multiplied and manifolded; here is where human experience is transformed into viable signs, symbols, patterns of conduct, systems of order. Here is where the issues of civilization are focused." Lewis Mumford, *The Culture of Cities* (New York: Harcourt Brace and Company, 1938), p. 3.

2. *Jacobellis* v. *Ohio,* 378 U.S. 184 (1964) (www.law.cornell.edu/supct/html/historics/USSC_CR_0378_0184_ZS.html).

3. Michael Lewis, *Moneyball: The Art of Winning an Unfair Game* (New York: W. W. Norton, 2003).

4. Bruce worked with Secretary Cisneros for four years and remembers him frequently using this expression.

5. See Louise Story, "United States of Subsidies," *New York Times,* December 1, 2012.

6. Angela Blanchard, "People Transforming Communities. For Good," Investing in What Works for America's Communities (www.whatworksforamerica.org/ideas/people-transforming-communities/#.USZCoFKmGyF).

7. Jessica Lee, "Advancing Innovation in States and Metropolitan Areas: Using Ballot Measures as a Platform for the Next Economy" (Brookings, forthcoming).

8. New York City, Office of the Mayor, "Mayor Bloomberg, Cornell President Skorton and Technion President Lavie Announce Historic Partnership to Build a New Applied Sciences Campus on Roosevelt Island," press release, December 19, 2011. See also Gale Scott, "Cornell Tech Gets Green Light from the Locals," *Crain's New York Business,* December 20, 2012.

9. See USAspending.gov.

10. See New York City Economic Development Corporation, "About NYCEDC: History," 2013 (www.nycedc.com/about-nycedc/history).

11. Neighborhood Centers, Inc., "100 Years of Caring," internal document, 2007.

12. See Philipp Rode and others, "Munich Metropolitan Region: Staying Ahead on Innovation," *LSE Cities Next Urban Economy Series* (London School of Economics, 2010). See also Andreas Koch and Thomas Stahlecker, "Regional Innovation Systems and the Foundation of Knowledge Intensive Business Services: A Comparative Study in Bremen, Munich, and Stuttgart, Germany," *European Planning Studies* 14 (February 2006).

13. "Less Energy, More Growth: Prosperity through Efficiency," Lean Energy Cluster and Monday Morning (www.leanenergy.dk/media/44595/less_energy_more_growth_lean_energy_publikation_printvenlig.pdf); "Copenhagen, Beyond Green: The Socioeconomic Benefits of Being a Green City," Green Growth Leaders and Monday Morning (www.sustainia.me/resources/publications/mm/CPH%20Beyond%20Green.pdf).

14. Bruce Katz, "Why the U.S. Government Should Embrace Smart Cities," Brookings, July 26, 2011 (www.brookings.edu/research/opinions/2011/07/26-cities-katz). See also Boyd Cohen, "Singapore Is on Its Way to Becoming an Icon Smart City," Fast Company, May 2012 (www.fastcoexist.com/1679819/singapore-is-on-its-way-to-becoming-an-iconic-smart-city); Greg Lindsay, "Cisco's Big Bet on New Songdo: Creating Cities from Scratch," Fast Company, February 1, 2010 (www.fastcompany.com/1514547/ciscos-big-bet-new-songdo-creating-cities-scratch).

15. "Latin America's Bus Rapid Transit Boom: Lessons for U.S. Public Transportation," panel discussion, Brookings, March 8, 2011 (www.brookings.edu/events/2011/03/08-bus-rapid-transit).

16. David King, Michael Manville, and Donald Shoup, "The Political Calculus of Congestion Pricing," *Transport Policy* 14, no. 2 (2007), p. 114.

17. Janna Anderson, Jan Lauren Boyles, and Lee Rainie, "The Future of Higher Education" (Washington: Pew Internet and American Life Project, July 2012).

18. See Techonomy website (www.techonomy.com) and Code for America website (www.codeforamerica.org).

19. Bruce Katz, "Why the U.S. Government Should Embrace Smart Cities," Brookings, July 26, 2011 (www.brookings.edu/research/opinions/2011/07/26-cities-katz).

20. Alan Berube and Carey Anne Nadeau, "Metropolitan Areas and the Next Economy: A 50-State Analysis" (Brookings, 2011).

21. Ibid.

22. In 1776 the United States had a population of about 2.5 million; Philadelphia was the largest city, with 40,000 residents. See Lawrence Yun, "Largest Cities in the United States in 1776, and in 2076," National Association of Realtors, July 3, 2012 (http://economistsoutlook.blogs.realtor.org/?s=Largest+Cities+in+the+United+States&x=0&y=0).

23. Benjamin L. Carp, *Rebels Rising: Cities and the American Revolution* (Oxford University Press, 2007).

24. Ibid.

25. Quoted in Benjamin L. Carp, "Fire of Liberty: Firefighters, Urban Voluntary Culture, and the Revolutionary Movement," *William and Mary Quarterly* 58 (October 2001), p. 786.

26. Carp, "Fire of Liberty," p. 55.

27. See Common Cause, "Elected Officials Search Take Action" (www.commoncause.org/siteapps/advocacy/search.aspx?c=dkLNK1MQIwG&b=4860375).

SELECTED BIBLIOGRAPHY

Ács, Zoltán J. *Innovation and the Growth of Cities.* Northampton, Mass.: Edward Elgar, 2002.

Addams, Jane. *Twenty Years at Hull House, with Autobiographical Notes.* New York: Macmillan, 1912.

Artz, Kendall W., and others. "A Longitudinal Study of the Impact of R&D, Patents, and Product Innovation on Firm Performance." *Journal of Product Innovation Management* 27, no. 5 (2010): 725–40.

Atkinson, Robert D. *The Past and the Future of America's Economy: Long Waves of Innovation That Power Cycles of Growth.* Northampton, Mass.: Edward Elgar, 2004.

Atkinson, Robert D., and Stephen J. Ezell. *Innovation Economics: The Race for Global Advantage.* Yale University Press, 2012.

Bender, Thomas. *The Unfinished City: New York and the Metropolitan Idea.* New York University Press, 2007.

Benkler, Yochai. *The Penguin and the Leviathan: The Triumph of Cooperation over Self-Interest.* New York: Crown Business, 2011.

———. *The Wealth of Networks: How Social Production Transforms Markets and Freedom.* Yale University Press, 2006.

Berube, Alan. "MetroNation: How U.S. Metropolitan Areas Fuel American Prosperity." Brookings, 2007 (www.brookings.edu/research/reports/2007/11/06-metronation-berube).

Berube, Alan, and Joseph Parilla. "Metro Trade: Cities Return to Their Roots in the Global Economy." Brookings, 2012 (www.brookings.edu/research/papers/2012/11/26-metro-trade).

Berube, Alan, and others. "The State of Metropolitan America: On the Front Lines of Demographic Transition." Brookings, 2010.

Burdett, Ricky, and Deyan Sudjie, eds. *The Endless City.* London: Phaidon, 2007.

———. *Living in the Endless City.* London: Phaidon, 2011.

Calvino, Italo. *Invisible Cities.* New York: Harcourt Brace and Company, 1974.

Castells, Manuel. *The Rise of the Network Society*. Cambridge, Mass.: Blackwell, 2009.

Chesbrough, Henry William. *Open Innovation: The New Imperative for Creating and Profiting from Technology*. Harvard Business School Press, 2003.

Chesbrough, Henry William, Wim Vanhaverbeke, and Joel West. *Open Innovation: Researching a New Paradigm*. Oxford University Press, 2006.

Chrislip, David D., and Carl E. Larson. *Collaborative Leadership: How Citizens and Civic Leaders Can Make a Difference*. San Francisco, Calif.: Jossey-Bass, 1994.

Cisneros, Henry, ed. *Interwoven Destinies: Cities and the Nation*. New York: W. W. Norton, 1993.

Davis, Allen Freeman. *Spearheads for Reform: The Social Settlements and the Progressive Movement, 1890–1914*. Oxford University Press, 1967.

Dempsey, Paul Stephen, Andrew R. Goetz, and Joseph S. Szyliowicz. *Denver International Airport: Lessons Learned*. New York: McGraw-Hill, 1997.

Fischel, William A., ed. *The Tiebout Model at Fifty: Essays in Public Economics in Honor of Wallace Oates*. Cambridge, Mass.: Lincoln Institute of Land Policy, 2006.

Fishman, Robert. *Bourgeois Utopias: The Rise and Fall of Suburbia*. New York: Basic Books, 1987.

Florida, Richard. *The Great Reset: How the Post-Crash Economy Will Change the Way We Live and Work*. New York: HarperCollins, 2011.

———. *The Rise of the Creative Class: Revisited*. New York: Basic Books, 2012.

Frug, Gerald E. *City Making: Building Communities without Building Walls*. Princeton University Press, 1999.

Frug, Gerald E., and David J. Barron. *City Bound: How States Stifle Urban Innovation*. Cornell University Press, 2008.

Gertner, Jon. *The Idea Factory: Bell Labs and the Great Age of American Innovation*. New York: Penguin Press, 2012.

Glaeser, Edward L. *The Triumph of the City: How Our Greatest Invention Makes Us Richer, Smarter, Greener, Healthier, Happier*. New York: Penguin Press, 2011.

Goldin, Claudia Dale, and Lawrence F. Katz. *The Race between Education and Technology*. Harvard University Press, 2008.

Hagel, John, and John Seely Brown. *The Only Sustainable Edge: Why Business Strategy Depends on Productive Friction and Dynamic Specialization*. Harvard Business School Press, 2005.

Hecht, Ben. "Revitalizing Struggling American Cities." *Stanford Social Innovation Review* 9 (Fall 2011) (www.ssireview.org/articles/entry/revitalizing_struggling_american_cities).

Istrate, Emilia, and Nicholas Marchio. "Export Nation 2012: How U.S. Metropolitan Areas Are Driving National Growth." Brookings, 2012 (www.brookings.edu/research/reports/2012/03/08-exports).

Jackson, Kenneth T. *Crabgrass Frontier: The Suburbanization of the United States*. Oxford University Press, 1985.

Jacobs, Jane. *The Economy of Cities*. New York: Random House, 1969.

James, Franklin J., and Christopher B. Gerboth. "Camp Divided: Annexation Battles, the Poundstone Amendment, and Their Impact on Metropolitan Denver, 1941–1988." *Colorado History* 5 (2001): 129–74.

Johnson, Steven. *Future Perfect: The Case for Progress in a Networked Age*. New York: Penguin Group, 2012.

―――. *Where Good Ideas Come From: The Natural History of Innovation*. New York: Penguin Group, 2010.

Katz, Bruce, ed. *Reflections on Regionalism*. Brookings Press, 2000.

―――. "Remaking Federalism to Remake the Economy: The Next President Should Harness the Power of States and Metros." In *Campaign 2012: Twelve Independent Ideas for Improving American Public Policy*, edited by Benjamin Wittes, pp. 61–72. Brookings Press, 2012.

Katz, Bruce, and Jennifer Bradley. "The Detroit Project." *New Republic*, December 9, 2009 (www.newrepublic.com/article/metro-policy/the-detroit-project#).

―――. "Divided We Sprawl." *The Atlantic Online*, December 1999 (www.the atlantic.com/past/docs/issues/99dec/9912katz.htm).

―――. "Metro Connection." *Democracy: A Journal of Ideas*, Spring 2011 (www. democracyjournal.org/20/metro-connection.php?page=all).

Katz, Bruce, Jennifer Bradley, and Amy Liu. "Delivering the Next Economy: The States Step Up." Brookings-Rockefeller Project on State and Metropolitan Innovation. Brookings, 2010 (www.brookings.edu/research/papers/2010/11/17-states-next-economy).

Katz, Bruce, and Mark Muro. "Remaking Federalism / Renewing the Economy: Resetting Federal Policy to Recharge the Economy, Stabilize the Budget, and Unleash State and Metropolitan Innovation." Brookings, 2012.

Katz, Bruce, Mark Muro, and Jennifer Bradley. "Miracle Mets." *Democracy: A Journal of Ideas* 12 (Spring 2009) (www.democracyjournal.org/12/6681.php?page=all).

Katz, Bruce, and others. "MetroPolicy: Shaping a New Federal Partnership for a Metropolitan Nation." Brookings, 2008 (www.brookings.edu/research/reports/2008/06/metropolicy).

Keating, W. Dennis, Norman Krumholz, and David C. Perry. *Cleveland: A Metropolitan Reader*. Kent State University Press, 1995.

Kretzmann, John P., and John McKnight. *Building Communities from the Inside Out: A Path toward Finding and Mobilizing a Community's Assets*. Chicago: Asset-Based Community Development Institute, 1993.

Lang, Robert E., and Jennifer B. LeFurgy. *Boomburbs: The Rise of America's Accidental Cities*. Brookings Press, 2007.

Liu, Amy, Brad McDearman, and Marek Gootman. "Strengthen Federalism: Establish a Regional Export Accelerator Challenge (REACH) Grant Program to Boost U.S. Exports and Trade Capacity." Brookings, 2013.

Liveris, Andrew. *Make It in America: The Case for Re-Inventing the Economy*. Hoboken, N.J.: John Wiley and Sons, 2011.

Luce, Edward. 2012. *Time to Start Thinking: America in the Age of Descent*. New York: Atlantic Monthly Press.

Ma, Zhenzhong, and Yender Lee. "Patent Application and Technological Collaboration in Inventive Activities: 1980–2005." *Technovation* 28, no. 6 (2008): 379–90.

Mann, Thomas, and Norman Ornstein. *It's Even Worse Than it Looks: How the American Constitutional System Collided with the New Politics of Extremism*. New York: Basic Books, 2012.

Marklund, Göran, Nicholas S. Vonortas, and Charles W. Wessner. *The Innovation Imperative: National Innovation Strategies in the Global Economy*. Northampton, Mass.: Edward Elgar, 2009.

McComb, David G. *Houston, a History*. University of Texas Press, 1981.

Mercier, Laurie. "Remembering and Redefining Deindustrialized Youngstown." *American Quarterly* 55, no. 2 (2003): 315–21.

Miller, Carol Poh, and Robert Anthony Wheeler. *Cleveland: A Concise History, 1796–1996*. 2nd ed. Indiana University Press, 1997.

Moretti, Enrico. *The New Geography of Jobs*. Boston, Mass.: Houghton Mifflin Harcourt, 2012.

Moynihan, Daniel P., ed. *Coping: Essays on the Practice of Government*. New York: Random House, 1973.

———. *Toward a National Urban Policy*. New York: Basic Books, 1970.

Muro, Mark, and Robert Weissbourd. "Metropolitan Business Plans: A New Approach to Economic Growth." Brookings, 2011.

Muro, Mark, and others. "Launch! Taking Colorado's Space Economy to the Next Level." Brookings, 2013.

Myers, Dowell. *Immigrants and Boomers: Forging a New Social Contract for the Future of America*. New York: Russell Sage Foundation, 2007.

Noah, Timothy. *The Great Divergence: America's Growing Inequality Crisis and What We Can Do about It*. New York: Bloomsbury, 2012.

O'Mara, Margaret Pugh. *Cities of Knowledge: Cold War Science and the Search for the Next Silicon Valley*. Princeton University Press, 2005.

Orfield, Myron. *Metropolitics: A Regional Agenda for Community and Stability*. Brookings Press, 1997.

Ostrom, Vincent, Charles M. Tiebout, and Robert Warren. "The Organization of Government in Metropolitan Areas: A Theoretical Inquiry." *American Political Science Review* 55, no. 4 (1961): 831–42.

Power, Anne, and John Houghton. *Jigsaw Cities: Big Places, Small Spaces*. Bristol: The Policy Press, 2007.

Power, Anne, Jorg Ploger, and Astrid Winkler. *Phoenix Cities: The Fall and Rise of Great Industrial Cities*. Bristol: The Policy Press, 2010.

Puentes, Robert. "Bridge to Somewhere: Rethinking American Transportation for the 21st Century." Brookings, 2008 (www.brookings.edu/research/reports/2008/06/transportation-puentes).

Rivlin, Alice M. *Reviving the American Dream: The Economy, the States, and the Federal Government*. Brookings Press, 1992.

Rusk, David. *Inside Game / Outside Game: Winning Strategies for Saving Urban America*. Brookings Press, 1999.

Safford, Sean. *Why the Garden Club Couldn't Save Youngstown: The Transformation of the Rust Belt*. Harvard University Press, 2009.

Sanker, Dan. *Collaborate: The Art of We*. San Francisco, Calif.: Jossey-Bass, 2012.

Sassen, Saskia. *Cities in a World Economy*. 4th ed. London: Sage Publications, 2011.

———. *The Global City: New York, London, Tokyo*. Princeton University Press, 1991.

Sennett, Richard. *The Craftsman*. Yale University Press, 2008.

———. *Together: The Rituals, Pleasures, and Politics of Cooperation*. Yale University Press, 2012.

Sørensen, Eva, and Jacob Torfing. "The Democratic Anchorage of Governance Networks." *Scandinavian Political Studies* 28, no. 3 (2005): 195–218.

———. "Making Governance Networks Effective and Democratic through Metagovernance." *Public Administration* 87, no. 2 (2009): 234–58.

Sorkin, Andrew Ross. *Too Big to Fail: The Inside Story of How Wall Street and Washington Fought to Save the Financial System from Crisis—and Themselves.* New York: Viking, 2009.

Sthanumoorthy, R. "Rate War, Race to the Bottom, and Uniform State VAT Rates: An Empirical Foundation for a Difficult Policy Issue." *Economic and Political Weekly* 41, no. 24 (2006): 2460–69.

Stiglitz, Joseph E. *The Price of Inequality: How Today's Divided Society Endangers Our Future.* New York: W. W. Norton, 2012.

———. "The Theory of Local Public Goods Twenty-Five Years after Tiebout: A Perspective." Working Paper 954. Cambridge, Mass.: National Bureau of Economic Research, 1982.

Sugrue, Thomas J. *The Origins of the Urban Crisis: Race and Inequality in Postwar Detroit.* Princeton University Press, 1996.

Torfing, Jacob. "Governance Network Theory: Towards a Second Generation." *European Political Science* 4, no. 3 (2005): 305–15.

Wallis, Allan. *Denver's International Airport: A Case Study in Large Scale Infrastructure Development.* New York: Panel Publishers, 1992.

———. "Denver's International Airport: A Case Study in Large Scale Infrastructure Development, Part 1." *Municipal Finance Journal* 13, no. 2 (1992): 60–79.

———. "Denver's International Airport: A Case Study in Large Scale Infrastructure Development, Part 2." *Municipal Finance Journal* 13, no. 3 (1992): 62–79.

Weisman, Steven R., ed. *Daniel Patrick Moynihan: A Portrait in Letters of an American Visionary.* New York: PublicAffairs, 2010.

Wilkinson, Richard G., and Kate Pickett. *The Spirit Level: Why More Equal Societies Almost Always Do Better.* London: Allen Lane, 2009.

Wood, Robert Coldwell. *1400 Governments: The Political Economy of the New York Metropolitan Region.* Harvard University Press, 1961.

Zeng, S. X., X. M. Xie, and C. M. Tam. "Relationship between Cooperation Networks and Innovation Performance of SMEs." *Technovation* 30, no. 3 (2010): 181–94.

INDEX

251

CPSIA information can be obtained
at www.ICGtesting.com
Printed in the USA
LVOW10s1340160517
534710LV00001B/1/P